HOW TO MAKE IT ON THE INTERNET

HOW TO MAKE IT ON THE INTERNET

POLLY SPRENGER

Virgin

First published in Great Britain in 2001 by
Virgin Publishing Ltd
Thames Wharf Studios
Rainville Road
London
W6 9HA

A catalogue record for the book is available from the British Library.

ISBN 0 7535 0510 X

Designed and typeset by Roger Kohn Designs
Printed and bound in Great Britain by
Mackays of Chatham

ABOUT THE AUTHOR

Polly Sprenger is a Silicon Valley ex-pat living in London. In 1999, she founded the London bureau of the Internet business magazine the *Industry Standard*, and joined the newly established *Industry Standard Europe* in 2000 as senior editor. Prior to the *Standard*, Sprenger was technology writer for *Wired News*, the daily news site of *Wired* magazine, where she wrote about the seamier side of the Net: pornography and hackers. She has written about technology and the Internet for the *Guardian*, the *Independent*, the *Daily Telegraph*, *New Media* magazine, *Internet World* and Playboy.com.

ACKNOWLEDGEMENTS

If you can make one generalisation about the Internet industry, it's that under no circumstances should you try to generalise about the Internet industry. Everyone sees it differently, and industry folks are fond of mocking any attempt to portray 'how it is' on the other side of the dot in dot.com. Without the help of countless industry brains, this book wouldn't even come close. First and foremost among those brains is Ramona Liberoff, who contributed whole chapters depicting life in the élite echelons of Internet business, things far beyond the ken of an industry hack like myself. Ramona's brain is on loan (at a stupendous amount per hour) to some of the leading companies in the Internet industry, so I'm deeply grateful and awestruck that she lent her grey cells to me and to this book. By her own account, she's on a single-handed quest to do all of the jobs listed herein, having started as a project manager for advertising agency Chiat/Day in New York, then joining a group of engineers with British Telecom as the European marketing manager of Concert, an international joint venture between BT and MCI. For the last few years she has been a consultant, first with multinational accounting firm KPMG, then as a freelance strategist. Her jobs have taken her into business development, marketing, and even the occasional recruitment as a sideline. 'I truly aspire to become a CEO, or alternatively party planner, because they sound like the coolest job in the book,' she says.

A big thank you must also be made to the more than seventy Internet industry workers, from CEOs to disgruntled programmers, who consented to give their view of things for this book. Thanks also to Bruno Giussani, James Glave, Jason Krause, Leander Kahney, Chris Oakes, Sean Geer, Lizzie Bailey, Scott Raynovich and all the other journalists and writers with whom I've shared such cynical exchanges about the state of the Internet industry over the past few years.

CONTENTS

INTRODUCTION

On a cigarette break outside our offices in Soho, having just finished compiling this book, I was approached by a smiling young man clad in what has become the uniform of the Internet industry: cornflower-blue pressed shirt (sometimes called 'new media blue' because of its prevalence in our industry) with rolled-up sleeves, khaki trousers and black leather shoes, probably from Kenneth Cole. He introduced himself as working for one of the many Internet-related venture capital companies that adorn Soho Square in London these days, and asked what I was working on.

I explained I had just finished writing a book about the Internet industry, and characterised it as 'an outsider's guide to the inside'. He said he looked forward to reading it, and I explained that for anyone who worked inside the industry, it might seem a bit simple, as though I were trying to teach Grandma to suck eggs.

'Ha!' he replied. 'You're assuming that there's anyone in the industry who actually knows anything!'

For anyone who has only seen the Internet industry portrayed in newspapers, magazines or on television, it might seem hopelessly baffling, complex, and as though it has turned the rules of business, and indeed of gravity, on their heads. How can companies that all seem to be unprofitable create so many young, good-looking 'dot.com millionaires'? Why is the collection of text and pictures that makes up the World Wide Web termed a revolution, for business, communication and society at large? And above all, how can the average Joe get a piece of the pie?

The dirty little secret of the Internet industry is that everyone, from the lowliest intern getting business experience to the most highly qualified CEO, is making it up as they go along. Sure, their years of running companies in other industries might be useful background, but Internet companies don't seem to follow the proper rules of business. Almost without exception, successful people working in the industry are not the most experienced, but the most flexible.

There's a whole other set of criteria that the Internet industry looks for when it goes searching for new employees, besides flexibility. Creativity is always a must-have, as is innate intelligence, boundless curiosity, and some kind of basic interest in our crazy revolution. In almost every job, Internet workers (or 'Net slaves' as a famous website of the same name has termed them) put in long hours, and tend to be obsessive about their jobs in a way that workers in other industries are not.

The pay-off, aside from the absurdly high salaries which are due to a lack of knowledgeable applicants, is that every person in the Internet industry gets to own a piece of the revolution. There's an understanding that we're not punching the clock, we're watching history unfold. Some day, when we're all old and grey, we'll be able to tell our grandchildren, 'We were there when modems were 28 baud, when Web pages first had pictures, audio and video, when 19-year-old computer geniuses made a fortune out of their dot.com, when the first adroit shopper bought their weekly groceries from Tesco's website instead of the shop around the corner, when a bright idea put down on paper (the ubiquitous business plan) was all you needed to raise millions from investors, when an Internet company made up of six people could topple its offline competition which employed thousands.' In short, as fellow Internet scribe Sean Geer, author of *The Pocket Guide to the Internet*, is fond of saying, 'when it was all trees round here'.

Of course, the trees are long gone in the recently paved parking lot of the Internet industry. Stock markets have crashed, companies have merged, been acquired, and quietly (or noisily) closed their doors. The glory days have gone for certain, bringing a disturbing note of realism to the young industry. But despite what the doomsayers predicted, the Internet industry didn't disappear, it just grew up. Most savvy observers think a kind of business Darwinism struck dot.comland, killing off the weak and clearing the way for the strong. The boom time for Internet enterprise, when anyone could launch a new company, has passed, but the core idea of the revolution – the idea that a network of computers can change the way the world conducts its business – has remained. Internet executives who used to jet around the world on 'the three Cs – Concorde, champagne and caviare' are now soberly discussing profit projections, cost cutting and good old-fashioned business theory.

But even in the new, grown-up Internet industry, we have a jargon all our own, particularly when it comes to job titles. Since Internet companies tended to be formed by young, entrepreneurial people who were into breaking the rules, many times they haven't bothered to conform to typical business titles. In what other industry would you have a 'Chief Yahoo' (chief executive officer of Yahoo!, one of the largest and most successful Internet companies)? The business of the Internet is simple: come up with a way to run a business on-line, raise money to build the business, hire a technical team to develop the website, hire a marketing team to promote the website, and off you go. But somehow, the people working in the industry have come up with a bizarre selection of job titles that all but obscures their function within the organisation. Check out these real-world examples, derived from an informal poll of industry luminaries, and *Fast Company* magazine's ongoing feature, 'Job Titles of the Future':

Job title	Company	Actual function
Chief Fool	Motleyfool.com	Chief executive officer
Chief Reality Officer	Zwirl.com	Making sure work gets done
Creator of Chaos aka Chief Concept Officer	eGreetings	Coming up with new ideas
Creator of Substance	eGreetings	Finance director
Culture Team Leader	Sapient	Human Resources
Director of Cool Stuff	ICL – an on-line ad agency	Developing online advertisements

Job title	Company	Actual function
Head of New Ideas	Lastminute.com	Planning future strategy
Networked Innovation Evangelist	Self-employed	Consultant
Ruler of the Free World	Freeshop.com	Chief executive officer
Vice-President of Deep Computing	IBM	Corporate manager
Virtual Reality Evangelist	Silicon Graphics	Speaker/writer about virtual reality

For more bizarre job titles and their descriptions, check out *Fast Company* magazine at:
http://www.fastcompany.com/online/resources/jobtitle.html

In the interests of ... well, reality, clarity, sanity and, to some extent, comprehension, this book covers what people in the industry actually *do*, rather than what their title might be. Don't be surprised if the next person you meet at a dot.com party has 'Eradicator of Office Paranoia' instead of 'Personnel' on their business card.

Good luck, and happy browsing!

Activist

Money: From nothing for volunteers through £12,000–£18,000 for work at non-profit organisations all the way to high-profile activists who can command £10,000 just for appearing at a conference.

Hours: As with money, hours range from very few for volunteers through typical 9–5 for those working in non-profits to a manic 24-hour schedule for those activists truly married to their cause.

Health risk: 2/10. Nothing in the activist lifestyle should pose a threat to your health, unless your activism angers the wrong company ... look out for concrete boots.

Pressure rating: 6/10. One prominent activist describes the pressure as 'more stressful than being a quantum physicist, but less stressful than being a short-order cook'.

Glamour rating: 8/10. One of the main elements of being an activist is making yourself into a media magnet. Getting on TV and into the papers should light up the glam-o-meter a bit.

Travel rating: 7/10. Travelling the globe is one of the perks of the position, but beware – you may spend much of your time in anonymous convention centres and business hotels.

On the Internet, the activist is a powerful force, presenting and protecting the rights of the populace from the encroaching forces of business domination and government control. Activists fight all types of causes on-line, but with expertise in their topic they become media spokespeople and have the ear of government.

In the beginning, at least in the Genesis story of the Internet, the worldwide network of computers was monitored, maintained and, yes, loved by that strange strain of humanity known as Geeks. Early Geek spent much of his time in seclusion, lovingly maintaining his computer and nurturing his Internet connection. He lived in universities, research laboratories or government agencies, and indulged the social side of his nature by communicating with others of his ilk through this new medium known as the Internet.

That was the good old days.

In the mid-1990s, the Internet found its way out of the universities, laboratories and government enclaves and into the world at large. Geek found himself suddenly exposed to the World, and found that his loving creation was suddenly being used for all manner of disgusting purposes. (Note: this is not a reference to pornography on the Internet; Geek was whole-heartedly in favour of that.) This was the invasion of the dreaded Commerce. Suddenly, the Internet was not a place of pure science and the art of computer programming, but a free-market economy replete with flashing neon signs, hefty advertising budgets, and a horde of marketeers, all foreign and intensely frightening to the Geek.

The Geek began to fight for his precious Internet and a whole culture of activism emerged as a central part of the Internet economy. These activists were fighting then and are still fighting today to maintain the Internet as a place where the average person has as strong a voice and as powerful a presence as a huge multinational corporation. They are struggling to prevent governments and businesses from exerting too much control over the Internet. With so much hype over making money through on-line businesses, the activists want to re-establish the Internet as a tool of the people for the purposes of communication, not a tool for simply making money.

A number of organisations were established to monitor the development of the commercial Internet. New issues began to crop up as businesses tried to come up with new and varied ways of making money on the Web. Although the US Government had funded much of the development of the Internet, no one wanted them to create the regulations that would govern it. The activists banded together to form their own organisations, and as the Internet has become more and more relevant to everyday people, those organisations have an increasingly important role in the industry as a whole.

One of the most critical issues that galvanises the Internet industry is privacy. As business transactions are conducted on-line, businesses have the capability to store incredible amounts of data about consumers. Companies can track the kinds of sites consumers visit, the types of goods they buy on-line, the searches they conduct in search engines, and the personal information users key into individual websites, such as their age, occupation, address, and date of birth. Each of these data is nearly useless by itself, but an increasingly common practice known as profiling has raised the ire of Internet activists. Profiling companies track all the moves a consumer makes on-line, and compile a database of those moves. By tracking the data over time, they can develop a near-complete image of what kind of interests users have, and what they are likely to buy. That data can be sold on for a profitable sum to e-commerce companies who can target advertising to the particular tastes of each consumer.

As quickly as profiling began to emerge, a massive backlash started against it. A number of organisations began lobbying government officials and companies to stamp out the practice. Among them were the Electronic Privacy Information Centre (EPIC), Junkbusters (a company which sells software to prevent companies from collecting information about you), and Cyber-Rights & Cyber-Liberties, a group working in the UK to prevent all manner of electronic infringements on citizens' rights.

Those groups now play a critical role in helping companies and governments establish rules for the

Internet. They are called upon whenever Internet policies are discussed, and since the electronic age is continually in flux, they are in constant demand. When not helping shape policy, Internet activists are fighting their chosen battles in the press, and in the courtroom, helping shape public and legal opinion about the field.

'With the rapid developments in electronic commerce, issues relating to freedom on the Internet increasingly dominate the interests of both businesses and consumers,' says Chris Ellison, the founder of the Campaign for Internet Freedom, an organisation dedicated to fighting censorship on the Internet. 'According to *Internet* magazine, that makes me one of the forty most influential people in the UK Internet industry.'

Although some of the larger organisations have full-time staff, home-grown efforts like Ellison's are mostly staffed by dedicated volunteers. He describes his average day as: 'Get up (7 a.m.). Travel to work. Give lecture at Brunel University's School of Business and Management. Write page on latest developments in multimedia computing for journal. Travel home. Plough through important Internet Freedom e-mails from my PA. Research latest developments on Internet free speech. Write monthly article for *Practical Internet* magazine. Eat dinner over keyboard. Edit latest article for Internet Freedom site. Post article to site. Reply to e-mails. Drink large glass of wine. Go to bed (midnight).'

So why would anyone bother to make a career out of activism? You can bet it isn't the financial rewards. Like most activists, the Internet variety are driven more by altruism and a commitment to a cause than by any promise of riches. 'I am not paid for doing this but I would be happy to do it as a paid job,' says Yaman Akdeniz, the head of Cyber-Rights & Cyber-Liberties. 'There is not much money involved with public interest groups or non-profits and no one is willing to fund organisations like mine. But there is a need for others to get involved and many do this on a part-time basis. However, this sort of job needs to be done professionally on a full-time basis for the protection and representation of the rights and liberties of the on-line users.'

Akdeniz, like Ellison, runs C-R & C-L on a volunteer basis. Many activists in the industry have second jobs, either at universities or large corporations that support their activism work. The benefit for the university or company is that Internet activists often command a great deal of public attention. Whenever an Internet issue hits the front pages, the press turns to these activists to get an opinionated comment. Having an activist on the staff gives credibility to the 'day job' institution. Akdeniz, a graduate of Leeds University with a law degree, also holds a Masters and is about to finish a PhD in Internet Governance. He's one of the few in the PhD programme who is on speed dial for the BBC, ready to serve as 'talking head' for any Internet story they are covering. Akdeniz says he treats the media carefully, making himself available for them so that when he wants an issue to get high profile treatment, they will pay attention.

'On the days that I need to issue press releases or reports it becomes very stressful because I am basically fighting for media coverage and you need to be very careful about when to issue the releases so as to maximise all your chances with daily newspapers, weekly supplements of daily newspapers, on-line media coverage, etc.,' he says.

Akdeniz tries to attract attention from international news outlets as well. Although Internet policy is generally local, all countries are formulating some kind of legislation related to it. As such, activists tend to have a voice both at home and overseas, particularly in the States. This can call for a lot of travel, when those shoestring budgets permit, to proselytise in other parts of the world.

'When funding is available for travel, it involves travel to all sorts of places as the policy debates on Internet regulation are very much international,' Akdeniz told me by e-mail. 'I am now in Toronto, and next week will be in Istanbul for another Internet related conference. I was supposed to be in Moscow the week after but that clashes with a meeting back in Leeds. After that, the Oxford conference is next. So a lot of travelling is involved and you need to show your face, give papers, and lobby and network with others.'

The conference industry may eventually produce some kind of financial support for the Internet activist. The industry is addicted to conferences, and all those conferences need full rosters of speakers. A qualified expert or activist can command a hefty fee. Activists who are particularly controversial, and therefore worthy of plenty of attention from the press, find their speaking fees increasing exponentially.

Ellison says, however, that he's still waiting for his ship to roll in. 'Some people might think that being in the eye of the media is glamorous, but I'm still awaiting that limousine and salary to match.'

For every cause on the Internet, there's an organisation somewhere fighting to change things. Far from being marginalised, these activists play a critical role in the way the industry develops, and in educating government and big business both in the way things are, and the way things should be.

SKILLS YOU'LL NEED

Excellent writing and speaking ability for presenting your views to the media and the industry at large. A full understanding of the machinations of the Internet, and how businesses and governments work together to monitor cyberspace.

GETTING THE JOB

- Enquire at organisations you are interested in as to whether they have positions available.
- Submit articles to journals covering the issue.
- Present yourself and your expertise to journalists reporting on the Internet. The more well known you become, the more valuable a spokes-

person you become for your cause.
- Attend all relevant conferences, and develop contacts within the field.

TIPS

- Keep current on issues facing the Internet industry. Read trade magazines and the business press to know what's making headlines, and what battles are being fought. Publications like *Wired* offer debate on how the world is affected by technology, while business publications like the *Industry Standard*, *Business 2.0* and *Red Herring* discuss how the commercial world is affected by the Internet.
- Develop an area of expertise. What issue on the Internet is most important to you? Read up on the subject, become familiar with the players involved, and begin contributing to discussion groups and publications on the subject.
- Become involved with the various groups that deal with Internet issues. All these groups have websites, and many hold conferences and meetings for concerned parties to air their views. While not all will have a job available, you can always volunteer to get your name out there and begin meeting figures involved in the struggle.
- Participate in on-line forums that share your concerns. There are hundreds of bulletin boards and chat groups for every issue of importance. Since the Internet is decentralised and global, much of the communication between interested parties happens on-line.
- Write to political figures and businesses. Familiarise yourself with which companies and government officials are relevant to your issue. If you intend to make an impact on policy, it's important to know them as your opponents and as your friends. As people in power, they can help you accomplish your goals.

USEFUL ADDRESSES

- Campaign for Internet Freedom, BCM Box 6237, London WC1N 3XX, UK.
TEL +44 (0) 20 7681 1559.
FAX +44 (0) 20 7681 1559.
www.netfreedom.org;
campaign@netfreedom.org
- Cyber-Rights and Cyber-Liberties, Centre for Criminal Justice Studies, University of Leeds, Leeds LS2 9JT, UK.
TEL +44 (0) 709 2199011.
FAX +44 (0) 709 2199011.
www.cyber-rights.co.uk;
lawya@leeds.ac.uk
- Electronic Frontier Foundation, 1550 Bryant Street, Suite 725, San Francisco, CA 94103 USA.
TEL +1 415 436 9333.
FAX +1 415 436 9993.
www.eff.org; info@eff.org
- Electronic Privacy Information Centre, 666 Pennsylvania Ave., SE, Suite 301, Washington, DC 20003, USA.
TEL +1 202 544 9240.
FAX +1 202 547 5482.
www.epic.org/; info@epic.org
- Foundation for Information Policy Research, 9 Stavordale Road, London N5 1NE, UK.
TEL +44 (0) 20 7354 2333.
FAX +44 (0) 20 7827 6534.
www.fipr.org; cb@fipr.org

● Junkbusters Corp., PO Box 7034,
Green Brook, NJ 08812, USA.
TEL +1 908 753 7861.
junkbuster@junkbuster.com
● Wired, 520 3rd St., 3rd Floor,
San Francisco, CA 94107-1815, USA.
TEL +1 303 945 1910.
FAX +1 303 684 9182.
www.wired.com/wired;
info@wired.com

Advertising Sales

Money: Sales managers at top sites make between £80,000 and £120,000. Entry-level sales jobs start at below £20,000, but a little experience goes a long way.

Hours: Up early for breakfast meetings and out late for cocktail parties. On-line salespeople work 'schmoozing hours'.

Health risk: See above.

Pressure rating: 6/10. Ads bring money in the door – the future of the company is in your hands.

Glamour rating: 7/10. If **schmooze-and-booze** is your cup of tea, this job has it all.

Travel rating: 10/10. It's a global economy, which means salespeople need to have a jet-set life. Get ready for frequent flyer miles.

Those annoying banners that pop up on Web pages are the life-blood of any Internet company; every click means another penny in the bank. But competition to sell advertising space on-line is fierce.

When the Internet was still a toy for researchers and university students, no one worried how it was going to be paid for. But as it moved into the commercial world, there was a flurry of attempts to make the Internet profitable. In those heady days, no one understood how a medium could be almost like TV, but without valuable adverts, and almost like magazines, but without someone paying a subscription fee.

Nowadays, the Internet industry is still figuring out how to make money. One of the most popular choices is to build a site, attract a load of visitors, get them to come back all the time, and then either 1) sell them things or 2) direct advertising at them.

'Money makes the world go round,' says Jonathan Bill, sales director for Real Media, a company that sells advertising for a variety of Internet companies. 'We generate one of the streams of revenue that enable dot.com companies to thrive.'

The most typical form of advertising on the Internet is the banner ad. The practice started in 1994, when the Internet was still in its infancy. One of the first banner ads appeared on the HotWired site, the website for the forward thinking *Wired* magazine. It was an ad for Zima, the briefly popular clear malt beverage aimed at young, hip people, the kind that Zima saw as flocking to HotWired. It was the first time a major company, and a major website, exchanged money for ad traffic.

By the end of 1999, on-line advertising spending had reached £50 million in the UK alone, and analysts predict it will reach £625 million by 2004 (Fletcher Research). Selling advertising has now become one of the most popular, and lucrative, ways to make money on the Internet.

Web companies generally fall into one of three categories: 1) those selling services, 2) those selling goods, and 3) those selling nothing, but offering some type of free entertainment, product or service.

The sites that sell nothing have several ways of making money. Some sell sponsorship, in which other companies pay to have their logo appearing somewhere on the page and most of the rest sell advertising.

A big part of the job is meeting and greeting. On-line sales people traverse the globe, attending conferences and industry events, ready at any moment to drop into a conversation about demographics. Advertisers will want to know everything about your site: how many people visit, how long they visit for, how often they visit, and what kind of people they are. There's also a curious statistic the industry has invented called the **click-through** rate. This relates to how many people visited your site and clicked on a banner ad while they were there. Click-through rates have been largely discredited as a **metric** for measuring the advertising appeal of a website, primarily because rates have been so low. The advertising industry decided that even though viewers weren't *clicking* on a banner ad they were *seeing* it, and therefore the ad made an impact. A newer metric emerged, that of the page view. A page view means not how long someone stays at a certain site, but how many times he or she performs an action while they are there. The new metric has come to be called an **impression**.

Another way websites measure their value to advertisers is the number of unique users they attract – in other words, not only how many times a person accesses the site, but how many different people access the site. But whatever metric happens to be the flavour of the month, ad sales people are reliant on a company called Media Metrix, which measures which site is servicing the largest number of users.

A conversation between two advertising sales people might sound something like this:

Online ad exec 1: 'How *are* you? We *must* do lunch! It's been *too* long!'
Online ad exec 2: 'Fab! Things are going great! Our user sessions are increasing, and page views are up twenty-five per cent.'
1: 'Fab! Our unique users are up twenty-eight per cent, and we soared four places in the Media Metrix ratings.'
2: 'We're not measuring unique users any more, we decided to measure by *fluidity*.' (Note: at the time of writing, this was still a fictional metric!)
1: 'Fluidity?'
2: 'Yeah, it's the measure of how many users travel through our site without changing the pace of their clicks.'
And so on.

All these details have to be stored in the advertising executive's brain, ready to be trotted out at the drop of a hat, or at least the sighting of a prospective client. With however many million websites out there, all fighting for a slice of the pie, the on-line ad exec has to quickly figure out how to distinguish him or her from the crowd.

'[The job] is a combination of face-to-face, cold calling, telephone sales, e-mail proposals, lunches and schmoozing at **networking** events in the evening,' says Davina Lines, who heads up advertising sales, among other things, at NetImperative, a Web company started in 1999. 'You have to be able to recall at any time what opportunities are available, where they will be positioned, the target audience of each area of the site, the amount of traffic, unique users and user sessions in any given period. Skills required – aside from a fundamental ability to sell – are persistence allied with patience, personality alongside professionalism, self-motivation and teamwork, understanding of your industry and a very good memory.'

Jonathan Bill says that a beginner in on-line ad sales can be successful more quickly 'by learning, absorbing and reading about the on-line ad industry, by approaching the right company and by realising that on-line sales is far more consultative and professional than other forms of ad sales – honesty, creativity and genuine interest are the key attributes. Obviously being able to sell helps, as does a cast-iron constitution.'

As with many jobs in the Internet industry, there's scarcely an average day. In fact, for advertising executives, there's scarcely an average hour. But from breakfast meeting to cocktail party, the life in ad sales is schmooze, schmooze, schmooze.

'Some would think that the fact that on-line sales people get to go out to lunch or dinner in the best restaurants on expenses, drink free drink at industry parties, travel abroad to meetings and stay at hotels would be extremely glamorous, and sometimes it is,' says Lines. 'What they don't see is all the crap and hard work that goes with it.'

Lines got into the field the same way many on-line ad sales people do: through traditional media. She sold ads for local newspapers and trade magazines, finally landing at *New Media Age*, a magazine that covers the convergence of media and technology. Here, she received a crash course on the Internet, and went on to co-found NetImperative, along with its feature website, netimperative.com – a news and information site for the new media industry which has a number of advertising clients well versed in what makes a website sell.

'[Selling] is an important role in any on-line business as the sales team act as the face of the company they work for, by being out and about more than most,' says Lines. 'However, I do not think that means the sales function is any more or less important than any other role within a company. I hate the tired, stereotypical retort of "Well, if we weren't out there bringing in the money you wouldn't have a job", as if the receptionist wasn't answering the phone or the accounts department weren't processing the invoices or the developers weren't developing, there would still be a product to sell. Sales people tend to play a huge role in communication throughout the industry generally.'

SKILLS YOU'LL NEED

A good memory, a people-friendly attitude, and a fearless willingness to ring people and ask them for money.

GETTING THE JOB

- Learn the difference between a website whose revenue is derived from advertising (i.e. a content site) and one which makes money from selling goods (an e-commerce site).
- The Internet makes job-hunting easy. Cruise websites that look interesting. Most sites have a 'Jobs' page for open positions.
- If sites don't have positions listed, try sending an e-mail asking about sales jobs.
- *New Media Age*, *Campaign* and other publications have jobs listings in the industry. Don't just consult them once, but regularly.
- Networking is a part of the job, but it's also a part of getting the job. Lots of advertising hiring takes place on the principle of 'it's not what you know, it's who you know'.
- Companies will expect you to sell yourself as hard as you will sell them. Remember this in the interview.

TIPS

- Familiarise yourself with the way advertising and marketing are different in a wired world. Understand what companies hope to get out of on-line advertising – i.e. brand recognition, and traffic from your website.
- Frequent industry events, remembering that the deal-making only starts after the second coffee and pastry or the third glass of wine.
- Stay current on the news of the industry. Publications like *New Media Age* and *Campaign* are crucial for finding out both who's hiring and who's buying ads.
- Be prepared to work on commission. Advertising sales in the on-line world is much like its off-line counterpart. With pay cheques based on results, you need to work hard to get rewards.

GLOSSARY

- **Click-through**

When a Web surfer clicks on an advertisement, taking the surfer through to the advertiser's site, this is termed a click-through. The number of click-throughs is one of many statistics (or metrics) sites use to determine the success of an on-line advertising campaign.

- **Impression**

A new buzzword in on-line advertising. Customers seeing your ad aren't supposed to buy something, they're just supposed to remember your company's name.

- **Metric**

A statistic used to measure the success of an on-line advertising campaign. A variety of metrics are used by the industry, since there is no firm agreement as to which statistic matters most.

- **Networking**

The leading activity at the schmooze-and-booze. The guy you're talking to may not buy an ad, but someone he knows might be dating the sister of the cousin of the on-line media buyer for AOL.

● **Schmooze-and-booze**
The unending string of cocktail parties advertising salespeople have to attend. All deals are done over cheap Chardonnay in this industry.

USEFUL ADDRESSES

● Campaign, Haymarket Business Publications Ltd, 10 Cabot Square, Canary Wharf, London E14 4QB, UK.
TEL +44 (0) 20 8845 8545.
FAX +44 (0) 20 8606 7301.
www.campaignlive.com

● The Net Imperative, 1st Floor, 40 Great Eastern Street, London EC2A 3EP, UK.
TEL +44 (0) 20 7684 8181.
FAX +44 (0) 20 7684 3481.
www.netimperative.com;
info@netimperative.com

● New Media Age, St Giles House, 49–51 Poland Street, London W1V 4AX, UK.
TEL +44 (0) 20 7970 4000.
FAX +44 (0) 20 7970 4898.
www.newmediaage.co.uk

ANALYST

MONEY: From £40,000 to £200,000 for run-of-the-mill analysts. A lonely few that attain stratospheric heights can make much, much more.

HOURS: Unlike in other parts of the Internet industry, analysts get to work a 9–5 day. Those on the financial side may put in more.

HEALTH RISK: 2/10. Good money, easy work. What health risk?

PRESSURE RATING: 4/10. As long as you don't make catastrophic mistakes, the pressure is minimal.

GLAMOUR RATING: 6/10. A range in this profession. Doing research has never been the sexiest of jobs, but those who make bold (and accurate) predictions find themselves getting plenty of attention from the industry and the financial press.

TRAVEL RATING: 4/10. The odd trip to industry conferences, but this isn't a jet-setting job.

No newspaper or magazine article about the Internet is complete without some variation on the phrase 'Edward P. Sangfroid, an analyst with Bigshot Investment Bank, said the company's actions were in keeping with their overall strategy'. These analysts spend their working days crunching numbers and studying corporate annual reports, making themselves into experts on Internet companies.

Analysts working in the technology world come in two flavours: those that cover the financials of Internet business, and those that examine the adoption and usefulness of new technologies. In general terms, the financial analysts come from large investment banks, and the technologists work for research companies.

Economists and bankers study every industry, but with the Internet changing so much of what is familiar in business and society, analysts in this sector are in much higher demand. They respond to a never-ending stream of companies, governments and journalists, all looking for answers to the questions How Big Is It? and What Does It All Mean?

The Internet seems to become more important all the time. More people are using it to shop, chat, learn, and conduct their business. More businesses are using Internet technology to become more efficient, increase productivity, and improve distribution. Even slow-moving governments are crawling towards the Internet, using the new medium to communicate better with constituents and revitalise their archaic systems. All these changes are measured in excruciating detail by an army of analysts. On a regular basis, they release their **findings** to an eager public, in **reports** with titles like 'E-commerce Growth in 2000' and 'Internet Telephony Expansion in Europe'.

Statistics are the life-blood of the

analyst. But their task doesn't begin and end with numbers. The second part of the equation is to figure out what the numbers mean.

Analysts who work for research organisations are generally beholden to a client, often a corporation, who wants to know if the product it's pushing will be well received in the marketplace. These analysts look at the industry as a whole, and try to help the client position the offering to the market in which it will be most successful. A number of research firms are generally held to be the leaders in the Internet and technology space, among them Gartner Group, Jupiter Communications, Forrester Research, and IDC (International Data Corp.).

These companies examine the Internet in minute detail, with analysts and researchers who specialise in every possible sector of the market. Although an analyst might be hired for a good general knowledge of the industry, they quickly develop an area of expertise. Some will study only companies that sell things on the Internet, and are given the title e-commerce analyst. Others work specifically on **ISPs** like AOL and Freeserve, and thousands more study smaller niche markets like on-line stockbrokers, travel, or business-to-business exchanges.

Research firms undertake specialised analysis for specific companies, but often a large part of their income comes from reports. These reports are compiled by teams of researchers and tackle general questions such as 'How much money is being spent on on-line advertising?' Most companies working through the Internet are interested in these numbers and the accompanying analysis, and so fork out hefty sums (as much as £1,000 for a 100-page report).

When not working on general research, or helping client companies with specific research needs, analysts spend a good portion of their time talking to the press. Journalists and analysts have a complicit understanding (although at times it's more like mutual loathing) about their relationship. Journalists need analysts to express an opinion and provide a useful perspective when something of importance happens in the industry. Analysts need to keep their name in the press to keep clients buying their research services and to promote their work. The mutual loathing part comes in when journalists resent the analysts for a) making more money for doing essentially the same job and b) getting free advertising. Analysts resent the journalists for a) getting for free what the client is paying thousands for and b) calling at the last minute and insisting on taking up valuable time in the interests of their deadline.

Noah Yasskin is Director of European Research at Jupiter Communications, one of the leading companies producing reports on all sectors of the Internet. He says that one of the major differences between industry analysts and financial analysts is that the financial types spend a lot of time crunching numbers, while the more cerebral industry analysts look at emerging trends.

'People use us for a variety of different business needs. At the highest level, they use us for strategic and tactical advice, and they use our data and forecasts to plug into their business plans, and to understand trends in the industry or to see through the hype.'

While a financial analyst might have a background in banking or finance, industry analysts come from all walks of life. Yasskin himself joined Jupiter Research as a research associate after abandoning his postgraduate studies in philosophy. He worked his way up into an analyst's position, before being promoted to Director of European Research. He didn't have any formal education or training in research or the Internet industry, but says that the skills he learned in his scholastic career have helped him develop an analytical approach to studying the Internet industry.

He explains that the foremost responsibility of the industry analyst is producing and writing reports, followed by briefing and advising clients and talking to the press. A less significant responsibility is making presentations at conferences and gatherings promoting the research the company has produced.

'You have to be able to write well and have some analytical skills, in terms of being able to see beyond the hype that clouds the market,' he says.

Analysts with investment banks have much the same relationship with journalists, but are less reliant on them for publicity. Most large investment banks will have teams devoted to studying the Internet. Significant players in this market have traditionally been large American houses, like Goldman Sachs, JP Morgan, Morgan Stanley, Merrill Lynch and Credit Suisse First Boston, but as the Internet economy takes off in Europe, large European banks are getting into the game as well.

Their work consists mainly of assessing the financial worth of companies in the Internet sector – their clients are investors who want to know if a certain company is a good investment. They are interested to a small extent in how technology works and how many people use it, but their primary focus is how much money it is likely to make. Investment analysts examine companies' management teams and strategies to see how likely they are to be successful.

'Analysts [in the finance world] come in three sizes,' says Huw van Steenis, an equity analyst covering e-finance and financial service strategy for JP Morgan Europe. 'Economists, who comment on macroeconomic trends impacting investment decisions; strategists, who advise on how to allocate assets between industrial sectors; and company analysts – the large majority – who make recommendations on between six to twelve companies which they follow day to day. My role sits between the last two as I cover some e-finance companies, such as the on-line brokers, and advise more generally on the impact of e-commerce on financial services.'

Internet companies have turned the financial world on its head. These companies, sometimes running up annual losses totalling millions of pounds, have been extremely popular when floated on public markets. The old rules of finance have been subverted, requiring analysts to be clairvoyant as they try to figure out which loss-making company should be valued at a billion-pound figure, and which should be tossed on the scrapheap.

'The role splits into four parts and any one day may have some mix of these,' van Steenis says. 'First, meeting and reading about the companies one covers. Second, thinking time – to formulate one's views and doing background research. Third, advising investors on what they should be doing with their investments. Fourth, periodically analysts will also get involved in the primary business of the bank such as bringing a company to the capital markets or supporting merger work.'

The old rules of the banking world still apply to analysts covering the Internet. When you're young, and just getting started, you slog away into the early hours of the morning trying to make your mark, and impress the boss. But as in many other areas of the Internet, the banking industry rewards workers who have an understanding of how the technology works, and where it can be successful. 'Starting salaries are typical investment banking salaries,' says van Steenis. 'The very best analysts on the street in a hot sector can be earning million pound bonuses. When investors are betting millions on your advice, stress levels can rise fast. The most stressful time is when you make an investment call which is quite at odds with current market orthodoxy. If you're right, clients will be delighted, but if it turns sour, then it's quite another matter.

'There's no avoiding the issue that it is hard work and you're really on the spot.'

SKILLS YOU'LL NEED

Research and analytical thinking skills, writing ability and a good presentation manner are paramount. An understanding of the Internet industry, which many analysts learn in an entry-level position, is also critical for moving ahead in the field.

GETTING THE JOB

- Leading Internet research firms usually have a number of entry-level positions in which a recent graduate can learn the ropes. Keep an eye out for job postings with titles like research associate and research assistant.
- Search the Web and periodicals for recent research by the company you are applying for a position with. Being able to mention their recent work can't fail to impress.
- Develop a speciality within the industry. Becoming an expert makes a you a hot commodity.

TIPS

- Brush up on research theory.

A big part of the job will be number collection and distillation, using statistics to analyse the industry and predict trends.

- Keep abreast of those trends by reading constantly, both trade and industry publications and mainstream media. Knowing which topics are hot will help develop the most relevant research.

● Hone your presentation skills. The better the pitch you make for your research, the higher your standing within the industry will be.

GLOSSARY

● **Findings**
The result of weeks of research spent crunching numbers and examining trends, all so that analysts can complete the phrase 'our findings show ...'

● **ISP**
Internet Service Provider – a company that sells consumers basic connectivity to the Net.

● **Research reports**
Fantastically priced compilations of research covering every aspect of the Internet industry. Statistics can prove anything, and this industry needs statistics by the boatload.

USEFUL ADDRESSES

● Credit Suisse First Boston, 1 Cabot Square, London E14 4QJ, UK.
TEL +44 (0) 20 7888 8888.
FAX +44 (0) 20 7888 2243.
www.csfb.com; info@csfb.com

● Forrester Research, UK Research Centre, 9–14 Windmill St, London W1P 1HF, UK.
TEL +44 (0) 20 7631 0202.
FAX +44 (0) 20 7631 5252.
www.forrester.co.uk

● Gartner Group, 56 Top Gallant Rd, PO Box 10212, Stamford, CT 06904-2212, USA.
TEL +1 203 316 1111.
FAX +1 203 316 6300.
www.gartner.com;
gginfo@gartner.com

● Goldman Sachs International, Peterborough Court, 133 Fleet St, London EC4A 2BB, UK.
TEL +44 (0) 20 7774 1000.
FAX +44 (0) 20 7774 2422.
www.goldman.com

● IDC UK, 6 Dukes Gate, Acton Lane, Chiswick, London W4 5DX, UK.
TEL +44 (0) 20 8987 7100.
FAX +44 (0) 20 8747 0212.
www.idcresearch.co.uk;
agleed@idc.com

● JP Morgan, 60 Victoria Embankment, London EC4Y 0JP, UK.
TEL +44 (0) 20 7600 2300.
FAX +44 (0) 20 7325 8689.
www.jpmorgan.com

● Jupiter Communications, 32 Haymarket, Piccadilly, London SW1Y 4TP, UK.
TEL +44 (0) 20 7747 0500.
FAX +44 (0) 20 7747 0510.
www.jup.com; jupiter@jup.com

● Merrill Lynch Europe, Ropemaker Place, 25 Ropemaker St, London EC2Y 9LY, UK.
TEL +44 (0) 20 7628 1000.
FAX +44 (0) 20 7867 4040.
www.ml.com

● Morgan Stanley UK Group, 25 Cabot Square, Canary Wharf, London E14 4QA, UK.
TEL +44 (0) 20 7513 8000.
FAX +44 (0) 20 7425 8990.
www.msdw.com

ANIMATOR

MONEY: £12,000 for beginning, low-level programmers to over £100,000 for high-end Web animation experts and producers.

HOURS: Animators work the hours other programmers work. Show up around noon and leave around midnight.

HEALTH RISK: 3/10, except that extreme exposure to **Shockwave** and **Flash** animations can cause epileptic fits and nausea.

PRESSURE RATING: 5/10. Until the £100 million pound failure of Boo.com, attributed to lousy animations, among other things, the pressure was only average. Post-Boo, things look a bit more severe.

GLAMOUR RATING: 4/10. With a few exceptions, not a job that guarantees a lot of black-tie exposure.

TRAVEL RATING: 1/10. It's almost guaranteed that your travel will consist of the commute from home to office.

Animators working on the Internet come in two flavours: those doing the dogsbody work designing advertisements and simple animations, and those in the more glamorous field of producing animations designed to entertain. Both camps, however, face an essential paradox: design it big and beautiful, and your website will crash; design it small and uncomplicated, and you'll get by, but at the expense of creativity.

Internet companies crave **bandwidth** like kleptomaniacs crave power shortages in security systems: there's just never enough. The promise of the World Wide Web was not just that it could distribute information around the world (the Internet could already do that before the Web came along) but that it could deliver multimedia around the world: audio, video, text, you name it. Website developers quickly came to realise that although it was theoretically possible to build a site that looked like something out of a hi-tech fantasy film, the reality was that massive multimedia files were bogging down the delivery times to the extent that they were impractical.

But what proved damaging for actual video was a boon to animation. Animation was low-bandwidth, and didn't necessarily need to contain an audio file. Off-line animators have found their skill set has a huge new demand in the on-line world.

'The biggest advantage that animation has today is in picture quality,' writes Jon Healey, a technology journalist with the *San Jose Mercury News*. 'A dial-up Internet connection delivers lousy video but vivid cartoons.'

But it wasn't only technical restrictions which helped animation succeed on-line; it was also the audience animation caters to. While a sophisticated adult audience might prefer a live video feed from CNN, the bulk of Internet users in the early days weren't necessarily the busy, news-hungry businessperson. Net users were predominantly teenage and young adult males, who would choose the foul-mouthed verbal lacerations of *South Park* over a live Web feed of *Panorama*.

Like every kind of entertainment, animation has morphed as it transitioned to a fully digital format. While in the old days, animators sat hunched over hand-painted, individual cells, new software programs and tools have helped make animation feasible in record time. The trick nowadays is to make the animation downloadable in small enough pieces that websites won't get bogged down. 'In these modern days, Web animators may not have to spend seventeen hours hand painting cells to make Dopey wink, but bandwidth, platform, and browser issues make animation for the Web its own special hell,' advises the website Animation Express in its on-line tutorial for website animation.

The key to becoming an animator on the Web today is a mastery of software tools. A horde of technologies has been developed in the last decade to perfect the delivery of animation on-line. The leading names in the field are Shockwave and Flash (from Macromedia) and **QuickTime**, but hundreds of others for more specialist development are available as well.

The Web animator is charged with the task of making sites more interesting, but not so interesting that the pages don't load. The highest-profile example of this was the briefly infamous Boo.com. Boo proudly told the world about its big plans for using animation on its retail sports site. Customers could visit the site and view items from any perspective, accompanied by an animated sales assistant known as **Miss Boo**. Unfortunately, Miss Boo and her accompanying animated features put such a drain on the resources of most customers' Internet connections that she ended up crashing the machines of more customers than she managed to sell clothing to. Only six months after the site was launched, the company had spent $130 million, went belly-up and called in the liquidators.

The gurus at Animation Express are familiar with the Catch-22 posed by animation. 'We've lived the paradox,' they write. 'Make it big and beautiful, and only some of your audience can see it; make it small and limited, and everyone can see it. We've been through the trials and errors of clunky first, second, and third versions of the hordes of graphics and animation programs. We've spent years muddling our way through new interfaces, finding workarounds for bugs, and struggling with the long way until we could forge our own short cuts.'

With the example of Boo.com looming large, animators' expertise and knowledge of the Animation Express 'paradox' are as important as ever. Animation is being used for everything from simple banner ads to virtual shop assistants to entertainment in the form of short films, and the whole field is expanding immeasurably.

Some Web animators were computer programmers who found their way into animation from a hi-tech or multimedia background. Others were exploring animation through film or television and found that the Internet could give them access to a broader audience than any other medium.

'From our point of view as a production company, we think the Internet offers some fantastic new opportunities for broadcasting existing work,' says Michael Rose, head of film and TV productions at Aardman Animations in Bristol, makers of the famous Wallace and Gromit cartoons. 'But it's also a new creative opportunity. There's a whole cyber universe opening up.' Aardman made animation history at the Cannes 2000 film festival when one of its shorts, *Angry Kid*, became the first animated piece only broadcast over the Internet to be nominated for an award.

'In the case of *Angry Kid*, the Internet is the best home for it,' Rose says. '[Each episode] is a lively little film in its own right. Because they're short [each episode is a minute long], they're easily compressible, and easily downloadable.'

Another hero from the animation world has found that his particular brand of humour is perfectly suited to the Net. Spike Decker, infamous in the US for his Sick & Twisted Festival of Animations, found that after more than twenty years of cult herodom, he's found widespread success on the Internet.

'The Internet has been a great thing to come along,' he says. 'I'm tired of being a pioneer and not getting a payday. We've got so much stuff that could be exploited.'

Short, animated films like Spike's are appealing in that they are suited to slow download speeds for the bandwidth-challenged, but they are especially suited to what is still the most dominant Internet audience – 18- to 35-year-old men. In fact, Spike's selections are so graphic that the Internet is the only place, aside from late-night cinematic screenings, where the Sick & Twisted Festival of Animation can get past broadcasting regulations. 'It's so sick and twisted, I can't even sell it to cable,' Decker says.

SKILLS YOU'LL NEED

Expertise in the various forms of animation software, but also knowledge of the technical limitations of the Internet and the connection speeds of people who will be accessing your site. Also an understanding of what types of content are best suited to the audience you are trying to reach, and the site your work will be featured on.

GETTING THE JOB

- First, make sure you have the skills. Website animationexpress.com has a series of on-line tutorials you can take to learn about Web animation and the various tools.
- Develop an on-line portfolio to showcase some of your animation. You can direct prospective employers to this site.
- Follow discussion groups on-line. Often employers will list job openings in discussion groups related to the position they are trying to fill.

TIPS

- Participate in on-line discussion boards addressing the newest developments in Web animation. You can increase your expertise exponentially by sharing with others in the field. On-line newsgroups like comp.graphics.animation, alt.animation and macromedia.flash carry running discussions on the latest and greatest in the field.

- Pay attention to animations used in fields other than the one you are working in. If advertising is your speciality, watch the artistic and entertainment world for new developments, and vice versa.
- Keep expanding your knowledge of software programs and other tools for producing animation. As with many areas of technical programming, you can never rest on your laurels for too long, or the technology will advance without you.

GLOSSARY

- **Bandwidth**

The Achilles' heel of the animator. This is the pipeline that supplies the Internet, and there's never enough of it to satisfy the dreams of multimedia producers.

- **Flash, Shockwave, QuickTime**

Web animation software that has become the hammer, screwdriver, and spanner of the web animator's toolkit.

- **Miss Boo**

The animated virtual personal shopper of Boo.com which has become a mascot for over-the-top Web animation that does more harm than good.

USEFUL ADDRESSES

- Aardman Animations, Gas Ferry Rd, Bristol BS1 6UN, UK.
TEL +44 (0) 117 984 8485.
FAX +44 (0) 117 922 7225.
www.aardman.com;
info@aardman.com
- Animation Express, 520 3rd Street, 3rd Floor, San Francisco, CA 94107-1815, USA.
TEL +1 415 276 8400.
FAX +1 415 276 8500.
www.hotwired.com/animation;
animation@hotwired.com
- Atom Films, Warwick House, 9 Warwick St, London W1R 5RA, UK.
TEL +44 (0) 20 7734 6161.
FAX +44 (0) 20 7734 6162.
www.atomfilms.com;
info@atomfilms.com
- Brilliant Digital Entertainment, 6355 Topanga Canyon Blvd, Ste 120 , Woodland Hills, CA 91367, USA.
TEL + 1 818 615 1500.
FAX +1 818 712 0810.
www.bde3d.com; info@bde3d.com
- Dotcomix, 2727 Mariposa, Studio 100, San Francisco, California 94110, USA.
TEL +1 415 522 6500.
FAX +1 415 522 6522.
www.dotcomix.com;
info@dotcomix.com
- Macromedia Europe, Pyramid House, Easthampstead Rd, Bracknell, Berkshire RG12 1NS, UK.
TEL +44 (0) 1344 458 600.
FAX 44 (0) 1344 458 666.
www.macromedia.com/uk/;
europe@macromedia.com
- Mondo Media, 135 Mississippi St, San Francisco, CA 94107, USA.
TEL +1 415 865 2700.
FAX +1 415 865 2645.
www.mondomedia.com;
content@mondomedia.com

BRAND SPECIALIST

MONEY: A **brand** specialist may earn from £25,000 to £60,000. They have usually been a designer or consultant first.

HOURS: Normal office hours prevail, with the odd late night spent creating the perfect presentation materials for the client.

HEALTH RISK: 4/10. Brand specialists tend to be cool, respected professionals who are held in some awe: they rarely have to slug it out with anyone over a logo.

PRESSURE RATING: 7/10. The pressure is high for brand specialists to be creative and innovative, and they are usually working for people who see the work as urgent.

GLAMOUR RATING: 9/10. Branding people and their offices are very trendy and glamorous (think *Wallpaper* magazine).

TRAVEL RATING: 4/10. Brand specialists will rarely travel far from the urban epicentre. They would lose their creative edge without enough espresso.

A good brand has always been one of the key assets of a large company, seen as inseparable from its reputation. A good brand is also vital for new Internet-driven companies who are launching in crowded markets. The company's challenge is to be remembered, and to promise prospective customers something significant enough so that they break their current consumer habits and relationships. Key to developing a good brand is the brand specialist, a cross between artist and priest. Branding is a weird science, combining the best marketing intellect with the keenest sense of design. In an atmosphere of new companies launching, and older companies realising they need to do things differently, branding is emerging as a key profession, and becoming a very popular career choice in the new media field.

You can't open a business publication without being confronted by someone speaking about 'brands'. Not just a logo, a brand in the age of the Internet is the general perception the public has of a company. Is the company cool? Dignified? Discount? Old-school? New-school? Left back a year? Class genius? A brand specialist decides how a company should be perceived by its public, and then sets about creating that perception with a combination of advertising, marketing materials, logos, and a catchy slogan. A brand specialist is the image consultant to the Internet industry. And as dot.coms vie with one another to be more than 'just another money-losing Internet company', brand is the battleground on which they've chosen to fight.

Seems abstract? Maybe so, but branding is big business. Internet companies spend millions on branding to inspire public sympathy or interest in their company, a new product, or even if they're not quite satisfied with the way their company is currently perceived. In Internet terms, if the company is doing poorly, it's not time to rethink the business plan, lay off some staff or attempt a merger: it merely needs to 'rebrand' itself to become something more trendy! 'Good brand strategy is the invisible force that makes communications, cultures and business great,' says Simon Mottram, head of strategy for branding specialist Sapient.

Most brand specialists, like Mottram, act as consultants to companies, usually working for specialist firms who focus on developing the ideas and infra-structure for a new brand, or for a division of an all-around Internet and e-commerce company. Developing a brand means they have to marshal a whole set of talents: people who can write, people who understand cultural change in organisations, and people who have excellent design skills.

Brand development affects far more than the external look and feel of the brand. Proper brand specialists are not acting as mere designers, changing logos and brochures, but are working with organisations to help them understand themselves so that they can communicate accurately, truthfully and meaningfully with the outside world.

Brand specialists actually come in several flavours, and from several backgrounds. The core of branding has often been seen as good design, although other relevant backgrounds may be in broader marketing communications, business consultancy or project management. Most brand specialists act as advisers on building or changing brands, but they have a client-side counterpart whose job it is to be the brand manager or steward. This person is responsible for how the brand appears to people. Brand specialists have coined a number of phrases for themselves; one example from Mottram: 'I think the term brand architect comes closest to describing what I hope I am doing at Sapient.'

So what exactly is the output of the brand specialist? The brand is a central idea or vision, which is expressed in a number of ways. Think about all the places where you interact with a company: you will see its advertising and public relations output; you will (if it has a physical presence) **experience** its store environments or possibly see its trucks or people in uniform; you will have an experience of buying its products or services; and you will have a relationship with people who represent the company. The sum total of these components is the **identity** of a corporation, in the same way that a combination of our natural attributes, name, looks, and choice of clothing constitutes our identity.

Although brand specialists started out as niche agencies, many are now owned by large communications conglomerates such as WPP (originally Wire & Plastic Products plc). Despite this, branding remains something of a specialist cottage industry. Branding consultants usually have beautifully designed offices, work in small teams, and exude a certain mystique and intellectual character that most marketing people do not. They have a special relationship with their clients, becoming involved at important times but keeping long-term advisory relationships. According to Louise Jorden of consultancy Rufus Leonard, a senior brand consultant will need to develop long-term relationships with key decision-makers in organisations in order to guarantee an understanding of the organisation in the event of branding activity taking place.

Although the atmosphere around branding is very intense, brand specialists themselves like to keep their cool. They don't want to ruffle their impeccably groomed exterior, and are very good at the cool put-down, such as, 'Of course, that is so 1973.' Also, branding tends to be a very local activity; as Mottram states, 'Brands tend to be highly culturally specific, therefore travel is unlikely to be significant. I usually get to the US and European countries a few times a year.'

How does one become a high priest/priestess of branding? There isn't one hard and fast career path, although it is certain that in order to make it as a brand specialist you need to prove adept at both creative and detail thinking, or, to look at it another way, be comfortable with elements of the arts and the sciences.

Looking at the most common backgrounds for brand specialists, you'll find design, computer science, mathematics, philosophy and humanities degrees. Some lucky people may jump over the fence from mainstream marketing services, although brand specialists tend to regard marketing people as executors, not visionaries. Mottram had an unusual start: he came from training as a chartered accountant with the firm that is now PricewaterhouseCoopers, decided that he wanted to work in branding and approached consultancies, including Interbrand, with a proposition involving the financial value of branding. Jorden, by contrast, did a graphic design degree at Camberwell College of Art, and then worked her way up through the design industry with a 'good aptitude for understanding what brands are all about and how to create them'.

What will a typical day be like? Expect to spend time explaining to people what you do, since branding is often seen as a black art. You will be involved at the beginning of projects, or at a time when there are major changes in a company, such as a merger. Mottram describes his most common challenges as: 'fighting for recognition in the boardroom, trying to move on from the outdated and increasingly inappropriate **FMCG** (fast-moving consumer goods) model of branding, persuading the conservative business community that, although it's intangible, branding matters, and staying focused when the influence of brands and branding can (and should) reach into every facet of organisations'.

Assuming you make it into the industry, what will it be like? From all accounts, most brand specialists are deliriously happy in their work. Mottram describes the job as 'using the right and left brain, the head and heart in my work every day and being at the bleeding edge of value creation'.

Brand specialists can see their market growing, as companies are buffeted by such forces as globalisation, increasing competition and media exhaustion. People are being bombarded by thousands of commercial messages a day, with the end result that money spent on media and marketing is delivering less attention and value. Strong brands make it easier to reinforce communication with an audience, and it's almost unthinkable that any new company would try to survive without one.

SKILLS YOU'LL NEED

It won't hurt to wear stylish Italian knitwear with panache, and say things like 'the brand essence speaks to me of refrigerators'. A brand specialist needs to be a clear and convincing communicator, reassure nervous clients, and balance design imperatives with business ones. The profile of a brand consultant is usually someone in their late twenties to mid-thirties with a certain amount of experience under their belt working with clients or in a design environment.

GETTING THE JOB

- Be clear about why you are interested in branding, and which aspects of it appeal to you.
- If you are entering from a design background, get a placement with an ad or design agency, attending conferences, and use the Web to build knowledge of the industry and what's happening.

TIPS

- Cultivate a genuine interest in companies and their internal structure, and the means of communicating that to the outside world.

GLOSSARY

- **Brand**

Originally the stamp that was put on cattle to indicate ownership, a brand has come to mean the sum of all the characteristics, tangible and intangible, that make a company or product unique.

- **Brand experience**

An individual's perception of the company, driven by contact with the brand through buying its products or working for the company.

- **Brand identity**

The outward manifestation of the essence of a corporate brand, product brand or service brand.

- **FMCG**

Fast-Moving Consumer Goods, e.g. detergent. Most marketing thinking came out of FMCG until other sectors like technology came along.

USEFUL ADDRESSES

- Interbrand, 111 Maiden Lane, San Francisco, CA 94108, USA.
TEL +1 415 989 7400.
FAX +1 415 989 7409.
www.interbrand.com
- Rufus Leonard, The Drill Hall, 57a Farringdon Rd, London EC1 M3JB, UK.

TEL +44 (0) 20 7404 4490.
FAX +44 (0) 20 7404 4491.
www.rufusleonard.co.uk;
info@rufusleonard.co.uk

● Sapient , 1 Bartholomew Lane,
London EC2N 2AB, UK.
TEL +44 (0) 20 7786 4500.
FAX +44 (0) 20 7786 4600.
www.sapient.com

Business Development Director

Money: From £35,000 to £100,000. Business developers are paid in different ways for different results, and there is often an element of performance-related pay.

Hours: At least 50–60 hours per week, not including the frequent travel, conference calls and late-night business dinners.

Health risk: 6/10. Business development folk are the creatives of business. Most describe their work as 'doing deals', which shouldn't pose too much threat to your long-term health.

Pressure rating: 8/10. It is a tough combination to think strategically and grow the business at the same time.

Glamour rating: 7/10. Business development people are as comfortable in Tokyo as they are in Reading, and they know where to get a martini in both places.

Travel rating: 7/10. Very travel-intensive, since you travel to where the prospective client or partner is, whether that's Scunthorpe or San Francisco.

'Business development' is a term invented in recent years by Internet companies and now accepted as a standard role in every dot.com.

*Shortened to '**bizdev**' (as in, 'Who him? Oh, he's the bizdev guy') in most companies, it refers to the process of growing very small businesses into very high-profile ones very quickly. This is done through an odd combination of '**partnering**' (i.e. making friends with other small businesses) and '**co-branding**' (getting other recently established Web companies to put your logo and name on their site and vice versa). Business development could accurately be described as 'doing deals'.*

In your classic twentieth-century company, sales people sold product, marketing people marketed the product, and executives made decisions about where the company would go in the future. The Internet industry, since in many cases it doesn't have a product to sell, has morphed these three roles into one, called business development (most often a senior role at the vice-presidential level).

For Web companies, success depends on a combination of clients and partners. For example, a website selling discount travel packages needs to get a number of customers on to its site in order to be successful: high traffic means lots of sales which mean higher commissions for the company. But how to attract traffic to the site? The company will probably go through traditional routes of advertising, attempting to attract publicity, and offering special discounts. In addition, they will use another business stratagem, partnering up with another Web company and agreeing to share traffic: Company A agrees to have a link to Company B's site in exchange for either a share in revenue or a similar link on Company B's site.

That's an example of the simplest sort of deal a 'bizdev' person might put together. As more and more money is involved, and the companies become more high profile, business development becomes part-alchemy, part-UN-calibre diplomacy. Success may not depend on the usual metrics (bringing in money or customers) but on other slippery measures: agreements signed for public relations purposes, client satisfaction and longevity.

'Essentially my core tasks are to acquire new customers at the least possible cost, and to drive sales,' says Emma Kane, business development director at Amazon.co.uk, the British arm of Amazon.com, the on-line bookstore. 'The way I do this is to develop and maintain relationships with other companies/sites who will drive well-targeted new customers to [us].'

Business development is a catch-all phrase for a new kind of role that is essential in Web companies, and delivers what they need most: speedy growth. Conventional wisdom in the Internet industry dictates that the first player in any kind of on-line business will be the most successful. This is called 'first-mover advantage'. The first on-line bookstore will have immeasurable advantage over the next one that attempts to start up. That's why companies want to get off the ground quickly, and why investors are often willing to sink a lot of capital into a venture long before it is profitable: they think that if they can build the business at a loss quickly, potential competitors will be staved off. The business developer's key contributions may include bringing in new clients, building long-term relationships with clients, negotiating **strategic alliances** and partnerships (which have a positive effect on reach in the marketplace and, if the company is listed, the share price), contribution to strategy based on what you see happening in the market, public speaking, and company profile-raising.

'Business development is all about making the right partnerships with the right players,' says Rick Jones, head of business development of Internet auction site QXL.com. 'Whether it's new technology (such as being able to bid at a QXL auction via your mobile phone) or a strategic partner who can add benefits to what we do – such as sports sites to help us promote memorabilia auctions of signed football shirts, cricket bats or whatever you want. The core reason for the job existing is the need for someone to focus on moving the business forward without getting too caught up in the day-to-day stuff – which means there are lots of speculative meetings and buzzy ideas flowing around.'

Although some business developers are naturals and have moved straight into the role, they are often people who have had experience working in fast-growth environments before, and are able to add a lot of informal support to the team. They also tend to be people with a high energy level, who inspire their colleagues as well as potential clients or partners.

'I would typically have enough to do simply reacting to e-mail and internal issues, without ever developing new business, managing relationships, handling contracts, and negotiation deals – the main parts of my job,' says Kane. 'A typical day involves two to three meetings, thinking up new promotions, touching base with promotional partners and contacts to make sure I'm getting the best value for money, clearing contracts with the lawyers, and deciding where the budget is best spent.'

Business development typifies the Internet industry more than most job responsibilities. Most bizdev folks say that their job changes on a daily basis. Although increasingly Internet business rules are taught in universities and colleges, most people in the role now learned as they went along, making up rules where there were none to fit. Antony Wolfson, business development director of the web advertising agency Traffic Interactive, says that the pressure to reinvent the wheel every day can take its toll. 'It can be incredibly stressful, particularly when you really want to win a project, but then it can also be one of the most rewarding roles as well when you win.'

Although a lot of the work that a business developer does can be seen as contributing to sales, often the benefits are not outwardly financial. Sales is a straightforward exchange of goods or services for money, while business development often includes an element of trade-off or barter. Web businesses, short on ready cash but long on enthusiasm, are especially prone to striking deals that have no financial impact but can raise their profile or make what they offer more valuable. Trading traffic between sites is an example of something that doesn't have a cost to either party, but which delivers value to both and helps bolster the value of advertising.

Nova Arnachellum, business developer for the Guardian Unlimited website, focuses on this kind of business development. Arnachellum manages a content distribution service that markets the *Guardian*'s core asset, news and other articles, to other website owners or managers. Part of Arnachellum's work is matching client needs to the capabilities and schedules of developers. 'It can occasionally get stressful,' Arnachellum says. 'Usually when I'm managing a particular project, like reconfiguring our crossword so that it's compatible with [other] technology, it will involve the client, myself, a project co-ordinator and a developer. Co-ordinating all these people can sometimes prove difficult, especially if we're working to a deadline or if we're short on technical human resources.'

Much of the business developer's time is spent in meetings, often highly speculative ones since they never know where key deals are going to come from. With all this partnering, back-patting and general attention to building relationships, the bizdev crowd are among the most social in the Internet industry: they start early with power breakfasts and finish late with drinks after work. According to Rick Jones, business developers meet everyone on earth, ranging from telecommunications suppliers to famous celebrities. Since a key part of their role is representing the company to outside players, they also spend a significant amount of time with people in the company who deal with marketing, product development and sales to figure out how they should be projecting themselves to the world at large.

'I fell in love with the possibilities of the Internet in my final year at university, when Mosaic and Netscape Beta version were the browsers of choice [translation: 1994], and knew it was the area I wanted to work in. I started a PhD in Electronic Publishing and the Internet in 1995, abandoned this after a year when I realised that trying to predict the future of the Internet was hopeless,' Kane says. 'I then spent four excellent years at a new media research group just as the Web was taking off, planning and managing Internet-related EU-funded projects.' Kane went from the public sector into working for start-ups, first at an incubator helping other companies, later joining Amazon.

There is no typical training or background for the business developer, and they tend to come from all walks of life. Some start in sales and marketing, others in public relations, and others in business planning or consulting roles. The job tends to draw a certain kind of person rather than depend on a certain kind of background: high-energy, socially supercharged, and with an endless supply of hearty handshakes.

SKILLS YOU'LL NEED

A hollow leg won't hurt, as you'll have to put away lots of martinis. Cultivate a resistance to jet-lag. Learn to pack clothing into a very small space (you never know how long you'll be away), and charm someone to do your ironing (business developers are a bit like James Bond: they always appear impeccably pulled together). Much of the skill comes down to personality: particularly the ability to be enthusiastic and excited, but very focused on the needs of the business. You need exceptionally high motivation and drive, and charisma is a key asset.

GETTING THE JOB

- This may be a case of creating the job in a company by pointing out the need for alliance-building and partnership.
- You may decide to move from sales into an area with a longer lead time and broader involvement.
- Networking will put you in touch with a number of people: if you can impress someone at a crowded event, then you have a good shot at being a business developer.

TIPS

- You will need to be a rare combination of someone who is commercial and strategic, able to negotiate deals but also have a clear view of where the company is going and how you can contribute.
- If you are developing business, you

will need to spend a lot of time inside the company getting to know people and gaining their confidence. Many of your ideas will come from informal brainstorms as well as a careful perusal of the company's strategy.

- Focus on milking and nurturing every contact you have ever met – you never know where help is likely to come from next.
- Get on the party circuit and network, network, network. FirstTuesday and others host regular networking events.
- Keep up with what other Web companies are doing by strict attention to industry trade journals like *New Media Age*, *Red Herring*, *Business 2.0*, the *Industry Standard*, and others.

GLOSSARY

- **Bizdev**

Industry-wide term for any activity engaged in to grow the business.

- **Co-branding**

Two companies agreeing to put links to one another's sites, a seemingly simple process that could actually require seven meetings, four lunches, and an eighty-page contract.

- **Partnering**

The process of joining up with other Web companies, usually in a deal that involves no cash changing hands, in a way that is mutually beneficial.

- **Strategic alliances**

Arrangements in which the business developer has promised something to somebody, usually the chance to address a customer or promote some joint event together.

USEFUL ADDRESSES

- FirstTuesday, 12 St James Square, London SW1Y 4RB, UK.
TEL +44 (0) 20 7849 6779.
FAX +44 (0) 20 7849 6226.
www.firsttuesday.com;
firsttuesday@egroups.com
- New Media Age, St Giles House, 49–51 Poland St, London W1V 4AX, UK.
TEL +44 (0) 20 7970 4000.
FAX +44 (0) 20 7970 4898.
www.newmediaage.co.uk
- Industry Standard, 315 Pacific Avenue, San Francisco, CA 94111, USA.
TEL +1 415 733 5400.
FAX +1 415 733 5401.
www.thestandard.com
- Business 2.0, 30 Monmouth St, Bath BA1 2BW, UK.
TEL +44 (0) 1225 442 244.
FAX +44 (0) 1225 732 262.
www.business2.com

Chief Executive Officer

Money: £100,000–£250,000. Executives also often own a piece of the company as an incentive for them to make it successful.

Hours: Often ten to twelve hours a day when the company is young. These hours may stick after the company is successful. The Internet industry never sleeps, and neither should you.

Health risk: 6/10. Although the stress is high, the pay-offs are big. Keep one eye on the prize, don't succumb to the temptation to go crazy, and you'll be fine.

Pressure rating: 7/10. The CEO is responsible for all aspects of a company's success. When the critics come a-hunting, it's your head they're after.

Glamour rating: 9/10. These are the people who made 'dot.com millionaire' first a catch-phrase, and then an oxymoron. They are still the glam merchants of the Internet world, the closest thing we've got to celebrities.

Travel rating: 10/10. The Internet is global, and so is the Internet CEO. Pack your bag.

At the top of the Internet heap are the chief executives. With them lies the final responsibility for the company. They oversee the staff, pursue the future of the business, liaise with investors and potential partners, and speak publicly both at conferences and to the press about what the company is doing and why it will be successful.

The Internet industry gets a lot of attention from the public and from the world's media. Few people understand how an industry made up of companies that all appear to be *losing* money can have so many young executives making a packet. Many of these companies, particularly ones that have been floated on the stock markets, are valued at prices well beyond their annual revenues or any multiple thereof. Responding to the charge 'Isn't it all just a giant rip-off?' is the task of the Internet chief executive, since they, like few others, have a unique perspective on what value, if any, the Internet holds for consumers and businesses.

Since the world has become so obsessed with chronicling the rise and fall of Internet companies, Internet executives, particularly at very famous companies, have become something akin to celebrities. They have their privacy invaded, speak only through publicists and make appearances on spotlight-flooded stages to cheering crowds who all want to know what it's like to be them. But while a celebrity's job begins and ends with this kind of glitz, for an Internet entrepreneur it is only the beginning. Behind all the attention, and the negative and positive publicity about the Internet, are real companies run by real businessmen and women, and the chief executive or managing director has a very real job to do. In addition to validating their existence to the world, they also have to recruit and manage a group of staff members in what is a very talent-hungry (and talent-depleted) industry, constantly refine the business in a changing marketplace, stay on friendly terms with the financial world in case new fund-raising is called for, and keep employees happy.

'Some might think it is glamorous as we tend to get a lot of press coverage, and they read stories about Internet millionaires,' says Fabiola Arredondo, managing director of Yahoo!'s European operations. 'But it does entail a lot of work and sacrifice, both professional and personal. If you are performance-driven, it is a terrific environment, as your results are constantly being measured. However, you are far more publicly exposed to both the ups and downs, to successes and failures. Gone are the corporate lunches, group perks, and private offices.'

Part of the difficulty in running an Internet company is that, since it is a young industry, it tends to be populated by young creative people. It is the younger generation which has grown up with computers, and understands the benefits of being able to shop, communicate and run your business over the Internet. On the other hand, it is older, more seasoned professionals whose wealth of experience makes companies run smoothly. CEOs, whether old or young themselves, need to make sure all of the staff can work together, reminding younger members that they need to knuckle under and wear a suit and tie once in a while, while delicately reminding the older staff that current professional etiquette doesn't let them pat the dishy new PA on the bum and ask her to fetch the tea. Internet executives, as a rule, are not the golf-playing suits that operate in other, more corporate industries. They do real work, and it requires a great deal more than six hours a week in the office.

'I am responsible for leading and driving our business in Europe across all fronts: production, engineering, sales, marketing, and business development. I do more in this role than in any previous managerial role I have held,' says Arredondo, who has also run the BBC's international television distribution business as well as held several executive positions at BMG Music. 'This is the same for all of our managers. They are required to "get their hands dirty" constantly in a way they might not have previously. Although the responsibilities have changed as we've got larger, we are still always doing, closing, launching ... the environment is a constantly changing, evolving, high-adrenaline, flexible one.'

Even though Yahoo!, as one of the world's largest and most successful Internet companies, is no longer a tiny **start-up**, Arredondo still treats it as one. She says that in addition to having more responsibilities, Internet executives tend to put in more hours than their counterparts in off-line businesses. 'It's not unusual to find me up at midnight on the phone or on mail at five in the morning. Without a doubt it is critical that you love what you do. If you love the industry, you don't focus on the hours. One thing that is a change is that partners or family need to get accustomed to seeing the PC and mobiles come out regularly in the evenings and at weekends.'

Many of the most successful Internet companies never lose the sense of urgency that they had as a start-up, and this atmosphere starts with the chief executive. If the CEO is still showing up for work early, staying late, and driving the same beat-up 1990 Ford Escort, the rest of the employees know that there's still work to be done, and the glamour times haven't yet come to their neck of the woods. Carol Dukes, founder of ThinkNatural.com, an on-line health and beauty supply company, stresses that, unlike many of her contemporaries, she spends more time building her business than worrying about getting her picture in the newspapers.

'Because we don't have London offices, a lot of meetings are held in coffee shops around town,' she says. 'In the office [in Berkhamsted; Dukes has eschewed a trendy and expensive London location], I share a small room with three other directors – there are only three desks between us! – and this room also functions as the office's server room, so it's hot, and the company's only meeting room, so it can be noisy.'

Dukes, who became an independent entrepreneur in her late thirties, doesn't quite typify the image of the twentysomething lavishly spending investors' money for some hare-brained scheme that will never make money. She spent sixteen years working in satellite and cable television, ending up as the director of Carlton Communications' on-line businesses. In July 1999, she left Carlton to found ThinkNatural. The move gave her the freedom to build a business on her own merits, but the move out of the corporate world had its own ramifications. 'I think most Internet entrepreneurs took a pay cut when launching out on their own – I know I did,' she says. 'And I would guess that we are typically earning less than half what we would earn in a corporate environment.'

One year after leaving Carlton, Dukes had seen ThinkNatural get funded to the tune of £2.4 million, the site was up and running and generating revenues, and the company was in the process of expanding into Germany. Her days had become the blur of routine that goes with running a business.

'I try to wander round the offices and especially the warehouse as soon as I arrive,' she says. 'This helps me get a sense of what's going on and "take the temperature" of the business. When I get to my desk there are always lots and lots of e-mails waiting for me, plus phone messages. I get very little post except junk mail and almost no faxes. The day tends to vanish in a blur of meetings, informal chats, e-mails and phone calls – it's all about communication. I find the only times I can spend reading, thinking, analysing and writing are evenings and weekends. I often come in on either Saturday or Sunday and find that I can achieve a huge amount. But all that communication during the week is vitally important.'

She focuses partly on the internal mechanisms of the business – keeping staff motivated, creating a pleasant working environment – and partly on the external impact ThinkNatural has on customers, investors, and the rest of the industry. This means deciding all too frequently that the company needs to change its strategy, and communicating those changes in the press, to investors, and at industry conferences.

Dukes says that running ThinkNatural isn't necessarily more demanding than working within a big corporate structure, but the constant threat of running out of money and needing to raise new finance adds 'a frisson of tension'.

'It's generally no more stressful than running a start-up company which is a subsidiary within a plc, which is what I was doing before,' she says. 'There are always a million things to do, lots of "people issues" and a sense that there are opportunities being missed. I guess it depends on what sort of person you are. If you're the sort of person who likes an organised routine with clear-cut work processes and objectives that don't constantly change, then you'd be very, very stressed doing this kind of work. If you thrive on change and newness and variety then it's easier to ride the waves.'

The job of the chief executive will change as the business does. At the beginning of a company's life, the CEO is likely to spend more time fund-raising than anything else. While the company is still technically a start-up, the CEO is also likely to have more hands-on contact with the employees and the business processes. As the company grows, the CEO becomes more tangential to its everyday workings and focuses on high-level issues like talking to the press and planning for the future: a thinking rather than doing job. When the company reaches that phase, the key word for the CEO is **delegation**. Rob Hersov, founder of a network of sport sites called Sportal, says that two years after he founded the company it has grown enough that he doesn't have to have a hand in every decision made. Founded in July 1998, by July 2000 the company had eleven offices and was publishing websites in seven languages.

'In the beginning I was involved in every decision and all aspects of the business,' Hersov says. 'Now that we have 250 employees and are growing rapidly on all fronts, I am now at **30,000 feet**.'

Hersov says his job has boiled down to seven basic responsibilities:

1 Keeping my head when all around are losing theirs (apologies to Kipling).
2 Dealing with shareholders, the board, strategic partners and the press.
3 Handling option grants and salary issues.
4 Ensuring the senior execs don't kill each other.

5 Acting calm and confident at all times (even when I'm not).
6 Doing the big deals.
7 Staying out of the way of the people who are doing the real work.

Things weren't always this easy. When Sportal was young, Hersov worked the obligatory twelve-hour days, complete with weekends. But he says that no matter how fast the pace gets, there's always a way to stay calm under pressure. 'Stress only applies if you do not have control over your own life,' he says. 'The best executives are competitive, fired up and edgy, but never stressed. I either deal with an issue immediately, or I pass the problem on to the executives around me. Delegation removes eighty per cent of the stress. A good diet, exercise and a sense of humour remove the remaining twenty per cent.'

SKILLS YOU'LL NEED

A clear understanding of the Internet industry and where your company fits in, ability to communicate clearly to the press and others what the company's vision is, a deft hand in dealing with people and keeping staff motivated, entertained and productive. Most importantly, the ability to be flexible, and operate in a fast-paced environment.

GETTING THE JOB

There's no easy way to this top job. You might start out as an entrepreneur, but you're just as likely to be removed from the CEO spot later on if you don't have the years of business experience that are now *de rigueur* for those with 'CEO' on their business cards. Any CEO should have several years' experience either in another executive position within the company or as chief executive in another company, even if it's an off-line one.

TIPS

- Don't ever think the job is done. In its short lifespan, the Internet industry has buried as many companies as it has made successful. The successes are the ones that can morph, chameleon-like, with every change in the industry.
- Stay current on the business. Publications like the *Industry Standard*, *Red Herring*, *Wired*, *Business 2.0* and *Tornado-Insider* cover what both your competition and your partners are doing.

GLOSSARY

- **30,000 feet**

A high-level perspective. This is a common piece of industry jargon that is synonymous with 'the big picture', an overall view of what is happening in the world or the industry at large. Correct usage: 'Don't give me the nitty-gritty details. Let's take it to 30,000 feet. Will we make money with this plan?'

- **Delegation**

Handing over responsibility to other people on your **team** so that you can spend more time focusing on the big picture.

- **Start-up**

A recently founded company. Most Internet companies still describe themselves as start-ups.

● **Team**
The staff. People who work in Internet companies dislike hierarchy, particularly if they are lower on the ladder than they'd like to be. Internet executives don't have staff, employees, underlings or subordinates. They have a team.

USEFUL ADDRESSES

● Business 2.0, 30 Monmouth St, Bath BA1 2BW, UK.
TEL +44 (0) 1225 442 244.
FAX +44 (0) 1225 732 262.
www.business2.com

● FirstTuesday, 12 St James Square, London SW1Y 4RB, UK.
TEL +44 (0) 20 7849 6779.
FAX +44 (0) 20 7849 6226.
www.firsttuesday.com;
firsttuesday@egroups.com

● Industry Standard, 315 Pacific Ave, San Francisco, CA 94111, USA.
TEL +1 415 733 5400.
FAX +1 415 733 5401.
www.thestandard.com

● New Media Age, St Giles House, 49–51 Poland St, London W1V 4AX, UK.
TEL +44 (0) 20 7970 4000.
FAX +44 (0) 20 7970 4898.
www.newmediaage.co.uk

CHIEF TECHNOLOGY OFFICER

MONEY: £60,000–£140,000

HOURS: 15-hour days, 6-day weeks.

HEALTH RISK: 8/10. Long hours and high stress – better stay away from fatty foods or this job is a heart condition waiting to happen.

PRESSURE RATING: 10/10. No one in the company except the chief executive has more responsibility for the success of the business.

GLAMOUR RATING: 3/10. Lots of credit from the staff internally, but not much exposure to the outside world ... or sunlight.

TRAVEL RATING: 5/10. Plenty of inter-office travel, but no glamorous junkets to Monte Carlo.

There's a saying in the building trade that a worker is only as good as his tools. Rusty saws and bent spanners don't make for well-built houses. In the Internet industry, companies are only as good as their technology, and as a result the chief information officer – in charge of all internal technology – and the chief technology officer – responsible for developing the site and the overall strategy – are at the heart of the company. Their jobs are finding ways to improve business processes and the customer's experience, all for the love of tech.

There's a world of difference between these masterminds and the so-called '**code jockey**', a desk-bound programmer whose only job is to do as he's told. Chief information officers and chief technology officers are likely to spend as much time in the boardroom as behind their computers. Creating a strategy isn't just about knowing how to connect a computer to a printer, but about predicting the ever-changing possibilities of technology and harnessing them for the benefit of the business.

Most Web companies are founded on a technological premise, the idea that the Internet can enable new efficiencies and create new short cuts not possible in the old 'bricks and mortar' world. An on-line bookseller is trying to use centralised distribution to serve a wider audience, allowing it to stock a greater selection than its off-line counterparts. Intelligent databases and searching capability make finding books a sure thing, and more efficient (though not necessarily more enjoyable) than wandering up and down aisles in a bookstore. As technology advances, so have the offerings of Web companies, with new and creative ways to exploit the advances for the good of the customer, and the good of the company.

The chief technology officer is the dream-weaver at the head of table, the brain responsible for assessing new technologies, and seeing how they might be applied to the corporate goals. Each new innovation holds a wealth of promise and potential hazard that could either be a path to riches or a fool's errand that could end up costing millions. Far from being the head techie on a crew of techies, the chief technology officer combines both technical and business expertise, having the technology savvy to understand what is possible and the business acumen to understand what is practical and potentially profitable.

For example, the Internet industry hasn't forgotten the notorious example of **push technology**. Push rode a wave of hype into the mainstream in 1996 and 1997. Promoted by companies like US-based PointCast, the technology was intended to thrust Internet content onto users' computers without them having to browse the Web, hunting for information like the proverbial needle in a haystack. For advertisers, this was a dream come true. Rather than trying to find which sites had the most traffic, and shelling out for adverts that might or might not get viewed, they could simply push their material at the users directly, via the PointCast software. Media companies were fascinated by the idea, and in late 1996 Rupert Murdoch's News Corp. attempted an acquisition of PointCast for some $450 million. FreeLoader, a PointCast rival, was sold for $38 million without making a single penny in revenue. But push technology was never meant to be. Industry perception turned against it, deciding that the medium would become so saturated with advertising that consumers would never be attracted in large numbers. In 1999, PointCast was sold to LaunchPad Technologies for a paltry $7 million.

Technologies like push which promise the moon and deliver nothing more than a stack of debts for unused research and development are the nightmare of Internet CTOs. The possibilities for building businesses on the Internet change more rapidly than teen pop icons. Given the plethora of new tools, software and platforms flooding the arena every day, it requires no small amount of prescience to decide what will work and what will fall by the wayside.

The successful CTO has an assortment of skills that range from business know-how, a keen understanding of the corporate product and management savvy for controlling the development team to an addiction to technology and a broad understanding of how it is used. They are almost always among the most highly paid executives within the company, since any Internet outfit relies on the solidity of its **technology strategy** to keep the boat afloat. The CTO will split his or her time between leading the developers and technology staff to brainstorming with the company management about what the future holds. The job is so varied that companies search long and hard for someone with the right set of skills. A fairly typical advertisement for a dot.com CTO might look like this:

'At least ten years' experience in software development and integration and a successful track record of managing large projects from development through deployment. A strong background in Information Technology, business management and leadership, and finance. An excellent understanding of current applications and trends in technology, specifically within the financial services sector. Experience with the fast-paced Internet business community. Experience with enterprise integration and networking. Excellent organisational and communication skills.'

CTO is also the job title of choice for entrepreneurs in start-up companies who are more Internet visionary than hard-nosed businessman. Marc Andreesen, the founder of Netscape, is a famous example of this, conceiving the idea for the company while still at the University of Illinois. Even though Netscape (and much of the revolution that followed) was credited to Andreesen, he was never chief executive of Netscape. That title was held first by Jim Clarke and then by Jim Barksdale, two long-time businessmen compared with Andreesen, a whiz kid.

In the carpeted halls of Silicon Valley these days, the word on every Web merchant's lips is **stickiness**. It's easy enough to get punters to arrive at your site (a few million pounds in advertising should do the trick) but how do you get them to stay? A sticky app (application) is what's needed, something to get them stuck, and once stuck, get them to spend. The favoured sticky app of the moment wasn't devised in Silicon Valley, but in the faintly eccentric, Oxford-educated mind of one Charles Cohen, founder of Beenz.com, a company founded on the inherent understanding that consumers will do almost anything to get stuff for free. (Cohen has followed in Andreesen's footsteps as a founder who also serves as chief technology officer.)

Beenz are an online currency, given out by sites in exchange for some action by a consumer. If a site wants to know more about their users, they offer twenty Beenz to those who will consent to fill in a questionnaire. If they want to send people to a certain under-visited part of their site, they offer an additional ten. Consumers can hoard their Beenz, or spend them, trading the virtual cash for free goods, discounts, and special offers. The killer app of the new economy, as it turns out, is bribery. Cohen, as CTO, spends his time figuring out new ways to distribute Beenz, and new ways to collect them, exploring everything from offering a Beenz-branded MasterCard to Beenz distributed and collected via a mobile phone.

'If this was a factory, I would be the person responsible for designing the production line and making sure it works,' he says. 'I spend my time deciding on the correct strategy, like developing products for mobile phones or smart cards, and then my job is to explain to the rest of the business what I've produced and how to maintain it. A really good CTO can explain very technical things to people who aren't technical.'

Despite the name, and the concept, Cohen was no bean-counter himself. At 29, he started his professional life as a speech-writer for a Liberal Democrat MP, then head of the party. This position of power enabled him to strongarm the other MPs in the party into making frequent use of e-mail and electronic bulletin boards.

At the end of three long years in politics, Cohen did some soul-searching and decided to enter commercial life. 'I did my duty,' he said. '[Then] I decided to make some money. I didn't want to go into lobbying, and I didn't want to be prime minister.'

Having assessed his qualifications as exactly none, thanks to his degree in philosophy and physics which he says 'prepared me for absolutely nothing', Cohen decided to pursue a career in public relations. 'I was good at dinner parties but I'm not a very humble person, which is not good for PR,' he says. 'You have to be polite, respectful, diligent. I was a workaholic, but not inclined to agree when I didn't.'

Lack of humility proved fateful for his PR gig, but the founders of the agency, Band & Brown, stood by him through thick and thin. 'It taught me a lesson in loyalty,' Cohen says. 'They stood by me even though I pissed off a lot of their clients.'

PR gave way to Web design, and finally to an idea that Cohen says just wouldn't leave him alone. 'I would buy *Wired* every month, and scan the index, waiting for someone to do it,' he says. 'It seems to have fallen into that "I wish I'd thought of it" category. That's kind of a weird feeling.'

Another type of chief technology officer comes from the embittered corps of the tech ranks, hardened professionals who've seen it all. Glen Jennison of Magex is such a CTO.

Magex is an on-line service which provides a secure way to buy and sell digital content like music, software, videos and games on the Internet. The service provides both copyright protection for the digital works and a secure payment facility for buying and selling the works. Digital copyright is one of the most hotly contested issues in the Internet space, and the technology advances almost daily, making Jennison's job a new adventure every day.

As a long-time tech worker, he's more than prepared for the barrage of technological upheaval that gets thrown at him on a daily basis. He has managed technological implementation programmes in Russia and central Europe, as well as South Africa, before coming home to roost at Magex in the UK. 'You could say that it's a school-of-life approach,' he says. '[My job] consists of developing new ideas for how to get more done in an ever shorter time frame.'

Jennison is in the pressurised position of working in an industry that faces a huge amount of public scrutiny. Magex has positioned itself to battle the growing problem of on-line piracy. Since Internet access has become so common, it has provided an easy avenue for anyone to distribute digital content, including content that hasn't been paid for. Billions of pirated works are exchanged on-line annually, ranging from music files to software and video games. Magex is trying to build a framework for distributing those works which guarantees they cannot be traded or sold on without remuneration coming back to the company. Needless to say, doing battle against a worldwide network of digital pirates can lead to some small amount of stress.

'Stress, what stress? I twitch like this all the time!' says Jennison. 'Seriously, the stress really gets the adrenaline going when you are trying to meet a live date and things go wrong and the date does not move. [But] in what other job could you get to take decisions that affect the whole business?'

SKILLS YOU'LL NEED

Expertise in a variety of Internet technologies, project management skills, ability to steer groups of people towards a common goal, understanding of the way the Internet industry is changing, and the ability to predict emerging trends.

GETTING THE JOB

- At executive levels, much recruitment is done through personal networks and headhunting firms. Signing on with one of these firms is imperative for a full range of job listings.
- Some job search sites cater to the technologically inclined, such as monster.co.uk. Posting your résumé with these sites is another, though less controlled, method of putting your name out there.
- Make sure you are in a position to discuss the company's business as well as their technology in the interview.
- This is an executive position – management skills should be highlighted as well as your vision for the company's future.

TIPS

- Learn your history! CTOs should have not only a comprehensive understanding of technology, but also of business, and what has been tried in the past.
- Keep abreast of the current trends by reading everything about the Internet business and new technologies you can get your hands on.
- Participate in industry events and conferences, but remember – all the interesting talk happens in the hallway, or in the bar.
- Listen to your staff. The Internet industry is about innovation with a long history of letting everyone have a good idea, regardless of internal hierarchy.

GLOSSARY

- **Code jockey**

The techie underlings that work under the CTO or CIO. Theirs is not to reason why, but to produce code.

- **Push technology**

A much-hyped technology of the late 90s which 'pushed' content onto users' computers. It never managed to deliver on its promise, although it did manage to suck up billions in research investment.

- **Stickiness**

The ability of a website to keep consumers within its pages. 'Sticky' applications are ones that manage to keep the consumer on the site for long periods of time, and keep them returning regularly.

- **Technology strategy**

A company's plan to use technology to fulfil the business's ambitions.

USEFUL ADDRESSES

- CIO.com, 492 Old Connecticut Path, Framingham, MA 01701, USA.
  TEL +1 508 935 4796.
  FAX +1 508 872 0618.
  www.cio.com; info@cio.com
- Korn/Ferry, 252 Regent St, London W1R 5DA, UK.
  TEL +44 (0) 20 7312 3100.
  FAX +44 (0) 20 7312 3130.
  www.kornferry.com;
  info@kornferry.com
- Monster.co.uk, 163 Eversholt St, London NW1 1BU.
  TEL +44 (0) 800 1695015.
  FAX +44 (0) 20 7391 4701.
  www.monster.co.uk;
  sales@monster.co.uk
- Search Partners Ltd, 38 Charterhouse St, London EC1M 6JH, UK.
  TEL +44 (0) 20 7253 1333.
  FAX +44 (0) 20 7253 1444.
  www.searchpartners.com/itheadhunting.htm;
  mail@searchpartners.com

CONSULTANT

MONEY: From £40,000 to £100,000 upwards: consultants should have valuable knowledge that people will pay significant fees to acquire.

HOURS: Long and hard, since you are usually at the client's beck and call working on important things.

HEALTH RISK: 4/10. No one has died yet from an attack of Post-It notes at a strategy session, although it is a fairly stressful lifestyle.

PRESSURE RATING: 7/10. You'll need to take the heat for some of the consequences of your recommendations to a company, and it's hard to have an 'off' day.

GLAMOUR RATING: 7/10. Watch for the equivalent of *Ally McBeal* (lawyers) or *E.R.* (doctors) for consultants. It's only a matter of time, as perceived glamour is high.

TRAVEL RATING: 8/10. Consultants live out of a suitcase. Choose a favoured airline to keep in business for the next few years.

Consultant is a general term applied to anyone who works in an advisory capacity with companies, generally on short- to medium-term projects (one week to two years), bringing a specialist knowledge. The Internet industry relies heavily on experts, and anyone with an expertise can slap on the label 'consultant', put a price on their hourly value, and set out to offer opinions. Only a cynic would point out the 'con-' in 'consultant'.

'Consultant' is one of the most abused words in the job lexicon, second only to 'strategy'. It's a vague term that can be applied to anyone with a specific function to perform, popular now with shop workers selling complicated merchandise ('Just a moment, madam, I'll get our electronics consultant for you').

The term is vague enough to encompass a number of other job functions, since it really only means someone who works for the company but isn't paid a regular, permanent, full-time salary. Some gurus do consulting work, in which they go into a company and dispense expert advice. Some analysts who work at large accounting firms might also spend a portion of their time as consultants to a specific company. And some strategists may work in a staff position, while others operate on a consulting basis. Even some PR people consider themselves 'media consultants', some brand specialists are 'branding consultants', and some janitors are 'custodial consultants'.

In the Internet Age, consultants have become to companies what psychologists are to anxious people: they can help you sort out your problems, or just give you someone to talk to, all for an exorbitant fee. Senior management might call in a market consultant when sales are improving for advice on how to maintain the trend, when sales are decreasing for advice on how to reverse the trend, or when sales are stagnant for advice on how to make something happen. An image consultant could be brought in to teach the company how to appear more friendly, more tough, more philanthropic, more frugal, more business-minded or more technology-driven. Company executives who are supposed to be planning the future of the company might bring in a strategy consultant to devise a strategy for the future of the company. Consultants do generally have some things in common: intelligence, analytical skills, and a set of qualifications, which may include an advanced degree or MBA. And despite the new rash of casual-dress offices, they are also usually keen to hang on to their suits.

Even with all manner of workers suddenly becoming consultants (à la electronics shop worker who used to be called a cashier), consulting is an expanding market. After the massive downsizing that many companies went through in the 1980s, many experienced business managers found themselves jobless. Companies, in turn, began relying on external help to make top-level decisions, having axed the portion of its workforce (i.e. middle management) that had specialist skills but wasn't necessarily a full-time requirement. In many ways, the consultant of today is the institutional fat that was trimmed from the corporate love handles of the 80s.

The life of the consultant is a good one. They are called in by companies only when needed. Their work consists mainly of examining someone else's efforts and pointing out where something has gone wrong. Consultants also have a healthy ego that manifests itself in their professional fees. This works out well for companies also. If they use a consultant, they don't have to keep someone on the staff whose expertise would inevitably cost more on a full-time basis than the consultant does on an as-need basis.

The main difficulty for consultants is explaining what they do to their friends. Most often, their area of expertise is so highly specialised that they are without a close group of peers. A consultant who is an expert on Implementing Middleware Strategies for High-End Multi-Cluster Server Farms isn't going to have a ready answer at the cocktail party when the good-looking blonde says, 'So, what do you do, then?' What's the default? 'Oh, I'm a consultant.'

Within this definition there is a huge variety of skill and experience. There are consultants who specialise in industry sectors such as mobile telephony, legislation such as EU competition rules, and esoteric subjects like specialist micro-economics or Web design. Consultants may specialise in certain kinds of processes, such as **business process re-engineering**, **systems integration** or **change management**.

Consulting is going through a boom time for another reason: the rapid growth of the Internet, and the set of skills required for companies to survive, means there is a growing need for urgent specialist help in such areas as e-commerce and new communications technology. These are new industries with a limited number of experienced practitioners. Those who know how the Internet industry works are in high demand, and may find they are more useful as a consultant helping many companies than as a staff member helping only one. In a climate of uncertainty and rapid change, people need business advisers. Often consultants are looking at problems where the specialist knowledge or experience doesn't exist in the company – or doesn't exist in the world, full stop.

There are two key aspects to becoming a consultant: acquiring a set of knowledge, and finding a way to convince prospective clients that your knowledge is valuable. Some consultants, like those who work at the larger consulting firms (Andersen Consulting, PricewaterhouseCoopers, KPMG), can acquire their expertise within the confines of the firm. They can then trade on that reputation after they leave the company and strike out on their own. ('Jack Spratt, formerly a consultant with Pricewaterhouse Coopers, can be reached at Spratt Consulting Group,' a consultant's publicity material might say.)

Christina Hastings, of Proteus, a new Internet consultancy, is on her second wave of consulting. She arrived at Proteus following a five-year stint with Andersen Consulting 'doing strategic and process analysis for a series of blue-chip companies'. This is a reasonably common path for consultants: learn at a big firm, then move to a smaller, more specialist firm where there is more autonomy and flexibility. Large consultancies such as Andersen describe their appeal as a trade-off: taking young people, training them very well and working them very hard, a background which then enables them to go on and do well elsewhere.

While many people are now doing as Hastings has done, and moving out of a big consultancy where you could be working on anything from feed manufacturing to aeroplanes, there's no question that a large consultancy for a few years is a good bet to give you the skills, confidence and client contacts that you'll need. Another approach is to spend over a decade in a fast-changing industry such as information technology, and become adept at recognising patterns, which is a key skill for top consultants. Nick Smith, the vice-president of vendor consulting within IT consultants the Gartner Group, has spent his entire career in technology: enough time to see it all, at least twice. 'Having failed to be spotted as an immense football talent (all I needed were skill, speed and strength) the obvious thing to do was to join IBM. Since then, I seem to have been involved in the interesting bits, such as PCs when new, desktop roll-outs, the Internet, and e-business.'

Consultants are expected to travel far and wide to wherever clients may be, and in the technology sector are often called upon to display their knowledge of what is going on in other markets. While frequent travel may add to the perceived glamour factor of being a consultant, the lifestyle can be wearing. 'I do silly trips, where I do a city during the day and move on to the next one during the evening,' says Smith. 'I eat dreadful room service meals, and some good restaurant ones. It's not glamorous to spend twenty-four hours in a forty-eight-hour period travelling.'

Despite the hassle of travel, the lure of the consulting life has called many. 'It's varied, challenging and fast-moving,' says Hastings.

And while a consultant's life may not be like a box of chocolates, it can be like a chocolate bar. 'The day of a consultant is like a Mars bar – work, rest and play, though not necessarily in that order,' says Smith. 'There're concentrated periods of project work, getting out and building networks, rushed lunches at the desk alternating with long lunches entertaining clients. You're away from home less than a long-distance lorry driver, facing hostility less than a policeman, and faced with new things, new places and new people.'

SKILLS YOU'LL NEED

Remember, a consultant is something of a teacher, and has to spend a fair amount of time in front of small groups explaining new ways of doing things. Needless to say, the ability to write legibly on whiteboards is paramount. Analytical rigour, commitment to clients, and an advanced degree (academic or business) are also assets. Consultants should be able to digest huge amounts of verbal and written information very quickly, and analyse what it means. Being a consultant is a quick way into understanding company politics and human behaviour: and it's a jungle out there.

GETTING THE JOB

- If you are a student, some consulting firms offer summer placements, which are a great chance to get your feet under the table.
- If you are a graduate, check out the consultants' websites, and try to speak with a recent graduate employee so you get a sense of the culture.
- When interviewing you for a consulting job, people will be looking for valuable, relevant experience showing you understand the industry or have a particular skill such as experience in implementing software.
- Consultants are often recruited by specialist headhunters such as LKRC. Check specialist Internet and e-commerce job sites, and sign up for industry events co-ordinator FirstTuesday's job postings, which always include a healthy sprinkling of consulting positions. On the IT consulting side there is another set of specialist headhunters. For freelance jobs, check on-line at www.guru.com or similar sites.

TIPS

- Develop a relevant skill set. This could mean years of experience in a related job, or simply being at the right place at the right time.
- Keep your name out there. Attend industry conferences, and submit articles for industry publications.
- Build up a roster of associates who can recommend you for work but are also helpful for researching new projects.

• Build up your intellectual stamina; be prepared to tackle numerous projects on multiple subjects in very short timeframes.

GLOSSARY

• **Business process improvement/re-engineering**
A common consulting project, which means taking a fresh look at the way a company does things, and figuring out how to do it better. Not as straightforward as it sounds: some of the people involved have never thought about how to do this, or have not been given the means to do anything about it.

• **Change management**
Consultants are often brought in during a time of change within an organisation, for example going through a merger or developing new product lines. During periods of change, companies have realised that it is essential to keep momentum and communication going, and consultants can help in this process, known as change management.

• **Systems integration**
When new systems are put in place to take over business processes, whether in accounts and finance or customer management, these all need to work with systems already up and running to share information and create one technology system. Systems integrators are practised at weaving together old and new technology.

USEFUL ADDRESSES

• Andersen Consulting , 2 Arundel St, London WC2R 3LT, UK.
TEL +44 (0) 20 7844 4000.
FAX +44 (0) 20 7844 4444.
www.ac.com; jobs@ac.com

• Cap Gemini/Ernst & Young, 130 Shaftesbury Ave, London W1D 5EU, UK.
TEL +44 (0) 20 7434 2171.
FAX +44 (0) 20 7437 6223.
www.capgemini.com

• FirstTuesday, 12 St James Square, London SW1Y 4RB.
TEL +44 (0) 20 7849 6779.
FAX +44 (0) 20 7849 6226.
www.firsttuesday.com; firsttuesdayjobs@egroups.com

• Gartner Group, 56 Top Gallant Rd, PO Box 10212, Stamford, CT 06904-2212, USA.
TEL +1 203 316 1111.
FAX +1 203 316 6300.
www.gartner.com; gginfo@gartner.com

• Guru.com, 639 Front St, Suite 200, San Francisco, CA 94111, USA.
TEL +1 415 693 9500.
FAX +1 415 837 1091.
www.guru.com; info@guru.com

• LKRC, 1st Floor, 184–186 Regent St, London W1R 5DF, UK.
TEL +44 (0) 20 7287 3500.
FAX +44 (0) 20 7287 3600.
www.lkrc.co.uk; info@lkrc.co.uk

CUSTOMER SERVICE

MONEY: £16,000–£30,000.

HOURS: If a company is in start-up mode, the hours can be more extreme, but in general customer service staff work office hours.

HEALTH RISK: 3/10. Minimal, except depression from extended exposure to abuse from irate customers.

PRESSURE RATING: 7/10. This position could be described as in the front line of the Internet economy.

GLAMOUR RATING: 1/10. Not a lot of glamour in being an anonymous question-answerer.

TRAVEL RATING: 1/10. None at all, unless a sudden trip to the warehouse counts as an exciting day out.

Customer service might be a rough way to make a living, but e-commerce companies are discovering that they can't live without it. With the Internet cutting out so much of the cost of doing business, companies are discovering that they can no longer compete just on the basis of price. Suddenly, service is the differentiating factor for customers, and the staff members answering the phone have a higher status.

In 1999, a famous e-mail was circulating around the Internet industry. It was in the form of a WAV file, an audio format that allowed the recipient to play back its contents. It contained a voicemail message left by an irate customer on an unnamed company's customer service helpline.

The message started out sedately enough. The man explained that he had bought a computer from the company, and that he was having problems with the hard drive; he had called the company that had manufactured the hard drive, and they had referred him to this company. Then the message just degenerated.

'And I've tried to reach you, and I've left messages, and I'd better GET A CALL BACK BECAUSE THIS MACHINE HAS ALL THE WORK I'VE DONE FOR THE LAST TWO [EXPLETIVE] YEARS OF MY [EXPLETIVE] LIFE, DO YOU UNDERSTAND ME, YOU [EXPLETIVE, EXPLETIVE, EXPLETIVE].'

His words weren't what resonated with people around the globe, who passed the file on as though it were the latest pirated film of celebrities *in flagrante delicto*, it was his hysteria. It's a hysteria that anyone who's ever purchased something over the phone, the Internet or by catalogue can relate to. A simple problem with the order, or a simple question that needs an answer, can require an endless tour through a voicemail system or endless e-mails to a company that seems to have made ignoring your missives a point of pride.

Slowly but surely, Internet companies have started to realise that customer service isn't an afterthought, but a critical way to beat the competitors. A Forrester Research report in 2000 found that 90 per cent of the 4.8 million individuals who shop on-line consider good customer service a crucial factor in choosing a Web retailer.

But even some of the largest Internet companies have a long way to go before they put the theory of customer service into practice. An *Industry Standard* survey in July 2000 tested the **response times** of some of the leading on-line companies, and found that, when compared with the results of a similar survey conducted a year earlier, most companies' service had got worse, not better. 'Customer service on these sites barely serves customers at all – and to make matters worse, top sites seem to be delivering more substandard assistance compared with service a year ago,' wrote Karen Solomon, author of the study. Solomon sent customer queries to ten of the largest Web companies, including Amazon.com, America Online, on-line auctioneer eBay, and Yahoo!, and found that four of the ten companies didn't respond at all. 'As a consumer, I don't care to help myself,' Solomon said. 'I am incessantly lazy. I want shopping to be fun and indulgent, and I want to be waited on quickly, hand and foot. I don't give a kilobyte about your costs. And I don't want to read the manual.'

Even experienced retail companies – the so-called '**bricks and mortar**' crowd – coming to the Internet have had difficulty translating their off-line know-how to the on-line world. Toys R Us, the American toy superstore, thought the Christmas of 1999 was going to be superb after the website toysrus.com got huge traffic before the holiday season. But they quickly discovered that they didn't have adequate customer service help to cope with all the queries and orders that were flooding in. As a result, the company made only $39 million in holiday sales, below their competitors Amazon.com and eToys, who commanded $95 million and $106 million respectively. For the following year, the company announced it would double its staff and expand operations, including building two new fulfilment centres to handle the demand.

All this investment in improving customer experience means that there is a burgeoning job market for tech-savvy individuals who also have a **human touch**. Whether it be staffing a call centre, or just responding to customer queries by e-mail, a growing proportion of the Internet economy is devoted to easing the angst of the customer.

Ben Cook, customer operations manager for a company called lastorders.com, has one of the more enviable jobs around. He answers questions about beer for a living. Lastorders.com bills itself as 'the on-line off-licence', but as the founders proudly tell people, 'We sell booze on-line.'

Cook, a New Zealander, joined the Edinburgh-based company several years after finishing university. 'At university I studied sciences – boring I know, but I kinda like them – and management,' Cook says. 'In between university and starting work at lastorders.com, I travelled the world for just under two years [spending] six months in North America, six months in Brazil, four months in Iran and four in Europe. I love travelling, seeing new places, meeting new people, learning new languages, etc. I think the main reason that I ended up at lastorders.com is because I am a people person.

'A little bit of luck was also involved. I never set out to be a customer services manager, but when I met [company founders] James [Oliver] and Ian [Gardiner], I shared their vision and excitement for lastorders.com, so I came on board the team and found that my strength was dealing with our customers, so I evolved into the position. Joining the company early on was a great advantage because I was allowed a lot of input into how our customer services department developed. I don't see customer services as rocket science, but I think it helps to be a dynamic person who thinks quickly on their feet.'

Stephanie Chapman is customer services manager with Nutravida.com, an on-line nutrition and vitamin retailer. Like Cook at lastorders.com, she joined Nutravida when it was a very young company and grew along with it.

'My background is in retail operations,' she says. 'I have been a personal assistant to senior members of staff for the past five years, moving to office manager of [Nutravida]. My move to customer services grew with the company, as after the launch I started dealing with our first customer enquiries and progressed from there.'

Cook says his job starts when a customer first visits the site, and carries on right up to the time when the customer receives their order and goes away happy. He oversees a crew of people who respond to customer queries, both by phone and e-mail, but also makes sure that orders are delivered on time, which involves co-ordinating between the corporate offices in London and Edinburgh, the London-based warehouse that holds the booze, and the Birmingham courier company that delivers it.

His day starts at 8.30, when orders dispatched the previous day are checked to make sure they arrived at the correct place. Cook and his staff verify that the right price was charged, the right amount of product was shipped, and that the names and addresses on credit cards match the names and addresses the orders have been shipped to. They also respond to questions from the warehouse and the courier service. Throughout the day, the team responds to phone and e-mail queries from customers as they come in.

'Making sure that my team is okay and coping with everything is a major part of my day,' Cook says. 'I believe that our customer services team look after the "nuts and bolts" of the company, making sure that everything is running smoothly. Our customers are our income, so we do what we can to make sure that they aren't just happy but ecstatic about our service.'

Chapman says she agrees with the conventional wisdom that customer service has become an increasingly important investment for Internet companies.

'It is imperative that an Internet company has a live person who the customer can speak to or e-mail,' she says. 'As the customer cannot meet us they may require some form of assurance that their order will be dealt with correctly and that their payment details are secure. As so many people are wary of the Internet, having a real person to speak to can ensure those customers place orders rather than being put off by on-line ordering.'

Since the customer service department may be the only human contact customers have with the company, Cook says it's crucial to have top-notch service – both at the end of the phone line and at the keyboard responding to e-mails.

'Being an Internet company means that we have very little contact with our customers, so the whole concept of good customer service is much more important,' he says. 'I am a consumer and like most people I like to know that there is someone on the other side of the computer. I order over the Internet a lot and like our customers I would expect someone knowledgeable to answer my calls rapidly should I need to know something, or answer my e-mails rapidly. I see customer service as the core thing that differentiates [us] from our competitors. Working in the booze industry with tight margins, there is often little difference in price between us and our competitors, so we use our customer service to get customers to continually come back to our site. We do this by employing genuine people who care about our customers. No one can fake good customer service. You've either got it or you haven't.'

Chapman agrees. 'The customer service department can make or break an Internet company ,' she says. 'If you deal with a problem well the customers are very grateful and will use the site again. A well-handled problem can be a real positive.'

Cook describes customer service as the front line of the Internet industry, where actual revenues start to pay back the huge amount of investment companies put into building their websites and background technology. Despite the importance of the task, he says, customer service is often underrated. 'Without customers, nobody including us would be in business, so I can't understand why some people pass off the job as menial. It's a job that you can sink your teeth into and really make something of it. I can express myself in the job and get a lot of satisfaction out of it. I am always learning new things, which is what I like the most. Within the company I am surrounded by a buzzing group of intelligent people who are always keen to share their knowledge and experience for the good of the company. I have never enjoyed a job so much in my life.'

But don't expect the job to be an endless stream of joyous interactions with customers, warns Chapman. 'The stress levels can be quite high when you are dealing with complaints,' she says. 'As you are the first point of contact for a customer you can be shouted at and get the full brunt of their complaint. You are on constant deadlines as orders must be processed and delivered within a certain timescale. Customer enquiries must also be responded to within twenty-four hours, and the stress to ensure these promises are carried out can be quite high.'

SKILLS YOU'LL NEED

The ideal customer service representative is organised, knowledgeable about the product, and able to deal quickly and efficiently with customer enquiries. A cool temperament and confident demeanour also go a long way towards keeping the customer happy.

GETTING THE JOB

- It's a growing market, and many e-commerce sites have positions to fill. Browse through some interesting ones, checking the jobs section to see what might be available. You can also e-mail the address for enquiries to see if there are positions open in the customer services department.
- Remember that your demeanour is what the job is about. Present yourself as calm, collected and, above all, pleasant!
- Familiarise yourself with the company's product or service before enquiring. A large part of customer service is having information at the ready, and demonstrating that in the job interview will make a good impression.
- Many e-commerce companies outsource their customer service to third-party companies. These call centres will have lots of openings, and help you get an understanding of how the job works.

TIPS

- Don't take abuse personally. If you understand that the customer is angry about his service and not with you personally, you can stay calm.
- Be confident in your dealings with customers, so that they will feel confident in you.
- Pass on customers' comments to upper management. The feedback you gather can help the business make decisions.

GLOSSARY

- **Bricks and mortar**

Off-line companies that are 'making an Internet play', in other words trying to morph their old business into an on-line success, either as a result of hype or common sense – often the former.

- **Human touch**

Although it will come as a surprise to some companies, this doesn't mean a recorded message on an answerphone or a website containing useless information or an e-mail address that no one responds to. Analysts say that companies with the most accessible help staff are more likely to succeed.

- **Response time**

The amount of time that elapses between when a customer sends a query to the company and when the company responds. The most common response time? Deplorable.

USEFUL ADDRESSES

- Call Centre Managers Ltd, The Old Brewery, Newtown, Bradford-on-Avon, Wiltshire BA15 1NF, UK.

TEL +44 (0) 1225 86 8888.
FAX +44 (0) 1225 86 2900.

www.callcentremanagers.com;
enquiries@callcentremanagers.com

- CyberCall Ltd, The Stone House, Parc Teifi, Cardigan SA43 1EW, UK.
TEL +44 (0) 800 0388388.
FAX +44 (0) 7050 55 5237.
www.cybercall.co.uk;
webmaster@cybercall.co.uk
- JobBox.net, 1st-Wave.com (Europe) Ltd, Internet House, Aston Lane North, Preston Brook, Cheshire WA7 3PE, UK.
TEL +44 (0) 1928 711000.
FAX +44 (0) 1928 717174.
www.jobbox.net
- Recruit Group, 10 Lloyds Ave, London EC3N 3AX, UK.
TEL +44 (0) 20 7480 7400.
FAX +44 (0) 20 7480 7411.
www.recruitgroup.co.uk;
info@recruitgroup.co.uk

DESIGNER

MONEY: Starting at about £15,000 for junior designers, growing to £70,000 for very senior professionals at the largest Web companies.

HOURS: A basic work day, 9–6 ... unless you're on deadline, in which case be prepared to bed down underneath your desk.

HEALTH RISK: 5/10. Making things look pretty is inherently good for the soul, but the hours and the terrible food (junk food is a staple of being a Web designer) take their toll.

PRESSURE RATING: 5/10. You are in the front line for the appearance of the site, but fortunately not for the business decisions.

GLAMOUR RATING: 2/10. The designer is a desk-bound worker bee – not much room for the jet-set lifestyle.

TRAVEL RATING: 2/10. See 'Glamour rating'.

Probably the most prolific group of Web workers, designers are nonetheless in high demand, and finding good ones is always a top priority of senior management. Understanding the limitations of technology and the principles of design is a rare gift, and a valuable one in an industry for which the website is the only interaction they have with customers or audience.

Old-school websites were about text, text and more text. The early technology prevented Webmasters from putting up anything more in the way of multimedia. In fact, it was only as technology evolved that it was possible for more visual elements to be incorporated into sites at all.

As a result, early Web designers were often better technicians than they were artists. Each new technological development meant a new option open to them, but few were designing their pages with appearance as the first priority.

Today, most of the technological restrictions have been overcome, but the legacy of oddball design still lurks. Habits that were developed to compensate for some shortcoming in Web browsers are still in evidence, even though the shortcoming has long since been eradicated.

A good Web designer still knows plenty about technology, but a new buzzword has crept into the vernacular: usability. Those subscribing to the cult of usability understand that it's not how many bells and whistles are crammed into a Web page that matters but how easy it is for an unsuspecting user to navigate through the site. In many ways, modern Web designers have had to overcome the legacy of distorted pages that came about as a response to temperamental technology.

'It is always important (and usually very frustrating for me) to liaise closely with the technical guys at our place right from [an] early stage so I don't go to the **client** with a beautiful, whiz-bang look for the site which looks fantastic on my printed visuals but won't work within the limitations of the Internet!' says Simon Cohen, a Web designer with RedBanner, a Web consultancy in London.

Cohen has been a professional graphic designer for more than fifteen years. He started off designing promotional materials for the music industry, eventually moving into packaging and print design. His Web design background started as an occasional freelance project, but gradually Internet projects became the focus of his work. Eventually he joined RedBanner, where a team of Web developers combined their technical skill with his artistic background.

Cohen works with the developers at all stages of the site building process. Designers are central figures in the early stages of any Internet project. They are involved from the very first planning meetings through to the final presentation of the concept. This is in contrast to other industries, where designers tend to be the last people to be brought in. In book publishing, for example, they are given a finished manuscript to massage into a visual form, as in magazine or newspaper production. But website construction is a combination of art and architecture. Site design isn't just about picking a colour and a font, but understanding how each page will be read, and how the user will navigate through it.

'There are a lot of sites out there whose design does nothing to improve the user experience, and therefore the business of the company,' says Cohen. '[This is] either because the company hasn't bothered enough with the visual design and it just looks plain boring, or because the designers have got so carried away with the aesthetics of the design that they have ended up sacrificing function for form!'

The Internet industry, though still in its infancy, has certain accepted conventions that guide most designers. Some are intuitive for any kind of design, others are unique to an on-line medium. Pages should be simple (Organic, one of the top UK Web design agencies, uses as its slogan 'Complexity recognised, simplicity realised'). Colours should complement one another, and not interfere with readability (e.g. no white lettering on a yellow background). Designs should be tested on multiple computers running different Web browsers to make sure that variations in the users' technology don't affect the way the page is viewed. Most importantly, the look and feel of the site (condensed to one word – **lookandfeel** – in Web designer speak) should be appropriate to the audience the site caters to.

'Who are you, and who's your audience?' says Jim Frew, Web design guru. 'Are you a twelve-year-old girl trying to communicate with other twelve-year-old girls? The director of a start-up company trying to get some cash from an investment bank? Hint: Purple and unicorns will work really well for one of these situations.'

These are the things the designer has to remind the clients. That client might be an outside company, if you work for a Web development agency, or it might be an internal client, a project manager who is using your services on some new area of the site.

'Essentially, it is my role within the company to oversee all the visual design aspects of a particular job. Normally, the first stage of any job will involve taking a creative brief from a new client, interpreting that brief in a way that is not only visually attractive, but also represents the core brand values of the company,' says Cohen. 'This generally means that I will come up with three proposed visual routes, which, through a process of meetings and amendments with the client, will end up as one approved design for the lookandfeel of the site.'

Once the client has approved this plan, Cohen produces a 'style guideline document' which shows how the design will be implemented and is echoed across all the pages of the site. He then works with 'the techies' (i.e. programmers) to make sure that, as the code for the site is written, all the pages have the lookandfeel that he has conceived and which the client has approved.

'When a client comes to us, as they often do, with their own designs, it is down to me to ensure that the design is consistent, and suitable for the Web, overseeing any changes to it to ensure that we can make it work without losing the integrity of their design,' Cohen says. 'This is normally way harder than doing the whole design myself!'

Satisfying the client can be a full-time job for any designer. The nightmare scenario looks something like this:

WEEK 1
Client: 'I'd really like to have the website greet all visitors by flashing their name in pink neon letters.'
Designer: 'A better idea might be to greet them with a discreet pop-up window.'
Client: 'I really want pink neon letters.'

WEEK 2
Client: 'These pink neon letters are too big. Can we make them smaller?'

WEEK 3
Client: 'These pink neon letters are too bright. Can we make them less neon?'

WEEK 4
Client: 'These pink neon letters are too pink. Can we make them a discreet blue?'

WEEK 5
Client: 'These discreet blue letters use up too much of the start page. Can we make them show up in a pop-up window?'

WEEK 6
Client: 'I love the way we greet visitors with a discreet pop-up window. You've executed well on my ideas. But why are we six weeks behind schedule?'
Designer: 'Sigh!'

'The stress of my job is related directly to the attitude of the client. When a client is clear about what they want their site to achieve, and what sort of image they are trying to project, the job tends to go smoothly, and the pressure on me is simply to produce visually exciting designs that satisfy those requirements within the timeframe,' Cohen says. 'The stress starts to increase when the clients themselves are not clear about what they are trying to do. It is not unusual for a job to change direction days from a deadline, and more often than not it is down to the designer to find a way of incorporating the new direction into a site design that may well have started from a radically different brief.'

Web designers are often depicted as a cultish crew, and strike fear into the hearts of managers. Good design talent is rare and valuable, and as a species designers generally get treated with kid gloves by the powers that be.

'Thankfully for the beginners out there, there is a shortage of skill, so some companies may take on college leavers without any experience,' says Brian Mann, a Web designer and founder of Fernhart New Media, an e-commerce consultancy. 'I was in print design for ten years, but [in 1995] I discovered the Internet. The design angle was just raising its head in the UK so I felt as a designer that I could make a good name for myself in this crazy sector. So with two other guys (one of a technical background and one with a sales background) we decided to jump on the Internet highway for ourselves. You may find this amusing now but at the time everyone thought I was mad! Who's laughing now?' Today, Mann's Web services company is thriving, and their clients range from Virgin Radio to Granada Media Group and ITV.

With demand so high, wages are going up all the time, and many designers are finding they can play the field as a freelancer or start their own company, charging exorbitant rates and avoiding work whenever they don't want to take on a project.

'As a freelancer, a designer will always earn a bit more, mainly because you get paid by the hour, and we tend to work long hours, but obviously there are no guarantees that you are going to be able to find work all the time,' says Cohen. 'When the workload begins to slow down for a company, it is always the freelancers who are going to be first to feel the pinch.'

The most successful designers are those who not only have innovative visual ideas, but who can also talk easily to clients and understand what their wants are. To make a gross generalisation, graphic designers tend to be introverted and withdrawn, preferring the company of their computer to that of the loudmouth marketing manager who is attempting to request the moon. As anyone who has ever worked on a freshly conceived project will tell you, getting drawn into interminable planning meetings can turn into the bane of the designer's existence. Most will try and keep meetings to a minimum, and actual time designing to a maximum.

'Ordinarily I will have maybe one or two client meetings, which I would hope would last no more than an hour or two each, and the rest of the day it's a case of sketching out designs, putting visuals together on the Mac, going through design implementation with the developers – the usual design processes, really.'

While some designers view their lot as that of a general dogsbody to the client's vision, they still appreciate that, as the Internet is a visual medium, they play one of the most important roles in the industry. 'My role is quite an important one really,' says Mann. 'My work is the first thing that a consumer sees when they enter the site.'

Cohen agrees.

'In a way, the role of designers within the Internet industry is the most visible one,' he says. 'The lookandfeel of a site is the first thing that most people will notice. What they possibly don't appreciate is the way a good design is integral to the success of a site as a business tool, not just visually but strategically.'

SKILLS YOU'LL NEED

Standard graphic design skills, knowledge of Web and Internet design tools, and an ability to discuss your ideas with the client and understand their ideas for the project.

GETTING THE JOB

- Prepare an on-line portfolio you can direct prospective employers to.
- Develop a list of possible sites to work on.
- Approach Web recruiting agencies for freelance or permanent work. Temp jobs often extend to something more permanent.
- Emphasise both your design skills and client skills in the interview.

TIPS

- Keep your hand in with developing technologies. Sites like Webmonkey and Builder.com offer sections on emerging tools for the innovative Web designer.
- Study the trends in Web design by browsing constantly. A new trick displayed on the South-East Asian Fish Sellers' Union website could be applicable to your client.
- Subscribe to industry publications that provide advice for Web designers, such as *New Media Creative* from Centaur Publishing, a UK-based publication, and *.Net*.
- Participate in on-line forums that discuss Web design issues. The design community on-line is a very active one, and spends a lot of time trading ideas and exploring new concepts. And hey, it's a great way to network and find new jobs.
- Web designers are in such high demand that recruitment agencies have a steady flow of work. Several of these specialise in Web creative work, like Monster.co.uk and Recruit Media. Register with these agencies.
- Top Web agencies are always on the hunt for new talent. From large agencies like iXL and Organic to smaller ones like RedBanner and Fernhart New Media, their current projects can be a good source of new ideas and their job listings can be helpful for finessing your career prospects.

GLOSSARY

- **Client**

Either your best friend or worst enemy, but every good designer should develop skills for making the client happy.

● **Lookandfeel**
Internet buzzword for the way a site looks and the message it sends to viewers.

USEFUL ADDRESSES

● Builder.com, 150 Chestnut St, San Francisco, CA 94111, USA.
TEL +1 415 364 8900.
www.builder.com

● Fernhart New Media, 87 Avenue Rd, Beckenham, Kent BR3 4RX, UK.
TEL +44 (0) 20 8659 2233.
FAX +44 (0) 20 8659 0618.
www.fernhart.com;
service@fernhart.com

● iXL, Tower House, 8–14 Southampton St, London WC2E 7HA, UK.
TEL +44 (0) 20 7632 4300.
FAX +44 (0) 20 7836 8929.
www.ixl.com; info@ixl.com

● New Media Creative, St Giles House, 49–51 Poland St, London W1V 4AX, UK.
TEL +44 (0) 20 7970 4000.
FAX +44 (0) 20 7970 4898.
www.newmediaage.co.uk

● Organic, 70 Salisbury Rd, London NW6 6NU, UK.
TEL +44 (0) 20 7644 2600.
FAX +44 (0) 20 7644 2609.
www.organic.com

● Recruit Media, 20 Colebrooke Row, London N1 8AP, UK.
TEL +44 (0) 20 7704 1227.
FAX +44 (0) 20 7704 1370.
www.recruitmedia.co.uk;
mailto:info@recruitmedia.co.uk

● RedBanner, 15/16 Steward St, Old Spitalfields Market, London E1 6AJ.
TEL +44 (0) 20 7456 0420.
FAX +44 (0) 20 7456 0421.
www.redbanner.com;
info@redbanner.com

● Webmonkey – Designers Resource, Lycos-Wired Digital, 660 Third St, San Francisco, CA 94103, USA.
TEL +1 415 276 8400.
FAX +1 415 276 8500.
www.webmonkey.com/designers;
Webmonkey@wired.com

EDITOR

MONEY: £16,000–£46,000. Some of the top jobs at the most famous websites (e.g. the *Wall Street Journal*, CNN) may exceed this, but the bulk of Web editing jobs fall in the £20,000–£30,000 range.

HOURS: Regular office hours, but expect them to be longer when crises erupt. Which they do. Every day.

HEALTH RISK: 2/10, except for the risk of heart attack when you see you've just published, by mistake, the graphic love letter to your significant other instead of an article about the hot new products from Sony.

PRESSURE RATING: 6/10. Not all of the responsibility falls to the editor, but a significant proportion does.

GLAMOUR RATING: 2/10. Forget the glamour, this job is about meeting deadlines and perfectionism.

TRAVEL RATING: 2/10. Another one of those chained-to-your-desk positions.

'Content is King.' That's the battle cry of the Internet. And when the revolution came, someone had to check the spelling. Enter the on-line editor, whom you can recognise from the squint, eyesight ruined by too many hours of staring at flickering computer screens. Although the World Wide Web originally had a reputation for poor-quality writing, and lousy design, today on-line editing has reached a level of sophistication equal to its off-line competition.

There are few more critical positions than the on-line editor in the production of a website. At heart, an Internet site is essentially a publishing and production endeavour, a new medium that combines the best of books, newspapers, magazines, radio and television. Since the early days of the medium, website producers have been fascinated by what technology can do, but as they've become more sophisticated, Web companies have realised that the old rules of publishing still apply. Sites still have to have correct spelling, be easy to read, contain pertinent and relevant information, and be written in an engaging style appropriate to a given audience.

That said, the job of the on-line editor is far more complex than that of their off-line counterparts. Not only do they have to master the written word, they also have to become technically competent in the tools of website production. Most on-line editors know enough **HTML** to program in links, have enough multimedia skills to embed graphics and sound files, and enough Web publishing skills to update pages and post new information to the site. They also have to have editing training to correct and perfect written **content**, and graphic design skills for overseeing the general layout of new content.

The job of the editor varies depending on what type of site they are working on. On news and information sites, the editor is responsible for choosing and editing stories, writing headlines and **blurbs**, and updating stories at an almost constant pace. On commerce sites, the editor's job can range from writing and editing descriptions of products for sale to commissioning **advertorials**. Government sites and company sites, which provide basic information to consumers and constituents, pose their own special challenges, a combination of news and promotional content that nonetheless requires sound knowledge of the basic rules of editing.

The Web changed the world of publishing immeasurably. Suddenly, the barriers to entry of producing a written work and offering it to a worldwide audience were reduced to almost nothing. Anyone who could lay their hands on a computer and Web address could tell the world almost anything. Gone were the days when a massive investment in paper, ink and printing presses served as a practical, if undemocratic, filtering system.

When it was more expensive to produce written work, more thought and time were given to making sure the work was as close to perfection as possible. Also, paper is more permanent than the Internet. Make an egregious typo or misspell a name on the Web, and the error can be quickly corrected. Do the same in a monthly magazine, and editors face a series of grovelling apology letters, published corrections, or even libel suits.

The immediacy of Web publishing also means that competition for news has reached an unstoppable pace. On a daily newspaper, deadlines happen once a day. But on the Internet, deadlines can happen all the time. This around-the-clock publishing schedule builds new stresses into the job of the editor, who can no longer look forward to a quick one down the pub after the 10 p.m. copy deadline.

The frantic pace, the open access and the impermanence of Web publishing have led to the medium being viewed with condescension by those in the print world. But after some embarrassing mistakes in the early days, Web editors have struggled to overcome the challenge of endless deadlines and the lure of being able to correct any error, and create some kind of standard of quality.

Editors on the Web today had two reasons to leave behind print publishing and pursue a career in the electronic medium: money and opportunity. Good editors are hard to find, and websites have to pay top dollar to get skilled editorial hands to move into the new medium. With the reputation the Web had for poor-quality editorial, most experienced editors were reluctant to view Internet jobs as worthwhile. This reluctance is starting to ebb, however, now that editors recognise it's possible to double their salary by moving to a Web position.

Some, like *The Register* editor Drew Cullen, take to the Internet as a chance to do real independent reporting without the need to raise loads of money. *The Register* reports on issues related to the computer and IT industries with such cheeky irreverence that many people outside those industries also read it. He founded the site with two friends, both of whom, like Cullen, had spent years writing for print magazines.

'We established a cult reputation – a kind of *Private Eye* of the computer industry,' he says. 'We set up as a proper business – with salaries, and an office, in April 1998, and started publishing daily in May. It's grown from there. It's less stressful working for something where you can make a difference. Large companies are OK if you have a civil service mentality – and if you like politics. And not getting things done.'

For young graduates just leaving school, the Internet has become a popular starting place as well. The world of newspaper, magazine or book publishing is extremely hard to break into, and with a shortage of staff on the Internet, young editors found they could make a decent living and enjoy more freedom and creativity if they sought work here rather than in print.

But if the barriers to getting an on-line editing job are lower, by no means is the job any easier. Most editors work long hours chained to their desk, and theirs is the first head on the block if embarrassing mistakes make it onto the website. Whereas a print editor might have one basic responsibility, Web editors often find themselves doing everything from tracking down errant writers to hunting up artistic elements for the site.

'I give assignments to freelance writers and edit their copy, decide (or am told) what other elements need to be part of the feature and obtain them, write all teases, headlines and captions and review the resulting pages with the Web designer before they go live. I also occasionally write an article or portion of a feature myself,' says Maribeth Bruno, senior editor of Playboy.com. '[My day] is a combination of reviewing features in the last stages of design so they can go onto the site that day, of editing and preparing other elements for scheduled features, of planning and assigning future features, and of trying to stay current with Playmate and technology news.' Granted, staying current with *Playboy*'s Playmate news isn't a feature of *every* on-line editing job, but you get the idea. *Playboy* was one of the first international publishing concerns to take to the Internet in a big way, and the website, despite the occasional appearance of scantily clad (or not clad at all) women, has been applauded for the way it's presented.

Stresses like those Bruno describes are present in any kind of publishing job, but she has to face hers on a daily basis. The pace of Web publishing can be relentless. 'Daily deadlines do create stress,' she says. 'And even if you and your co-workers pull off a great job on a particular feature, you know that in a couple of days it will be pushed off the front page in favour of fresh stuff.'

Editors are often the unsung heroes of a Web publishing enterprise, keeping the daily machinations of the production of content running smoothly. Sadly, there's not a lot of glamour in the job, although the pay compares favourably and the opportunities for advancement are strong.

'There certainly is a level of glamour in arriving at the Playboy Mansion and being allowed in, even if you're there just to provide editorial for a webcast, and I'm not going to say it wasn't fun to follow six Playmates around South Beach for a weekend,' says Bruno. 'I don't think editors get a lot of respect in the Internet industry, but visitors to our site seem to appreciate a well-written article as much as they would if it were on paper, so I'm hopeful for the future of the job.'

On the glamour side, Cullen agrees. 'It's not glamorous, unless you think being an editor with a computer Web mag is glamorous – in which case I would urge you to get out more,' he says.

Like many who end up as Web editors, Bruno left university looking for a job in print publishing. 'The year I graduated from college was reportedly one of the worst years ever for finding a job, so after many fruitless attempts at employment I went back to school,' she says. 'I got a lot of good practical skills out of that and also some good contacts, but a graduate degree is hardly necessary for this business. I started with *Playboy* as a proof-reader, but also took freelance writing jobs and taught myself some HTML, so when *Playboy* began expanding its on-line division I was ready to make the jump.'

The crucial thing for someone seeking a position in Web publishing is to develop both technical and editorial skills. 'Be a good writer and for goodness' sake a spelling and grammar whiz, because hardly anyone you work with will be,' says Bruno. 'Know a little about a lot of different subjects, understand the Internet's strengths and weaknesses, and be willing to learn new skills – HTML, **FTP** and what have you. Then work your way to the top, baby.'

Even more importantly, says Cullen, no matter how awful your job is, remember that it could always be worse. 'Running *The Register* is a hell of a lot easier on the mind than working on, say, a conveyor belt churning out meat pies,' he says. 'I speak from experience.'

SKILLS YOU'LL NEED

Strong editing skills, familiarity with HTML and Web publishing programs, knowledge of Web publishing conventions and page design, good organisation, and an interest in the content you're developing.

GETTING THE JOB

- Build a website that highlights your ability. Post stories you have written or edited, along with supporting elements like art or audio and video files. Refer prospective employers to this site when applying for jobs.
- Prepare an electronic version of your portfolio and CV. In the electronic publishing industry, many employers are accustomed to viewing materials on-screen. Rather than sending your application through the post, check first and see if they would prefer an electronic version e-mailed to them.

- Many sites hire on a freelance or contract basis that can lead to permanent work. However, it's not impossible to make a decent living as a freelance editor as well. Check out www.freelancers.co.uk for ideas.

TIPS

- Just because it's new media doesn't mean the old media rules stop applying. Words still need to be spelled right, stories need to be well written and engaging, and art elements need to support the story. Keep your editing skills sharp.
- Study Web publishing by browsing many different sites. Observe how different elements of a page fit together, and how static (unchanging) parts of the page work with dynamic (changing) elements.
- Keep current on new Web technologies and techniques. New technologies for managing and producing content emerge all the time. The on-line editor is a 'creative', but this is one area where technology and creativity are intertwined.

GLOSSARY

- **Advertorials**
Website content designed to promote a specific product, and placed on the site in exchange for a fee if it's a third-party site or by the company themselves if it is their own site.
- **Blurbs**
Sharp, pithy and – above all – short phrases on the home page of a website designed to entice the user to click through to another page. An art form in and of itself.
- **Content**
The mass of information that makes up a website: words, pictures, video and audio files. Basically things to look at and listen to.
- **FTP**
File Transfer Protocol, a format for exchanging files over the Internet.
- **HTML**
Hyper Text Mark-up Language, the basic programming language for writing Web pages.

USEFUL ADDRESSES

- Freelancers.co.uk (on-line only).
www.freelancers.co.uk/;
queries@freelancers.co.uk
- Media Guardian, 119 Farringdon Rd, London EC1R 3DJ, UK.
TEL +44 (0) 20 7239 9685.
FAX +44 (0) 20 7837 2114.
www.mediaguardian.com
- Mousetrap Media, 8–12 Middle St, Brighton BN1 1AL, UK.
TEL +44 (0) 1273 384293.
FAX +44 (0) 1273 384291.
www.journalism.co.uk;
www.mousetrapmedia.co.uk;
jobs@journalism.co.uk
- NetJobs (on-line only).
www.netjobs.co.uk/;
info@netjobs.co.uk
- New Media Age, St Giles House, 49–51 Poland St, London W1V 4AX, UK.
TEL +44 (0) 20 7970 4000.
FAX +44 (0) 20 7970 4898.
www.newmediaage.co.uk
- Recruit Media, 20 Colebrooke Row, London N1 8AP, UK.
TEL +44 (0) 20 7704 1227.
FAX +44 (0) 20 7704 1370.
www.recruitmedia.co.uk;
info@recruitmedia.co.uk

● UK Press Gazette, 19 Scarbrook Rd, Croydon, Surrey CR9 1LX, UK.
TEL +44 (0) 20 8565 4200.
FAX +44 (0) 20 8565 4462.
www.pressgazette.co.uk

Entrepreneur

Money: £0 to millions. Entrepreneurs starting out often work for nothing, but with success comes the pay-off.

Hours: a minimum of ten hours per day – often more – and one weekend day at least in start-up phase.

Health risk: 8/10. The hard-working entrepreneur can easily become a slave to the vision.

Pressure rating: 8/10. From raising money and keeping investors happy to finding employees and keeping them happy to actually making your business work: the weight is on the hearty shoulders of the entrepreneur.

Glamour rating: 5/10. When it works, you're golden. When it flops, you're a lunatic. The heady heights of fame and the dolorous depths of mediocrity have all been scaled and plumbed by the Internet entrepreneur.

Travel rating: 10/10. Always on the go. Learn to love it.

The Internet has minted its own breed of heroes, and they are the entrepreneurs. These are the idealistic, wildly ambitious, frantically driven architects of the Internet economy. They could alternatively be described as selfless visionaries or greed-driven opportunists, but they have carved out a new way of doing business that takes power away from the old corporate structure and have established a new perception of successful business people as young and smart instead of old and experienced.

The culture of Internet businesses gave rise to a new kind of fashion: busy chic. The less time you have to eat, sleep, bathe, watch telly and attend to the demands of nature, the more respect you command. This is a far cry from the old model, where success meant you had earned a life of leisure. The successful businessman didn't rise at 5 a.m., down a banana and a cup of tea, rush to the office, take meetings and draft e-mail until 6.30 p.m., rush to a cocktail party, grab the red-eye to New York or the Eurostar to Paris, take more meetings, and start the process all over again.

It is virtually compulsory that conversations with colleagues start out with a litany of how busy you've been. Here's a quick quiz to see if you'd make it as an Internet entrepreneur. Tick one answer to the following questions:

Question: 'Hello, how've you been?'
Answer A: 'Great, never better.'
Answer B: 'Really busy. I just flew in yesterday from Munich where we had a meeting with our **mezzanine investors**, but I had to stop over in Paris on the way home to sit on a panel with four other start-up founders to discuss the impact of mobile phones on the industry. Oh! And I met with Jan Jorgensen at

Heathrow to talk about our strategic partnership as he was on his way to Baghdad to meet with his outsourcing partner. How're you?'
Question: 'Want to have lunch this week?'
Answer A: 'Sure, how about Thursday?'
Answer B: 'Well, I've got to be in Stockholm on Monday for the International Web Summit where I'm giving a presentation. I'm back on Tuesday but I've got to meet with the design group to finalise the lookandfeel for the beta launch as well as put the final touches to the strategic marketing survey to help ascertain our target demographic. Friday morning I've got a meeting with the investors to close our second round but I have to be back in the office by one for a meeting with the branding expert to go over logo concepts. Wednesday I'm in Milan to meet with our content partners. Um, how about Thursday?'

If you chose answer A to either question, forget it, baby, you're old economy all the way. Any entrepreneur worth his salt knows that it's not the initials after your name or the money in your bank account but the number of entries in your diary which counts in this industry.

The modern Internet entrepreneur has become something of an icon. In the olden days of the Internet (early 1990s), it was the young and the restless who pioneered development of the medium. The Internet, early on, was a phenomenon found primarily in universities, so it was young people who were exposed to it. As the Net started to get commercialised in the mid-90s, it was the same young people who made up the bulk of a new wave of experts in the field. Early pioneers like Jerry Yang from Stanford University, who founded Yahoo!, and Marc Andreesen from the University of Illinois, who founded Netscape Communications, won massive recognition in the press for being millionaire whiz kids. Later, in the UK, Martha Lane Fox of Lastminute.com and Kajsa Leander and Ernst Malmsten of Boo.com were glorified for being young, adventurous and savvy. All this media attention attracted copycats who wanted their own hour in the sun.

But for all the attention entrepreneurs get, most will tell you that it's a lot of hard work with no guarantee of a pay-off in the end. In the early days, there's the thrill of raising money, and the promise of somehow launching the next great Internet company. Later on, if everything goes as planned, there's a comfortable routine of doing business. But in the interim, a business has to get built, customers found, employees hired, and, for most Internet companies, investors kept happy.

At the outset, choosing an investor is one of the most critical decisions a budding entrepreneur has to make. In industry parlance, there's 'dumb money' and there's 'smart money', and conventional wisdom is split over which is better. Dumb money, usually from wealthy outfits that just want to get into the Internet game but aren't really sure why, can be ideal. They provide the cash, and you get to spend it. They don't ask too many questions, and they don't attempt to run your business. The downside is they probably can't offer you anything except cash. Smart money, which could come from venture capital companies or a growing horde of 'incubators', may be a bit more high-maintenance in terms of justifying your business proposition, but the industry contacts and know-how they can offer may more than make up for the rigorous going-over they'll give you pre-investment.

Incubators, although they've developed a bad reputation, held a lot of value for Internet companies when the concept was young. One of the most famous, Idealab, was founded in 1996 by a **serial entrepreneur**, Bill Gross. Its idea was to help bright business ideas and their conceivers get started by dealing with the administrative details like office space and fax machines. They also invested small amounts of cash, and introduced entrepreneurs to the industry. Idealab saw its fair share of copycats as dot.com mania spread and more people were looking for ways to make a quick buck. One of the more successful was Garage.com, founded by a long-time Apple Computer executive, Guy Kawasaki. Kawasaki and Garage.com founded a series of conferences known as 'Start-up Bootcamps', which ostensibly teach the entrepreneur everything they need to know for founding their business in a few short days.

These days, enough Internet companies have got off the ground for there to be something of a formula for launching businesses. As more publicity becomes focused on the industry as a whole, the formula has become so familiar that you can refer to each stage by a catch-phrase and your peers will know what you're talking about.

Entrepreneur checklist:
- Have idea for company
- Write business plan
- Raise **seed financing** from **angel** investors or other financiers
- Hire staff
- Build site
- Raise first-round financing
- Issue press release about funding
- Hire more staff
- Expand site
- Launch site
- Issue press release about launch
- Get first customer
- Issue press release about first customer
- Raise second-round funding
- Issue press release about funding
- Expand site
- Issue press release about site expansion

And then either:
- Sell company
- Issue press release about selling company

Or:
- Go public
- Issue press release about going public

Entrepreneurs may refer to their early-stage investors, particularly if the investor is an individual, not an investment company, as 'our angel', as in 'I'm having lunch with my angel'. The various stages on the list are significant markers. 'I remember when *we* were pre-launch, I didn't sleep for a week.' 'Post-expansion we've really had to rewrite the whole business plan.'

Often, entrepreneurs will be the idealistic, visionary types that come up with a great idea but don't have the business acumen to run the company beyond its infancy. It is an accepted practice to bring in an experienced businessman or woman to run the company after it is up and running. Josh Hannah, the entrepreneur who co-founded Flutter.com, an on-line betting site, says that he and co-founder Vince Monical planned on this happening from the beginning.

'I have two roles: I'm the co-CEO and do all the external stuff and Vince does the internal/COO [chief operating officer] kind of stuff,' Hannah says. 'In addition, I'm the vice president of business development. Vince and I took functional roles in addition to co-CEO roles so that when the day comes to bring in an experienced CEO, we'll have a place for ourselves in the company.'

But in the early days of Flutter, the company was too young to have a rash of lengthy, hyphenated titles on the organisational chart. The co-founders and the early employees all worked together to get the company up and running. A start-up in any industry has lots of ill-defined roles, with everyone taking responsibility for everything, until the company reaches maturity and figures out that their staff list is an organisational nightmare and needs to be rationalised. This is where that experienced CEO comes in handy. 'What do I do?' asks Hannah. 'It's an endless list ... everything! Prepare and manage board meetings, set the overall strategy, networking, PR, interviews, financing and fund-raising, business development, setting international strategy, strategic partnerships ... it's a long list.' How long is the entrepreneur's day? Usually from 8.30 in the morning until midnight in the early life of a company, Hannah says.

Obviously, a lot of the success of the company will depend on how hard the entrepreneur works, and the Internet industry has come to depend on start-up CEOs working every daylight hour and quite a few of the darker ones as well.

Michael Zur-Szpiro, co-founder of Moov.com, divides his time between internal and external responsibilities to keep the company moving. 'I spend about a quarter on things like corporate finance and strategy, a quarter on website development, a quarter on selling development projects, a quarter on team and colleagues. There are numerous meetings, either at our offices, at partners' offices (advertising, bank, lawyers) and a lot of phone conferences which link up colleagues from all over. The mad stream is interrupted by countless cappuccinos and espressos and toasted focaccias, but by evening I'm dehydrated and starving and exhausted.'

Not a few entrepreneurs have burned out from the endless amount of work that requires them to promote their company in the press, network endlessly with potential partners, always thinking about where the next round of financing is going to come from, while in the meantime keeping the business running. Lots of what the Internet entrepreneur spends time on isn't related to the day-to-day functions of starting a business, like building the product and getting customers. The industry tends to require spending a lot of cash early on to establish a presence in the market, putting off until later worries about becoming profitable. Because of this, entrepreneurs need always to be worrying about where their next investment is coming from, and this means keeping a high profile in the press, with the entrepreneur spending a lot of time networking.

Philip Orwell, Zur-Szpiro's partner who helped found Moov.com, says the Internet entrepreneur will be superhumanly flexible. 'My job consists of keeping lots of different people happy,' he says. 'As well as keeping our team on track, reinventing the track each month and making sure there's money for what we want to do.'

Hannah says the need for money is the one constant in the life of an entrepreneur. 'The potential for stress is extremely high. We had fifty employees when we were doing our second round – financing went smoothly but the actual cash didn't come in until eleven days before we ran out of money. If you're prone to stress, then that kind of thing will get to you. I am pretty stress-free – don't really know why, it's not like I have some planned activity like a yoga hour to get rid of it or anything, I just work hard on what I can control and don't sweat what I can't – so I stay pretty sane.'

Although many of the early Internet entrepreneurs came from a technical background, increasingly they tend to come from the ranks of business school graduates and management consulting firms. The Internet as an entrepreneurial playground has moved from being the province of the techies to that of the MBAs. Some Internet entrepreneurs will proudly tell you that they don't know anything about technology at all!

Hannah is one who came from both business school and the management consulting side of things. He worked at the management consulting firm Bain & Co. for six years, getting his MBA while working there. 'I got into this because I looked at a bunch of friends running and founding Internet companies and said, I can do that!' he says. 'It looked more challenging and rewarding than what I was doing, so I found a couple of kindred spirits to bolster the determination, we came up with a fun idea and went for it.' Orwell's story is the same: a background in consultancy, and then deciding with his co-founders that they'd had enough of doing someone else's bidding and wanted to strike out on their own. 'We wanted to start our own thing and do something new.' Zur-Szpiro, as well, came from management consultants, in his case Boston Consulting Group.

But while it may seem like a lark at first, entrepreneurs come face to face with reality quickly. Once you have staff in the company, and customers using your product, and investors looking for a return on the money they've sunk into the company, responsibility starts to pile up. Zur-Szpiro offers this advice to the budding entrepreneur: 'Dream and then work to realise the dream. And then change the dream to adapt to reality.'

SKILLS YOU'LL NEED

Ambition, creativity and boundless confidence. Understanding the industry and the capabilities of the Internet is paramount, as is the management talent to attract and motivate staff. Don't forget good health, and physical and mental strength to keep on going when the going looks dreadful.

GETTING THE JOB

- You can't get into the game if you don't start playing. A famous axiom of the Internet industry is 'first-mover advantage', meaning that the first one out of the gate has exponentially greater impact than the seventeen that follow. Or, as a famous footwear company would say, 'Just do it.'
- Be at every cocktail party, and every industry conference. Every person in the room is a potential golden contact for the eager young capitalist.
- Presentations are critical. Perfect your pitch before you do anything else.

TIPS

- Start smart. Get your business plan read by people who you can trust but who also know the industry well enough to offer pertinent suggestions.
- Do market research. Venture capitalists want to know what market need your plan will satisfy. The time is past when any business plan with the word '.com' in the title will get funded.
- Stay current on the news of the industry. Publications like the *Industry Standard*, *Red Herring*, *Wired*, *Business 2.0*, *Tornado-Insider* and *New Media Age* cover what start-ups are doing and who is succeeding.
- Choose your venture capitalist or incubator carefully. Make sure that the equity you give away is equal both to the investment you receive and the support your investor gives you in the form of connections and expertise.
- Attend industry conferences like Garage.com's Start-up Bootcamp to mix with other entrepreneurs and meet investors. You're only as good as your collection of business cards.

GLOSSARY

- **Angel**

A monied individual who gives a start-up its first investment. There are a number of angel investors in the Internet industry who got in and made their money early on their own start-up, and now act as angels to other companies.

- **Incubator**

A company that helps other companies get started by providing office space, equipment and business acumen in exchange for a stake in the start-up.

- **Mezzanine investor**

A mid-level investor. Funding to keep

a company afloat is usually raised in rounds. The first round will be to get the company started, but a large second round might be required later on to help the company expand. Mezzanine funding is raised in between those two rounds, and is usually a smaller amount to keep the company going until the large second round is raised.

- **Seed financing**

The initial financing a company receives to get operations up and running. This is usually much less money for much more equity than any other round of funding.

- **Serial entrepreneur**

The entrepreneur who just can't stop making companies. They build one, sell it, build another ... and so on.

USEFUL ADDRESSES

- Apax Partners, 15 Portland Place, London W1N 3AA, UK.
TEL +44 (0) 20 7872 6300.
FAX +44 (0) 20 7666 6441.
www.apax.com
- Business 2.0, 30 Monmouth St, Bath BA1 2BW, UK.
TEL +44 (0) 1225 442 244.
FAX +44 (0) 1225 732 262.
www.business2.com
- Garage.com, 90 Long Acre, Covent Garden, London WC2E 9RZ, UK.
TEL +44 (0) 20 7849 3014.
FAX +44 (0) 20 7849 3200.
www.garage.com/europe
- Idealab, 130 West Union St, Pasadena, CA 91103, USA.
TEL +1 626 585 6900.
FAX +1 626 535 2701.
www.idealab.com
- Industry Standard, 315 Pacific Ave, San Francisco, CA 94111, USA.
TEL +1 415 733 5400.
FAX +1 415 733 5401.
www.thestandard.com
- New Media Age, St Giles House, 49–51 Poland St, London W1V 4AX, UK.
TEL +44 (0) 20 7970 4000.
FAX +44 (0) 20 7970 4898.
www.newmediaage.co.uk

Evangelist

Money: From £40,000 for corporate evangelism to much, much higher for industry evangelists.

Hours: But for the travel, the life of the evangelist would be a piece of cake. Take away hours spent on a plane and it's cake city.

Health risk: 2/10. Other than a sore jaw from talking all day, the evangelist has little to fear in the health department.

Pressure rating: 3/10. As long as the evangelist continues to believe what they're evangelising about, everything should be low-key.

Glamour rating: 6/10. It's less glamorous than being a movie star, but some evangelists have actual groupies, which should increase the glam factor.

Travel rating: 7/10. Get out a calculator, and start clocking those frequent flyer miles.

Internet evangelists, like their Southern Baptist brethren, spend their days preaching the Word. Unlike the Baptists, they get paid handsomely for their rhetoric. Evangelists are usually associated with a particular product or company, and trot the globe telling people how wonderful that product or company is. An evangelist isn't a sales person, since they never close a deal, and they're not a marketing person, since they don't buy advertising space or come up with funny slogans to put on T-shirts.

Evangelists are a strange concept that the Internet industry has revolutionised, if not invented. Their job is to advocate a certain product, service or company, and although that may involve lobbying government bodies, most often it is simply spreading goodwill throughout the industry by word of mouth.

Nowadays, evangelist has become yet another catch-phrase of the Internet industry. Any sales person who is talking up his product is 'evangelising'. Any headhunter trying to recruit business school graduates is 'evangelising'.

But among the old school, evangelism was a real practice, with a real need.

The Internet industry is based on standards. The only reason we have a World Wide Web at all is because a group of academic and government technologists, in the 1970s, agreed that they would all make their computers talk the same language. In other words, a standard was established. In order for all those technologists to agree, they had to do a certain amount of talking among themselves, and promoting one standard over another. Some technologists who felt strongly about a specific standard devoted considerable time to contacting their colleagues, and talking them round to their way of thinking. This was evangelism, and it has become a way of life in the Internet industry.

Computer and software companies quickly realised that standards could work for them, since 'standard' is just another way of saying 'monopoly'.

They saw that if their product could become the 'de facto standard,' then it could mean big profits, as they would have an almost guaranteed marketplace. Companies, particularly Apple Computers, **Microsoft** and Sun Microsystems, adopted the practice that had started in the government institutions and universities, by hiring people to talk up their products and promote their use.

These 'evangelists' were a hugely successful ploy. They were trusted in the industry because they weren't trying to sell anything, merely trying to point out why Product A would be better than any other product. Apple, Sun, Microsoft and their ilk went out of their way to hire evangelists who were already well known in the computer industry, and so would command greater respect from their audiences. The industry tends to respect people for what they know, and with so much brainpower concentrated in one field, they expose charlatans quickly. An evangelist who isn't up to snuff won't last long, and isn't likely to garner much acclaim unless his or her technical prowess or business acumen is on a par with the salary they are receiving.

These corporate evangelists speak at conferences, write papers about their field, and generally spend their time communicating with other people in the industry to promote their company, cause or product. This means travelling all over the world, giving speeches, networking and talking to the press as an expert source. The fact that corporate evangelists are on a company payroll doesn't detract from the respect they are given by their peers. As mentioned, in many cases they hold a position of influence in the computing world already, and were hired by their corporate sponsors because of this. The non-corporate computer community, which includes research outfits, government bodies and academic institutions, is full of people who had expertise in specific niche sectors of emerging Internet technology – the companies have a wide body of experts to choose from.

While some of those non-corporate programmers and computer chieftains went corporate, many stayed in the public sector or in academia. By no means did they stay out of the arguments over what product or platform was better, though. Like their corporate counterparts, the public sector developed its own kind of evangelist, ones driven by a passionate belief in a specific technology or standard, not necessarily one owned by the company who paid their salary.

Take Eric Raymond, a computer programmer who has spent his whole life behind a keyboard. Raymond is Geek personified. Although he had spent his professional career in computers, it wasn't until 1993 that he became involved with an international network of Über-Geeks who spent all their free time coding software ... for fun. These programmers shared all their work with each other, and as a result built some of the best software programs in the world. They communicated with one other via the Internet, and posted all their work on-line. This decentralised, somewhat amorphous effort is known as the Free Software Movement or the **Open Source Initiative**. Its main product is **Linux**, an operating system like Microsoft Windows that many industry people think may be the one product that can unseat the might of Microsoft.

'I'm a long-time Internet **hacker** who happens to think like an anthropologist,' says Raymond. 'In 1993, I noticed a big question that nobody else saw the importance of. How was the Linux community managing to produce high-quality software while violating every rule of conventional software project management?' In other words, how did a decentralised group of programmers who didn't know each other except in an on-line, virtual capacity manage to produce such innovative software code when no one was paying them to do it and nobody was in charge of the project? (Note: When Raymond says 'hacker', he doesn't mean a spotty thirteen-year-old who tries to break into websites with his father's computer. In old-timey computer terminology, a 'hacker' is just your average, run-of-the-mill programmer. In fact, one of Raymond's roles as an evangelist for the Internet community is to discourage the media from using the word 'hacker' to describe the criminal activities of teenage computer enthusiasts. For anyone wanting the politically correct vernacular, those with criminal intent are **crackers**, while people who write code for a living are hackers.)

Raymond studied the open source movement for three years, fascinated partly as a programmer and partly as a nascent anthropologist. He wrote a paper about his observations entitled 'The Cathedral and the Bazaar', a seminal work that has been adopted as a bible by Geeks the world over. He then became a spokesman for the programming community, travelling the world to promote the cause of Open Source software, and the importance of publishing software code (Microsoft, by contrast, keeps the code to its Windows products a well-guarded secret).

'One of my functions is to be sort of a roving ambassador from the Internet hackers to the industry,' Raymond says. 'The development method the Linux and Open Source community have made visible is the same one the Internet community has been using for thirty years.' Programmers working on Linux projects share all their ideas on on-line bulletin boards and in discussion groups, much the same as programmers who work on Internet software.

Raymond is credited within the Internet community for understanding the needs of both his hacker compatriots (who, delicately speaking, tend towards the anarchic) and companies that need to ... well, turn a profit. Linux has gained a huge amount of popular recognition in the media, and corporate recognition on the part of companies starting to use the software Raymond's hacker pals have developed. Many on both sides of the fence say Raymond has helped this uptake by evangelising Linux to the corporates, and convincing the hackers that just because a piece of software makes money doesn't make it unworthy.

'The things I talk about are products of the Internet culture, but until recently they have only been understood unconsciously by techies, and not at all by the Internet industry's management,' he says. 'My job is to remedy both kinds of unawareness.'

As Linux became more popular in the late 1990s, programmers who worked on the project started forming companies to produce commercial versions of the software. One of these was VA Research, later renamed VA Linux. Raymond was appointed as a director of the company, and issued an allotment of shares, valued at the time at around $6,450. More and more press attention focused on Linux, and VA Linux readied itself for an Initial Public Offering (IPO) on the stock exchange. With so much interest in what this collection of volunteer Geeks had developed, the float was hugely successful, setting a record for the largest first-day run-up in the history of the Nasdaq, the American index of high-tech companies. At the end of the first day of trading, Raymond's 150,000 shares were worth $37,387,500.

But that princely sum wasn't achieved by a drive to make money, Raymond says. 'All of the effective Open Source evangelists I know are really motivated by a desire to change the world. They'd be advocates whether they got paid or not – you'd have to club them senseless to stop them, and even then I'm not sure but that they'd restart their spiel before fully regaining consciousness.'

SKILLS YOU'LL NEED

Strong analytical skills, and a convincing gift for rhetoric. Evangelists must also have a passion for their topic, and a strong understanding of the industry as a whole. Good speaking skills and charisma are also on the menu.

GETTING THE JOB

Becoming an evangelist isn't about going down to the local job centre and applying for a post. Evangelists develop over time, and gradually become recognised.

TIPS

- Be opinionated, but be prepared to back up what you say. The industry makes short work of those who attempt to bluff it.
- Keep current on what the industry is talking about. You should be prepared with a thought on every hot topic of the moment. Read trade magazines and the business press to know what's making headlines, and what battles are being fought. Publications like *Wired* offer debate on how the world is affected by technology, while business publications like the *Industry Standard*, *Business 2.0* and *Red Herring* discuss how the commercial world is affected by the Internet.
- Develop an area of expertise. What issue on the Internet is most important to you? Read up on the subject, become familiar with the players involved, and begin contributing to discussion groups and publications on the subject.

GLOSSARY

• Cracker

Criminally minded computer experts who try to break into other people's networks. Honourable computer experts resent the 'hacker' tag being given negative connotations by the media, and so are trying to rebrand those vandals as 'crackers'.

• Hacker

A programmer who writes code, not a teenage criminal. Real hackers are fighting back against the media using their preferred term to describe what they see as pre-pubescent, unskilled vandals.

• Linux

An operating system like Microsoft Windows or Unix. Linux was devised by Linus Torvalds, who wrote the kernel, or heart, of the operating system and then published his work. Because the code is publicly available, software programmers around the world could examine it and try to perfect it, as well as write software programs that would work with it.

• Microsoft

The enemy of Geeks everywhere. This juggernaut of a software company inspires derision from programmers, who say the company has bound the world with buggy software, then collected lucrative support fees for making said software work.

• Open Source Initiative

A backlash against Microsoft, this worldwide volunteer initiative is fighting back against 'black box' software like Microsoft's, in which the inner workings of the code are a mystery to all but Microsoft itself. Linux is an Open Source project.

FINANCE DIRECTOR

MONEY: From £60,000 upwards. Expect a bonus if you save the company money or make its numbers look good.

HOURS: Fairly normal 9–6, except during important times, when the finance director can go several days straight with no sleep.

HEALTH RISK: 6/10. You might get rotten tomatoes hurled at you by investors when your financial results are lower than expected.

PRESSURE RATING: 7/10. Internet companies often take a while to become profitable, so their financial structures are unusually complicated. This means high stress for the person in charge of managing that situation.

GLAMOUR RATING: 2/10. FDs are deliberately low on glamour, since glamour is usually expensive.

TRAVEL RATING: 5/10. You go where the board goes when money is involved, which means the round of London, Frankfurt, Tokyo and New York.

Lots of people think the success of an Internet company relies on a marketing genius or a technical whiz. However, there's someone just as important who's usually in the shadows of the office: the finance director. Even though what they do doesn't seem very exciting, as it usually involves lots of spreadsheets and meetings with people in grey suits, they hold the health of the company in their hands. Money plays the same role for companies that blood plays for people: without enough circulating, there's a major risk of death. Finance directors are there to make sure the money is managed well and never runs out.

Finance directors manage all the money affairs for a company. Although the average finance director has spent a long time climbing up the ranks and learning how to handle a company's financial affairs, nothing can prepare an FD for the pressure involved in working in an Internet company, where all the rules appear to be upside down. The only rule that hasn't changed is that money has to be very carefully managed and accounted for to investors and other interested people.

Most people have become finance directors by training as chartered accountants and working at one of the big accounting firms such as PricewaterhouseCoopers or KPMG. While there, in addition to drinking lots of beer on Friday nights to relieve the boredom, they also tend to work on teams sent out as **auditors**. Auditors are neutral finance professionals who make sure that companies have not misplaced expensive equipment or bought everyone a Ferrari and charged it to 'expenses'. They go through the company's financial affairs very carefully, every year. The finance director in training has plenty of opportunity to see what makes a well-run company and what is a bankruptcy waiting to happen. While they are doing this, they are also learning all the arcane practices of accounting and tax that make up the rule book for finance directors.

Once they have qualified as an accountant, if they decide not to stay at a big accountancy house, they will usually spend a few years with a company in junior or niche positions under the command of a finance director. Their jobs might include:

- purchasing (buying all the stuff a company needs, and dealing with the contracts and payments for these things)
- treasury management (handling the amount of money that the company has in cash or investments)
- controller (which is just what it sounds like – controlling and approving money coming in and out).

It is not until a prospective finance director understands all the above that he or she can really make the next step into understanding how money makes the company tick. The process is similar to becoming a doctor: medical students have to understand all the functions of the body, and do a medical internship in a hospital under experienced doctors, before they are allowed to pick up a scalpel and take the patient's life in their hands.

Once someone gets to the lofty position of finance director, they are effectively responsible for all the operational management issues that affect the company's day-to-day health. The position is challenging in an Internet company, since the company is often borrowing large amounts of money from investors to get going without the immediate likelihood of bringing things into balance with lots of customers and revenue.

The finance director might seem like the guy to feel sorry for. The CEO is usually at conferences in Monte Carlo telling everyone about the great future of Internet shopping. The CTO is in the basement, happily tinkering with a giant database. Meanwhile, the finance director is trying to figure out how a few people in North London buying frozen peas add up to the amount the marketing people need in their budget to tell everyone why they should buy frozen peas on-line. Once he or she has done that impossible calculation, the finance director is usually the one managing nervous investors, who want to see their money again some day. The FD gets to explain why it is necessary to pay for a celebrity dressed up like a green pea to stand outside supermarkets talking about your website to anyone who will listen.

It is an enormous challenge to balance risk-taking with prudence. Because the job is so important, and people who have the right balance of skills and personality are so rare, there is an enormous demand for good finance directors at start-ups, which have realised that having someone talented as finance director may mean extended survival both with investors and with key suppliers.

A good finance director is worth his

or her weight in gold. Not only will he or she be intent on making the company as healthy as possible, but they will be the respectable grey hair outside the company which justifies people's faith and their investment. Finance directors don't always have the easiest time of it. In a company headed by young managers who think that all they have to do is grow, and all they have to do to grow is spend, the FD can seem like an obstacle instead of a solution. In fast-growing technology companies, the finance director is often known as the 'sales prevention officer'. Indeed, the finance director might even veto taking on a large multinational client, because they will recognise that the amount of money and people you need to serve them will entail spending huge amounts of your cash and seeing a very slow return.

An Internet company may seem like a finance director's worst nightmare: constant cash flow issues, a distant prospect of profit, and nervous investors. However, to some finance directors it is the ultimate challenge, and they revel in the Internet company's lack of hierarchy and structure, and their own ability to do more than just balance the books: indeed, the fact that they are the most important person in difficult times. Finance directors in Internet companies are younger than the norm, and are well paid for their responsibility.

Most people in Internet financial roles have the ability to work with both the old and new economies. Martin Greenbank, CFO (Chief Financial Officer) of @rk Investments, says an attribute of young management teams is that they don't have a history of dealing with problems in a professional way: 'The job can be stressful when the management team try to work round problems rather than confronting them.'

The stress level will also rise when exceptional events become the norm, as they do for many Internet companies. Although the typical finance director's calendar resembles that of a farmer, with set planting and seeding times during the year, the Internet company finance director will often find other things upsetting the plan. The company may be short of resources, in which case he or she will end up doing things that are not at all in the job description – typically operational roles like human resources, legal issues or keeping up with health and safety regulations.

As a finance director, you need to be very good at telling the truth, since a good FD will be scrupulously honest and fair in dealing with investors. However, finance directors have their own variety of spin, just as politicians do. Within the accounting rules, and during the budgeting process, the finance director must do what he or she feels is best for the company. If that means understating a certain amount of money due because it isn't guaranteed, that's what he or she has to do. And if he or she can see clouds on the horizon, there's nothing wrong with telling the marketing director to delay the frozen pea celebrity until after the end of the financial year. And a good finance director should always keep a bit in the bank for emergencies, such as having to pay off a member of staff or investor who departs the business prematurely.

The time when a finance director really gets tested in an Internet company is when one of two things happens: a **market** (public) **listing** or a merger or acquisition. A company goes public when it chooses to open its doors to outside investors, a process which is harrowing and expensive. The benefits of being a listed company are those of greater access to money (so key to many rapid-growth Internet companies) and higher visibility. The downsides are greater pressure and openness: all your investors now have a right to know a lot more about you than they did when you were private. Not all big companies go public, despite the benefits: Richard Branson's Virgin Group is a key example of a complex business that chose to stay private to avoid the level of exposure that public companies are subject to.

Mergers occur when the company combines with another, when everything from job titles to accounting systems have to be glued together. Acquisitions are when a company buys another company, usually in the same or a related sector. Both mergers and acquisitions are frequent events in the changing Internet landscape, and prove a real challenge for the management team as a whole: often most difficult for the finance director, who is stuck sorting out all the pieces of a complex jigsaw puzzle.

Martin Greenbank has seen companies through sale and market listing, which is where the finance director stops being Clark Kent, steps into a phone booth and emerges as Superman. Suddenly, the FD is the centre of all activity, and the focus of a lot of pressure from outside the company. His or her natural prudence and calm become major assets in an environment of relentless pressure. The key task is to negotiate the best position for the company while maintaining integrity and sorting through issues that might be as varied as the details of a customer contract or the cost of the company's paper clips.

Clearly, this job isn't one that you can just stroll into. Anyone who wants to become a finance director has to put in at least five years before they acquire the skills (and the acronyms) necessary to do the job. As Greenbank stresses, 'The industry can always make use of intelligent, articulate and hard-working individuals with a "can-do" attitude who are not **risk-averse**.'

SKILLS YOU'LL NEED

The ability to remember where lots of different pieces of paper are. You'll also need to be a spreadsheet wizard, and able to draw graphs of the company's performance which start at the lower left-hand corner of the page and go up rapidly, with one exception – the company's expenses. The ability to count, at least to a hundred, is desirable, but since the finance director's role is lofty, you might be able to hire someone (called a controller) to do that for you. Nearly all finance directors will be expected to be qualified accountants, and to have held a controller position in a company or been an auditor with one of the large accountancy firms.

GETTING THE JOB

- Be qualified: there are no short cuts to becoming a qualified accountant with a big firm of accountants. Choose an accounting firm that has some Internet exposure, whether investments or clients.
- Try taking on a financial role with an incubator: this will give you the chance to work with a group of companies without some of the pressure.
- At interviews, highlight your initiative and the ability to think 'outside the box'.
- Try to build your contact network outside the finance profession at gatherings like FirstTuesday, where you can meet people on the business side who might take a shine to your (discreet) style.

TIPS

Understand if you're the type of person to flourish or be crushed under the pressure. Also ask yourself whether you feel comfortable dealing with lots of different kinds of people, from big City investors to young Internet techies.

GLOSSARY

- **Auditors**

Auditors spend time each year with companies above a certain size in order to make sure the business is reporting its results properly. They are usually a team of serious young people in blue suits who trawl through files looking for the receipts for last year's coffee supplies, which, of course, no one can find.

- **Market listing**

The process of taking a company 'public', or seeking inward investment from a group of outside shareholders. Usually involves a set of criteria such as revenue levels, time in business and compliance with the individual market's rules. Markets for Internet companies may include small-company ones like AIM (the Alternative Investment Market), or the US-based Nasdaq, where Microsoft lives.

- **Risk-averse**

Opposed to taking risks. This is generally used to describe prudence, and can be a deal-making term. Whenever someone suggests there are too many problems with a particular deal, the opposition will suggest they are merely being 'risk-averse', a no-no in the Internet industry.

USEFUL ADDRESSES

- Andersen Consulting, 2 Arundel St, London WC2R 3LT, UK.
TEL +44 (0) 20 7844 4000.
FAX +44 (0) 20 7844 4444.
www.ac.com; jobs@ac.com
- Deloitte Touche Tohmatsu, Stonecutter Court, 1 Stonecutter St, London EC4A 4TR, UK.
TEL +44 (0) 20 7936 3000.
FAX +44 (0) 20 7583 1198.
www.deloitte.co.uk
- Ernst & Young, Rolls House, 7 Rolls Buildings, Fetter Lane, London EC4A 1NH, UK.
TEL +44 (0) 20 7951 2000.
FAX +44 (0) 20 7951 4001.
www.ey.com; info@ey.com

- Institute of Chartered Accountants in England and Wales, Chartered Accountants' Hall, PO Box 433, London EC2P 2BJ, UK.
TEL +44 (0) 20 7920 8100.
FAX +44 (0) 20 7920 8547.
www.icaew.co.uk;
comms@icaew.co.uk
- KPMG Audit plc, 8 Salisbury Square, London EC4Y 8BB, UK.
TEL +44 (0) 20 7311 1000.
FAX +44 (0) 20 7311 3311.
www.kpmg.com; info@kpmg.com
- PricewaterhouseCoopers, Plumtree Court, London EC4A 4HT, UK.
TEL +44 (0) 20 7583 5000.
FAX +44 (0) 20 7822 4652.
www.pricewaterhousecoopers.com

GOVERNMENT ADVISER

MONEY: From £20,000 to about £55,000. Generally, the longer you've been there, the more you get.

HOURS: Civil hours in the civil service, about 40 per week.

HEALTH RISK: 2/10. Civil servants don't lead too stressful a life. The worst danger you'll face is lousy coffee – but you can get that in the private sector, too.

PRESSURE RATING: 4/10. This job is slightly removed from the front line of the Internet industry, and as such doesn't maintain such a high nail-biting factor.

GLAMOUR RATING: 1/10. People do not do these jobs for the glamour. You're anonymous, not particularly well paid, and wear a grey suit.

TRAVEL RATING: 2/10. Public sector work tends to be local – if you're in London, you might get to Northumberland. The exception is working on international committees, when you'll live on a plane.

Entrepreneurs are not the only people forging their way in the brave new world of the Internet. Governments have had to change too. Both governmental and non-governmental organisations have been formed to 'deal with' the changes the Internet has wrought. Some organisations help fund new Internet companies, others help governments adjust old laws to reflect Internet issues, and still more help governments – the oldest of old-school institutions – change their practices to take advantage of the Internet. All these 'public sector' groups rely heavily on advisers who are experts on the Internet, and can offer an objective point of view since they're not attached to a particular company. They are the people who work in Internet-related roles in the public sector. They are concerned with informing government, and making sure government makes the right moves to encourage businesses to succeed on the Internet.

Today, the Internet seems like it was made for capitalism. Dot.coms abound, selling everything from cat food to discount holidays. It's easy to forget, especially when the press is full of reports of 'dot.com millionaires', that this communications revolution was originally the work of stodgy, slow-moving governments. The American military built the original Internet, and the World Wide Web was conceived at the Swiss research organisation CERN. Although the Internet has moved from being an open-access, free network for the exchange of ideas to its current incarnation as the communications network for electronic mail and transactions, there are still a number of people in the public sector who concern themselves with Internet questions.

They may not be getting rich from a dot.com scheme, but Internet companies pay them special attention, since regulation will shape the way the industry evolves. Governments around the world are trying to ensure that they are supporting business by encouraging competition on-line, supporting equal access to the Internet for their entire populations, and making sure that they take their own medicine by using the best of modern technology and making it accessible to enhance the public's interaction with government. There are a number of governmental, quasi-governmental, and quasi-private sector bodies who enable these things to happen. Some are organisations set up and funded by the government, some are set up by the industry to lobby the government, and some are set up by independent bodies to serve as the consumers' voice, neither industry nor government.

One of the most critical organisations in the Internet field is OFTEL, or the Office of the Telecommunications Regulator. OFTEL handles such meaty questions as fair pricing for high-speed Internet access, and fair pricing for lifetime Internet usage. OFTEL's role is also to keep close tabs on British Telecom and make sure that it is not preventing other people from succeeding in the Internet market. Although it is a powerful organisation, it is very small. Since it spends public money, OFTEL has an incentive to keep its structure lean, and employs fewer than 200 people.

There are also relevant parts of the Cabinet Office, the Department of Trade and Industry and the Confederation of British Industry (a quasi-governmental institution) which take on different Internet-related issues. The Department of Trade and Industry is particularly concerned with establishing the right commercial infrastructure for e-commerce to succeed. Patricia Hewitt is currently the e-minister within the DTI. She works together with an 'e-envoy' and the minister for e-government, who advise the Prime Minister about what tack to take in promoting the use of the Internet both inside and outside government.

The Internet has thrown government for a loop. It is widely recognised in government circles that the need for modernisation is critical. Hefty targets have been set for this (fifty per cent of all interactions with government, particularly for routine transactions like getting a driving licence, should be available on the Internet by 2002). All the same, government has been at something of a loss as to how to make this happen.

A new post was created in 1998 for someone to broker between business and government, and to make sure that the government's modernisation was taken in hand. Alex Allan, the former British high commissioner to Australia and IT consultant, became the first e-envoy. Although he lasted only six months in the job, he set ambitious goals for the government. 'Successful businesses are based on quite a lot of individual initiative,' he says. 'That's difficult for government.

Government has trouble coming to grips with things that move fast.'

This problem could also be said to apply to the non-governmental organisations in the public sector, which is often mired in red tape and lengthy procurement processes. Therefore, for projects like information technology, there are a group of consultants who specialise in public sector projects. Deirdre Pappalardo is a consultant with Kable, a research consultancy that focuses on public sector IT and telecommunications projects. Prior to joining Kable, Pappalardo had a strong background in public sector work. 'I have worked in Congress, for a public affairs firm in the US and one in the UK, and have a Masters' from Cambridge,' she says. 'All of this required research and analytical skills, and through my previous jobs I gained a solid background in telecoms and e-government: a topic that is impossible to avoid these days.'

Many of these organisations have little public visibility but are filled with extremely committed people who believe in public sector infrastructure as supporting and, indeed, making possible the current Internet and e-business revolution.

Although much government activity seems to be taken up with big business and Westminster, there are many local and regional development groups which make sure that everyone can maximise their Internet potential. Business Link is a DTI-funded initiative that helps small businesses get started, and there are a number of Internet and e-commerce specialists within local Business Links.

There is also a group of regional development agencies that make sure that the new media revolution is not confined to major metropolitan areas. Sarah Turner is the executive director of one such group, Wired Sussex, which 'works with over five hundred companies in Sussex to establish the area as one of the leading centres in Europe of new media production and e-commerce'. Turner has a Masters' degree in multimedia, and worked for a training organisation before joining Wired Sussex in 1997.

Other groups are making sure that there are not two socio-economic groups: IT haves and have-nots. The concern has arisen that the Internet, although creating many opportunities, is contributing to a less than equal society. Only those with enough income to support a PC or interactive television and to pay the phone or service provider bills may take advantage of the wealth of resources the Net has to offer. Initiatives such as the government's Social Exclusion Unit have, as part of their mission, the mandate to make PCs and Internet training available to those who need it the most and who currently can't afford it.

People who choose careers in the public sector often have a naturally serious outlook and a sense of vocation, which makes up for the lack of external prestige and high salaries that many dot.com employees enjoy. 'People look at you as the "expert" in government policy and developments – and often use your research to make business decisions,' says Pappalardo.

'The job isn't glamorous, but rather, well respected.' Turner agrees, and says that Wired Sussex uses its information 'to influence what's going on locally, nationally and internationally'. She speaks enthusiastically of the effects of Wired Sussex's work, which include 'the creation of hundreds of high-value jobs in the area, and Brighton's image in the national press as Silicon Beach'.

The public sector values substance over style, and the path to becoming a respected figure in a public sector career means you have to pay your dues. Respect and opportunities depend on academic achievement, prior track record, and a certain level of networking among public sector organisations.

People in these roles have put a great deal of thought into their position and impact on the Internet industry. '[We are] the outsiders who step back and observe, analyse, and criticise what politicians and civil service are doing, help industry figure out what government is up to, and, on good days, actually influence policy because we can step back and look at the big picture and analyse issues in depth,' Pappalardo says.

The public sector tends to be parallel to but separate from the private sector. Most public sector employees working in the Internet arena have a degree in politics, economics or mathematics, have worked in a consultancy or for an organisation like OFTEL, and have then moved elsewhere in the public sector.

SKILLS YOU'LL NEED

- A detailed understanding of government policy and its impact on business.
- A degree in economics, mathematics, government or politics.
- Some experience working with a consultancy or the public affairs department of a major company.
- A desire to make the world a better place for consumers, and an interest in how government helps to achieve that.

GETTING THE JOB

- While policy organisations tend to keep a low profile, all public sector bodies do advertise available jobs.
- Contact the careers office of the Civil Service.
- Find out what regional development agencies are operational in your area, and look on their websites for job opportunities.

USEFUL ADDRESSES

- Department of Trade and Industry (DTI), 1 Victoria St, London SW1H 0ET, UK.
TEL +44 (0) 20 7215 5000.
FAX +44 (0) 20 7222 0612.
www.dti.gov.uk;
dti.enquiries@dti.gsi.gov.uk
- Kable Ltd, The Courtyard, 55 Charterhouse St, London EC1M 6HA, UK.
TEL +44 (0) 20 7608 0900.
FAX +44 (0) 20 7608 0901.
www.kablenet.com
- OFTEL, 50 Ludgate Hill, London EC4M 7JJ, UK.
TEL +44 (0) 20 7634 8888.
FAX +44 (0) 20 7634 8943.
www.oftel.gov.uk

- Wired Sussex, 23 Old Steine,
Brighton, East Sussex BN 1 1EL, UK.
TEL +44 (0) 1273 666 830.
FAX +44 (0) 1273 666 832.
www.wiredsussex.com;
info@wiredsussex.com

Guru

Money: From £160,000 for gurus on staff at a company to £7.5 million for expert independent management and financial gurus.

Hours: 50–60 per week. A busy guru has to stay on top of new developments as well as jet around the globe dispensing wisdom.

Health risk: 4/10. Getting the star treatment from corporations around the globe isn't too taxing, depending on how averse you are to free Dom Perignon.

Pressure rating: 5/10. The most stressful part of guru life is deciding which lucrative offer to accept and which to reject.

Glamour rating: 9/10. As close as the Internet industry gets to rock stars, gurus are the celebrities of Geekdom.

Travel rating: 10/10. Most gurus spend a significant portion of their time on a plane, seeing every corner of the globe.

In the youthful Internet industry, many business decisions are as much guesswork as they are a result of thoughtful, rational deliberation. In this climate of uncertainty, experts with a proven track record are a hot commodity. Gurus are a staple of the industry, the cream of the crop, the most in-demand, highly qualified and experienced experts. How can one evolve from simple expert to fully fledged guru? Read on.

To a Hindu, a 'guru' is a spiritual leader or a teacher. To a worker in the Internet industry, a guru is also revered, but more as a guest speaker at conferences than as a religious figure.

The Internet has a long history of reverence for experts in the field. As a bizarre confluence of media and technology, the industry tends to refer to itself as a 'knowledge economy'. In the knowledge economy, ideas and information are respected as much as, if not more than, money and power. Gurus sit at the head table in the knowledge economy, rewarded financially for what they know.

A guru can come from any field, but almost always has a long history in the industry and a wealth of experience, having been around long enough to gain a reputation for knowing more than anyone else. Most were around 'in the early days' (i.e. the early 90s or before), and have developed an expertise related to one specific corner of the industry. Some, like the famed *Wired* columnist Nicholas Negroponte, are futurists or visionaries. Negroponte is a 'big picture' guru, who proselytises on how the Internet and technology are changing the world at large. Other gurus have more specific areas of expertise: there are programming gurus and Web design gurus and public relations gurus and branding gurus and financial gurus and database gurus.

There's no licensing board or entrance exam for admittance into guruhood. It's an ephemeral process that no one can quite quantify.

Basically, a proto-guru will gradually gain recognition from his immediate circle. Then he might publish a few articles that garner some critical acclaim. Articles might be followed by a few appearances at conferences and other industry events. If his area of expertise becomes particularly popular or important, he might be asked to author a book. The book will be followed by more lucrative speaking engagements and requests to write articles for more important publications.

Guruhood escalates from there, but a would-be guru will know they have arrived once the industry starts to pay out ever increasing sums for their opinions and expertise. They will be brought in by corporations to expound on their expertise, and perhaps offer a critique on the way the company addresses particular issues, and how it could change for the better. The rest of their days are spent in contemplation (not unlike the gurus of Hindu extraction), or promoting their writing and themselves through speaking engagements, or getting quoted in the trade and business press (not quite like those other gurus).

Jakob Nielsen is a Danish Internet guru who has won international acclaim for his work as a 'usability expert'. Usability refers to the science and art of making Web pages easier for us lazy and dumb consumers to use. The process might sound simple, but if you think of all the times you've banged your head against your computer screen in frustration while screaming 'Where is the customer service link on this [expletive] website?' then you'll know why Nielsen's services are in demand.

'To a great extent I am just an evangelist trying to convince Internet executives to do what users *actually* want,' he says. 'There is another part of the job which consists of trying to predict the future and tell people how the Internet will be next year and in ten years. Contrary to those of most other futurists, my predictions are at least based on knowledge of user behaviour, which does not change nearly as fast as technology.'

Nielsen has followed what has become the textbook route to guruhood. He spent nearly twenty years in the computer science field before striking out as an independent consultant (the 'official' job title of many gurus).

'I have been doing the same work for twenty years, though the first many years were not at all in any kind of guru capacity. I started out studying computer science but quickly realised that I was more interested in making computers easier than in doing the actual programming,' he says. 'Besides usability I also got into hypertext and on-line information systems in the early 1980s. These topics were considered to be of very limited use back then and did not get much attention.'

In the late 80s and early 90s, personal computers were becoming ridiculously popular, but the computer industry was struggling to keep up. Since so many people wanted to use computers, and most of these people were not experts, the industry had to redesign its software and systems to make them easier to use. Enter Jakob Nielsen, usability expert.

'People had great difficulties using software and large amounts of money were spent on technical support hotlines to answer simple questions that would have been obvious with a better design,' he says. 'Because of this situation, my work got more recognition and I got a very prestigious job as Sun Microsystems' usability guru with the title Distinguished Engineer. Shortly after I joined Sun Microsystems, the Web took off big time, and I decided to change the focus of my job from making software easier to use to making the Web easier to use. Luckily, the definition of the Distinguished Engineer job title is "you are the world's leading expert, so you figure out what is most important to the company in your field".'

After four years as the Web usability expert for Sun Microsystems, Nielsen concluded that he wanted to tackle bigger issues than just how Sun could improve the usability of its Internet products, and decided to found his own company. He started the Nielsen Norman group with Don Norman, a usability expert from Apple Computers who has also attained guru status.

Since then, Nielsen and Norman have lived the life of the guru to the fullest, jetting around the world to speak at conferences for thousands of pounds per day, writing books, publishing articles, and offering opinions to the many journalists who contact them for an objective opinion on a variety of issues.

'There is no true average day in the guru business,' Nielsen sighs, not altogether sincerely. 'There are many days spent visiting clients or lecturing at conferences. Travel days typically only involve one or two events per day since it is hard to get time for more when you have to provide an intense and energised performance. There may be one or two hours speaking in front of a big audience and a few more hours meeting with smaller groups. In the case of a client visit, the small groups will typically be individual teams working on projects that need help. In the case of a conference trip, the small groups may be potential business partners or prospective clients. When staying at home, a typical day would involve loads of e-mail since that is the main way to keep in touch with colleagues and business partners. Most days there will also be a short one-to-two-hour meeting with a local client or a short meeting with my staff to plan future projects. The rest of the day consists of reading, thinking and writing in order to develop new material.'

The bread and butter of the guru is the **conference circuit**. The Internet industry attends thousands of conferences every year, from tiny events for a few hundred people to massive circuses attended by thousands. The big draw at these conferences is the chance to hear well-known industry figures expound on what's new in their field. Most organisers try to have a mix of independent gurus and corporate executives.

'Event organisers want their event to be special, and one of the main ways of standing out is to offer the local audience an opportunity to be in the same room as an international celebrity and ask their own questions,' Nielsen says. 'I have offered to present lectures at a substantially reduced fee through a video link, but almost nobody takes me up on this offer. The words may be the same, the slides may be the same, but it is *not* the same when the guru is not physically in the room. I have estimated that it is typically worth between $100,000 and $250,000 in extra registration fees to an overseas conference organiser when they can feature a prominent international guru as their lead speaker.'

All this publicity puts a hefty strain on a guru to keep their presentations fresh. Some conference speakers have been known to recycle speeches from one conference to the next, drawing groans from the ground as soon as their **Power-Point** slides hit the screen behind the stage. 'Oh no, here we go with the "Digital Nervous System revolution" speech again,' these seasoned conference-goers will groan.

'As a guru, you can never rest on past accomplishments, you always need new material since mid-level people "borrow" everything you do and include it in *their* seminars and articles,' says Nielsen. 'The proper attitude in these cases is to be happy that you have made your mark and to spend the time thinking about the next big thing rather than trying to prevent others from using your material.'

Of course, the pay-off for all that hard thinking is in the cash you can bring in. Nielsen says that the low end of the income spectrum for an established Internet guru is around a quarter of a million dollars per year (£166,000), a typical figure if the guru is employed by a specific company. 'When going independent, there is a potential for higher earnings, and one or two million dollars per year would be about right for a successful independent guru like myself,' he adds. 'A few very famous gurus may go beyond ten million dollars per year, but that's more common for management gurus than for Internet gurus, and I am not at that level myself yet. Independent gurus have income that derives from a combination of consulting fees, lecture fees and book royalties, and there is never any guarantee that next year will be as good as the current year. You can never rest on your laurels as a guru since you have to keep on top of new developments and in front of up-and-coming new people who would like to take over your status.'

The downside of the guru job isn't only the constant threat of losing your edge, but also dealing with a never-ending stream of requests for your time. Although this might seem a bit like crying all the way to the bank, Nielsen says that for a job that basically consists of doing whatever you want to do the stress is surprisingly high. 'The vast freedom of having the world as your playground implies the need to stay in touch with everybody and having to prioritise the huge number of opportunities and requests that come in every day,' he points out. 'There are always too many attractive offers and interesting things to do.'

Keeping up with all the attractive offers, and the constant self-promotion, means that most of a guru's life is spent in some form of transportation. Nielsen says he racks up some 100,000 airline miles per year. Being the world expert in your field means making appearances in many countries on every continent across the globe. 'Travel is necessary because my fans around the world demand to see the guru in person,' he says. 'The more everything else becomes virtual, the more the guru business becomes one of fans wanting to touch the famous person. In my native country of Denmark, there is a saying that "people want to see the giraffe". You can see plenty of nature films on television, but people still go to the zoo.'

As the Internet becomes more important to all industries, and all facets of life, the people who have become famous within the industry find that their fame is suddenly much broader-scale. Such is the respect for the expertise of Nielsen and his ilk that he is beginning to break into product endorsements and even pose for some packaging, although mainly for software, websites and other industry-related products. 'Endorsements and merchandising will be a tricky business, though, since a guru needs to be above the fray and seen as an impartial authority. Actors and sports stars can promote bad products without blemishing their reputation, but gurus need to maintain a high level of integrity and restrict their endorsements to products that they actually believe in,' he says. Nielsen rues the fact that he has yet to make an appearance on a breakfast cereal, but who knows – Webbieos could be the next big thing, and he could be the ideal poster boy.

SKILLS YOU'LL NEED

Years of experience, proven expertise in some sector of the industry, the respect and admiration of thousands, endless energy and an unabashed appetite for self-promotion. Also, a guilty conscience will absolutely preclude any success as a guru, since the work entails accepting vast sums of money simply for offering an opinion.

GETTING THE JOB

- Only years and years of experience can ensure guruhood. Start there!
- Of course, there's always Guru.com, a network of up-and-coming gurus who help each other find jobs and trade information.

TIPS

- Build up an expertise in a certain area, and cultivate an unhealthily obsessive interest in that topic. After twenty years of this, you could be eligible to be a guru.
- Choose jobs that relate to long-term strategy or futurism. Nielsen advises that this will force you to think deeper thoughts than the average, rushed Web project.
- Establish a website catering to other people interested in your given area of expertise. If you gradually build up a profile within the field, you can eventually become *the* source for information on the topic, a must for any would-be guru.

GLOSSARY

● **Conference circuit**
The endless stream of events held every year catering to the Internet industry. No conference is complete without a guru in attendance, and no guru is complete without a trip round the circuit.

● **Power-Point**
A software program from Microsoft that allows people to create slide show presentations. Power-Point presentations are the central weapon in the arsenal of the guru, and no conference appearance is complete without one.

USEFUL ADDRESSES

● Guru.com, 639 Front St, Suite 200, San Francisco, CA 94111, USA.
TEL +1 415 693 9500.
FAX +1 415 837 1091.
www.guru.com; info@guru.com

● Nielsen Norman Group, 2704 Fairbrook Drive, Mountain View, CA 94040, USA.
TEL +1 650 210 9690.
www.nngroup.com;
info@nngroup.com

Headhunter

Money: From £20,000 up to six figures. Depends on the level and salaries of those people you place.

Hours: A basic office day, plus evening meetings, early morning meetings and weekend phone calls.

Health risk: 4/10. You're usually in a position to make people happy, except when you tell someone they haven't got the job.

Pressure rating: 6/10. Companies are desperate to hire staff, and will see the headhunter as being slow if they don't have the perfect someone today, right now, immediately.

Glamour rating: 4/10. Expect little glamour: the headhunter just finds the business stars a job.

Travel rating: 3/10. Unless you work for an international agency, you tend to stick near to home in your search for candidates.

The Internet industry has a bottomless hunger for good staff. These need to be people who are well educated, commercially aware, experienced and willing to work for lower-than-average salaries today for the chance of jam tomorrow. The headhunter finds people for companies who need them. Sounds simple, but finding good people is getting harder all the time. There are many vacancies, and few suitable candidates. Worse still, headhunters don't tend to get paid until they've found the person and they've been placed for a few months. Recruiters for Internet jobs need to work hard, understand the jobs they are offering, and, the hardest part, be able to judge who will do the job well.

In Silicon Valley in 1999, there was an apocryphal story doing the rounds that concerned a headhunter's phone technique. Headhunters were well known for scanning phone lists of hot companies in order to ring all their employees and try to **poach** them away. As a joke, one Web design company allocated phone numbers to everyone in the office – including Dennis, the office's black Labrador. Sure enough, the dog got several phone calls from hungry recruiters, who couldn't understand why a request to 'speak to Dennis' was so funny.

While this is amusing, the state of the Internet job market is no joke. There are thousands of unfilled job vacancies in Europe for qualified technology and new media people. A recent survey estimates that the Internet will have created over three million jobs in key European markets by 2004. Demographically, this is a disaster – there simply aren't enough Web-savvy, creative-minded professionals to fill all the slots.

Many prospective employees assume that jobs are most commonly advertised in classified job sections of newspapers, and others assume that the thing to do is approach a company directly for a job. While this is true for many lower-level positions, most senior positions with Internet companies (say, above senior manager, earning more than £40,000 per year in the private sector) are filled through headhunters, or **executive recruiters**. Candidates know how rare they are, and act accordingly. A good candidate will expect a great deal more in pay and responsibility than they would have ten years ago. Also, they will be less loyal, and more likely to jump ship, meaning that headhunters will often end up having to fill the same job twice in one year.

Headhunting is not typically a job with a high profile or a lot of respect. Alistair Lamont is a founder and director of new media specialist recruiter Where it's @. He founded Where it's @ partly because of the negative image that most people had of recruiters – with his consulting background, he felt he could provide a better service to those looking for and those offering jobs. Lamont says that 'most people see recruiters as one step up on the food chain from estate agents. However, if you do your job right, that perception can change.'

Headhunters exist for a number of reasons. For one thing, advertising a senior position with specialist skills in a newspaper would have a very small chance of reaching the right people. Also, many companies don't like to let the world know what senior jobs are available in the company, since the vacancy might be interpreted as a weakness. Companies also prefer to give a recruiter first shot at interviewing candidates to save time. Recruiters can claim, with some degree of truth, that they keep in touch with certain markets and people and have a better chance of finding the best person for the job.

For the person who is looking for a job, dealing with a headhunter can be a frustrating experience. Recruiters are often juggling many people, with the result that they make the candidate feel like 'one of many'. No one likes the experience of sitting across from someone who is struggling to remember your name, and skimming your CV desperately as they say, 'Umm, so I see here that you worked at ...' The job is even harder when the recruiter is dealing with a highly technical or specialist position: it is almost impossible to win the candidate's respect without asking the right question.

There are hundreds of recruiters around the UK, and those that specialise in staffing Internet companies are one of the fastest-growing sectors. Internet specialist recruiters now number more than 200 in London alone. Some of these handle freelance talent or project teams for a fee. In the attempt to differentiate themselves from other staffing agencies, recruitment firms are dreaming up new marketing techniques: one company, for example, Aquent Partners, calls itself a 'talent agency for the Web', appealing to the sense that many Internet creatives have of being on a par with movie stars.

While some recruiters like Aquent work for the people seeking positions, more often they are paid by companies who use them regularly to staff vacant positions. They help find these clients people for their vacancies, and sometimes advise on other human resources issues. Clients pay the recruiter a scale of fees for working on the search, with the biggest chunk of the fee usually being success-based (person found, person installed in the job, person staying in the job and delivering). When a headhunter is looking for someone to do a job, they either research and build up a short list of candidates (particularly if it is an executive or senior position), or advertise in relevant publications. They handle the interview process and help the client work through the short list. If these more scientific methods are exhausted, they're likely simply to start polling their friends and professional acquaintances to see if anyone in their personal network knows a suitable candidate for the position they're trying to fill.

This sounds relatively straightforward. However, Internet jobs are confusing for everyone concerned: the company, the recruiter and, often, the candidate. Jobs are not clearly defined, salaries are wildly variable for what sound like identical jobs, and many of the employers are entirely new, without the track record or prestige to convince someone to leave their job. Many clients and job-seekers alike are dissatisfied with traditional recruitment companies. A third of clients in a recent study interviewed candidates put forward by their UK recruitment agency who were 'totally inappropriate for the job', with lack of relevant experience and necessary skills cited as the most common reason. Some of the larger global executive search firms like Spencer Stuart and Korn/Ferry, have adapted well to the Internet age. Many now take equity in start-up companies as part of their fees. Some have launched their own Web services for mid-level executive searches: Korn/Ferry and the *Wall Street Journal* put together a joint venture, FutureStep, to target junior execs on their way up the ladder.

Some executive search consultants build long-lasting relationships with companies and get to know their business nearly as well as the executives they work with. They build up great relationships with the company's board, and are generally paid consulting fees rather than recruitment success fees. They justify this by investing in a significant amount of resources, technology and people, to help them do their job better. They also spend a lot of time understanding the individual company's needs: it is easier to find the right person for the job if you also understand what context and culture they will be going into.

Recruitment jobs, even at the executive search level, are not glamorous jobs. Although you are frequently dealing with people who will be important for a company's future, you will often be earning far less than they are. Recruiters need to have a lot of patience with people who are rude: both prospective candidates and prospective clients. You need a thick skin! In addition, headhunters need to be well connected within an industry. Entry-level recruiters start either for a small firm or for the research department of a large one. Research people build up a database of contact resources that they can use as a job or idea pool when they receive a request from a client. Consultants, who are generally more senior to the researchers, handle clients directly, conduct important searches, and build the relationship with a client over time.

Even for headhunters who are finding candidates for important, high-profile companies, the job is not particularly well paid. A headhunter has to justify their value over time. How good is their network? How quickly did they fulfil the client's needs? How appropriate were their prospective candidates, and was the successful candidate still there in six months? All of these affect the recruitment consultant's pay packet: he or she will generally be paid a low salary with potentially large bonuses on the success of their job searches.

SKILLS YOU'LL NEED

- A great phone manner for all those tricky conversations when you're trying to persuade someone to give you something very important (their attention for five minutes, or the chance to find them a new job).
- A knack for understanding people.
- An ability to network like mad, and keep in touch with hundreds of people, one of whom might be your perfect candidate now or next month.
- Excellent communication skills. You'll need to be a company's ambassador in order to attract scarce talent.
- Great organisational abilities. You are dealing with hundreds of people on a regular basis, and all of them will have high expectations of you.

GETTING THE JOB

- Education is less relevant than for other jobs, although you may want to consider a degree or some training in psychology or the social sciences.
- Apply directly to the recruitment consultancy, executive search firm or specialist who interests you. There are not many vacancies, but bringing a good network and plenty of energy will help you.

TIPS

- Decide whether it is more attractive to you to work in a firm that handles long-term senior searches, where there will be a more structured career path, or whether you'd enjoy the rough-and-tumble world of acting as a 'talent agent'.
- Build up your network over time by working for an Internet specialist. It turns out to be a small world, once you're in it.
- If you want to become a recruiter, have a short spell working for a company that might be your target client. It will give you a valuable understanding of what life is like 'on the inside' for all those people you'll be placing.

GLOSSARY

- **Executive recruiters**
Companies that specialise in only senior management and board-level positions, usually for multinational corporations, but occasionally for

start-ups.

• **Poaching**

The practice of companies stealing talented employees from their competition. A familiar practice in the Internet biz.

USEFUL ADDRESSES

• Aquent Partners, 1 Bedford St, London WC2E 9HD, UK.
TEL +44 (0) 20 7836 8200.
FAX +44 (0) 20 7836 4034.
www.aquent.com

• Major Players, The Banana Warehouse, 5 Langley St, London WC2H 9JA, UK.
TEL +44 (0) 20 7836 4041.
FAX +44 (0) 20 7836 4009.
www.majorplayers.co.uk

• Spencer Stuart, 16 Connaught Place, London W2 2ED, UK.
TEL +44 (0) 20 7298 3333.
FAX +44 (0) 20 7298 3388.
www.spencerstuart.com

• Where it's @, 111 Camden High St, London NW1 7JN, UK.
TEL +44 (0) 8707 333 111.
FAX +44 (0) 8707 333 222.
www.wia.co.uk;
info@wia.co.uk

INCUBATOR

MONEY: From £25,000 to £60,000. Top deal-makers at incubators may get some extra if the incubator has successful investments.

HOURS: You work the same hours as your start-ups, although you probably sleep better than they do.

HEALTH RISK: 5/10. Be prepared for eye strain while you read hundreds of business plans from hopeful entrepreneurs.

PRESSURE RATING: 7/10. With so many small, fast-moving companies in the same space, there's always something that needed doing yesterday.

GLAMOUR RATING: 6/10. Incubators were once quite glorious reminders of the decadence of Internet business. Sadly, they've fallen from grace a bit.

TRAVEL RATING: 6/10. Internet businesses will be global one day, and incubators are forming international alliances. Pack your bag.

The incubator is the most common name for a company that helps small Internet start-ups get off the ground fast. Working in an incubator has all the highs and lows of start-up life: stress, frequent brainstorms, and lots of learning – without some of the risks, like going bankrupt.

Although the pressure on Internet companies for them to accomplish a lot in a small amount of time is intense, they still have to face the same issues as any other growing small business. Dot.coms run into difficulties getting office space, buying equipment and getting staff in so they can keep on growing the business. Incubators have sprung up as a way of overcoming these problems, and as a way of investing in potential high-growth companies early on. They usually offer desks, equipment and support over a set period of time during the company's early period of growth, and in exchange usually receive a chunk of ownership in the start-up. If the company succeeds, the incubator can sell their stake for a big profit. And if the company fails, as many do, the incubator has only risked some office space and the use of their fax machine.

An official definition of an incubator is a safe, controlled environment that helps something young to get to a position where it can grow on its own. In Internet terms, incubators nurture fledgling Internet businesses and give them a head start. Companies taken in by an incubator are usually missing some key elements: not just office space and equipment, but often some aspect of their business idea. Incubated companies are often little more than a business plan and one or two people. The companies come into the incubator, are given technology, space and help, and benefit from the knowledge of people around them who have done and seen it all before.

Incubators started to spring up in 1997 after savvy finance people realised two things: there was a lot of money to be made from Internet companies, and the earlier you got a piece of them the better off you were. A few entrepreneurs, many of whom had set up Internet companies before, realised that it would be a good idea to put together a bundle of services to help get Internet companies up and running, and get them out to market quickly.

The incubator was, at first, a US phenomenon, but it quickly spread to Europe, where the need was actually greater than in the US. Gung-ho American entrepreneurs, dealing with a sophisticated financial market, were often able to steer their companies to success quickly. Young entrepreneurs in Europe, however, struggled to get even the basics, like city centre offices, and found getting financial and moral support extremely difficult. Imagine, if you will, the following conversation between a Euro dot.com entrepreneur and his parent:

Parent: 'So, child, you have secured your MBA from a prestigious European business school. Which well-paid consulting firm or major industrial organisation will you grace with your presence for the next twenty years, by which time you will be well positioned to take a seat on the board?'

Child: 'Well, actually, Papa/Pater/Père, I'm planning on starting an Internet company. I've seen a huge opportunity: no one supplies those long straws with bends in them to cocktail bars at the moment. I will be able to grab that market with my website, bendystraw.eu.com, and will be an Internet millionaire: *voilà!*'

Parent (thunders): 'You will be excommunicated from this family, and your alumni association, and the church, and the family bistro! No one, in the history of this family, has ever been a lunatic failure! Go from this house and do not ever call on me for help!'

Child slinks off, and looks up Incubator in the local Yellow Pages (*pagine gialle, pages jaunes*).

There is little familial tradition or support for entrepreneurs in Europe, most of whom are first-generation. Young businesses, because of the risk-averse nature of city-centre landlords, also find it difficult to get offices, and hard to attract people. (This is opposed to Silicon Valley, where it isn't unknown for landlords to take stock in the company in lieu of rent!) Therefore an incubator may be their first port of call to get their businesses started.

Incubators themselves are staffed with people who have an entrepreneurial background. They tend to attract those who have started their own business – or may do one day, when they get a bright idea. Incubators are likely to hire from the business schools or consultancies, which help with business plans. They are also likely to have a couple of experienced entrepreneurs, like Jerome Mol, who started a software business as a student before setting up the multinational incubator GorillaPark.

Although the role of an incubator

seems like that of an expert adviser, in truth incubators are often learning themselves about what their start-up companies need through working with them. For one thing, helping one kind of business succeed doesn't mean the same formula will work for the next kind of company. Companies come to incubators for very different reasons, and sometimes don't know what they'll need a few months down the road. Also, the financial markets are very fickle when it comes to Internet companies, so the incubator takes a serious risk when they take on another company: there may not be an investor there after a few months to receive them out into the world. Jamie Mitchell, CEO of e-Start, a 'launch network', helps entrepreneurs start businesses in Europe. Mitchell says that deal-making is one of the most rewarding experiences in working with start-ups. 'Losing a deal after putting in weeks of effort is the most frustrating part of the job. Conversely, the signing of an investment agreement is the highlight, perhaps only being beaten by seeing your investment **exiting** at a huge multiple to your initial investment!'

Incubators are a lot like start-ups themselves, and have seen their value and reputation tarnish as Internet companies have lost favour. In view of this, companies that formerly referred to themselves as incubators are trying on new names and new models. Incubators are renaming themselves **accelerators**, **value catalysts** and **venture architects**, among other titles. Several are also looking at their business model, and instead of taking a chunk of the company in exchange for office space are charging fees like ordinary consultancies for introductions to potential staff or investors.

Although the future of incubators (or venture architects, or value catalysts) is uncertain, there's no doubt that it's a great environment in which to learn. Incubators see several hundred business plans a week, from which they choose very few. Many people in incubators have been in start-ups before, and have valuable knowledge to pass on. The incubator may provide a good service to its start-ups, but may offer even more to those entrepreneurs who choose to learn from others in such an environment before they strike out on their own.

SKILLS YOU'LL NEED

There are a number of jobs available in an incubator. Many of them are administrative, and there are usually several that are financial in nature. An important skill is the ability to sniff out successful entrepreneurs. Clearly, one of the key capabilities is the ability to judge people and ideas, based partly on experience and partly on instinct.

GETTING THE JOB

Approach incubators directly. Most are eager for people, especially if you're energetic and have good business judgement. If you can analyse a business plan, have training in psychology, or have got websites up and running, then incubators will want to hear from you.

TIPS

Work for a venture capital firm first, get some skills, and wait to see which incubators develop a good track record over time.

GLOSSARY

- **Accelerator, value catalyst, venture architect**

Assorted names for Internet incubator-type companies. All these companies take a certain reward in either fees or an equity stake for helping companies get to market quickly, by providing either services or people.

- **Exit**

Venture capital term for getting your money back from an investment. All venture capital investments, which incubator investments are a form of, should have an exit strategy for when and how the investor gets their money back. How much is due depends on the success of the company.

USEFUL ADDRESSES

- Antfactory, Prospect House, 80–100 New Oxford St, London WC1A 1HB, UK.
TEL +44 (0) 20 7947 5000.
FAX +44 (0) 20 7947 5001.
www.antfactory.com;
international@antfactory.com
- Esouk, 32 Brook St, London W1Y 1AG, UK.
TEL +44 (0) 8700 111030.
FAX +44 (0) 8700 111040.
www.esouk.com
- E-Start, 1st floor, 20 Soho Square, London W1V 5FD, UK.
TEL +44 (0) 20 7440 5400.
FAX +44 (0) 20 7440 5421.
www.e-start.com;
info@e-start.com
- Garage.com, 90 Long Acre, Covent Garden, London WC2E 9RZ, UK.
TEL +44 (0) 20 7849 3014.
FAX +44 (0) 20 7849 3200.
www.garage.com/europe
- Idealab, 130 West Union St, Pasadena, CA 91103, USA.
TEL +1 626 585 6900.
FAX +1 626 535 2701.
www.idealab.com

JOURNALIST

MONEY: From £16,000 to £40,000 at most publications/sites. A scant few journalists can reach a six-figure salary, but only after years of blood, sweat and tears.

HOURS: When a story's on the burner, be prepared to chase it till it breaks. But since most of your sources work office hours, you're likely to do the same.

HEALTH RISK: 5/10. The obligatory rounds of free drinks parties can take their toll.

PRESSURE RATING: 6/10. Not the most stressful job, but it does keep the heart rate up.

GLAMOUR RATING: 6/10. You can be a bigwig to the industry, but try explaining to your grandmother why it's exciting writing about 'technology 'n' stuff'.

TRAVEL RATING: 7/10. Get ready for press **junkets** which companies use as not-so-subtle bribes in an attempt to get coverage.

*The Internet industry relies on a horde of business and technology publications to keep track of who's wielding influence and who's gone down the tubes. Journalists, because of their access to a wide audience of readers, are courted by the industry, and coverage is coveted. Even the most junior reporter is treated to lunch, dinners, drinks and overseas trips. Of course, if the news is negative, phone calls mysteriously don't get answered, and executives are eternally 'on holiday', expected to return some time conveniently after your **deadline**.*

Those of us who trained as journalists before 1996 were told horror stories about life after University. Lecturers waxed nostalgic about writing obituaries for weekly newspapers in places like Motherwell for six years on an annual salary of peanuts and crab apples, forced to sleep under the managing editor's desk, unable to afford a place to live, writing till their fingers bled – and they were happy to do it! Most of us aspired to little more than the chance to write for nothing, develop a habit of whisky and cigars, burn out before the age of forty, and in short live out the romantic Fleet Street ideal. We expected to scrap for an opportunity to work on any newspaper, let alone one that was actually read, instead of used as a fish wrapper.

What a disappointment to find that the development of a new medium meant that jobs were plentiful, salaries were on the rise, and the Fleet Street ideal was now a mineral water and watercress salad for lunch, then home to the other half in the two-bedroom semi near the park.

After all that preparation, journalism went through something of a revolution after the Internet. From the invention of the printing press until the invention of the Internet, journalism evolved at a pace much the same as in other industries. A few innovations over the last several hundred years caused subtle changes in the way newspapers were printed and distributed, and in the way they were sorted and cut, but those technological changes had little effect on the way newspapers were written. Journalists have been conducting the business of writing and reporting relatively free from the influence of technology.

The Web had a dramatic effect on the way news was collected and distributed. Not only could journalists do research in minutes that would take days in the off-line world, but they could also publish their news almost instantly, changing the daily deadlines that had been the norm in newspaper journalism for decades. News organisations – newspapers, magazines, television broadcasters and wire services – faced a serious shake-up in the status quo.

By 2000, most news outfits had developed some sort of plan to take advantage of the Web. In almost every case, this meant publishing the news they put out regularly in an on-line format as well, but many also published additional content on-line. Since the rest of the world was changing, and more workers were deskbound (and in front of a computer terminal for much of the day), news organisations found that the way their readers consumed the news also changed. Rather than just buying a morning or afternoon paper, consumers were also checking websites during the day for interim updates.

Established groups like the BBC, the *Guardian*, Sky News, the *Financial Times* and CNN invested millions in building up their on-line news corps. But established journalists were hesitant to risk their reputation by writing for the website, which was generally perceived as less glamorous than television or newspaper journalism. It was only recent graduates, anxious to get experience and build up a CV, who jumped at the chance to work in on-line journalism.

'I was there very early on with the on-line reporting thing,' says Adam Penenberg, a former senior editor with *Forbes*, one of the leading business magazines in the United States. 'I came from hard-core print [journalism] and knew how they felt about on-line journalism.' The fact that so many Web journalists were young, and eager, guaranteed that anyone working in the medium was treated with no small amount of derision in the early days. In a column in 1998, John C. Dvorak, a long-time Silicon Valley columnist, ranked all journalists in order of importance. He placed on-line reporters at the end of the list, above only tabloid reporters. (Interestingly, he ranked magazine columnists, of which he was one, as the most important of all scribes.)

But Penenberg was part of a movement of serious journalistic talent to move from old media to new. In the mid-90s, he was writing for Wired News, the on-line news site of the famed *Wired* magazine. He moved from there to reporting for *Forbes*' site, Forbes.com. In 1998, a major change of attitude was taking place in the United States, although it had yet to make its way across the Atlantic. Some of the big-name journalists, particularly those who wrote about the Internet and business, were leaving high-profile jobs to work on websites. Web companies, highly valued on the stock market at the time, were able to pay much larger salaries than the 'old media' companies, which were still subscribing to the 'treat 'em mean, keep 'em keen' theory – that treating journalists badly left them hungry and made them better reporters.

Penenberg was recruited by the *Industry Standard*, a magazine in San Francisco that was paying top dollar for high-profile journalists to leave more established publishing outfits. 'I was involved in one of the first tugs-of-war over an on-line reporter, between *Forbes* and the *Industry Standard*,' he says. 'Back then, it was unheard of for an on-line journalist to be offered a six-figure salary to move from a magazine's on-line publication to its flagship magazine. Nowadays both print and on-line publications are paying six figures and getting into poaching wars over top talent. How long this will last is anybody's guess.'

Penenberg is a well-known figure among a growing group of journalists whose professional lives are centred around the Internet: we write about it, we use it for research, and we publish on-line. As Internet technologies have a greater and greater effect on the world at large, more journalists are devoted to covering the industry, and the industry has come to rely on us to publicise any and all new developments.

'Like most journalists who cover technology, I get about a hundred e-mails a day, most of them from publicists pushing this company or that product, begging me to meet the CEO of Client A, "a hot new middleware company", or asking me to consider quoting Client B's top geek as an "expert" source,' says Penenberg. 'Since so many people across the country from all walks of life own stock in technology, good press is key. Which means every single company publicist, to justify his or her salary, has to place stories in the big publications. Sometimes start-ups that don't even have a product out will have their **flacks** approach reporters in an attempt to get press. It's crazy. They want to have their company **profiled** in a major publication yet they haven't done anything to justify press coverage.'

In many cases, journalists who cover the Internet play a central part in the way the industry functions. Companies are reliant on publicity to increase their public profile, both to boost their valuation if they are listed on a stock exchange and to bring more attention to their site in the form of Web traffic and on-line customers.

'Nowadays, good journalists make good money and have become mini-celebrities,' says Penenberg. 'A far cry from the 90s, when writing gigs were few and far between and people were prognosticating the death of newspapers and magazines. I know reporters who haven't paid for their own lunch in three years. In exchange for this good treatment, however, publicists demand access: we are under constant assault from them. I had to put a message directed at "flacks" on my voicemail greeting: no PR pitches by phone; send them by e-mail. If you've ever gotten back from a week's vacation only to be met with 250 voicemails, 200 of them from publicists, you'll know why I only accept story pitches via e-mail (they're easier to organise and keep track of that way, too).'

The Internet is a crucial tool for all journalists these days. E-mail is the preferred form of communication, and a great way to reach sources, like the CEOs of large companies who were previously accessible only through a cavalry of assistants and PRs. Web searches are critical for gathering information and investigating archived stories from other publications. The Web contains lots of hidden information as well, information that journalists are increasingly savvy about accessing and using. For Internet industry journalists, the Internet *is* the story, but it's also where we find the story.

'Some days I have to travel, but others I spend my time in on-line databases, surfing the Net, composing e-mails or following discussion threads on lists I subscribe to,' says Penenberg. This combination of on-line sources and typical journo tricks like hanging out in pubs getting sources drunk, and letting PRs buy them lunch, is how most journalists get ideas for the pieces they write.

For the daily news reporter working on-line, similar processes are followed, only things move much faster. Guy Middleton, who has written about technology and the Internet for several British news sites and magazines, produces stories on an hourly and daily basis, rather than weekly.

'I roll in around nine o'clock, check my e-mail and sniff around a few of my favourite news sites,' he says. 'Usually what I write will be original, but it's fairly common for Reuters or the *Financial Times* to get given announcements pre-embargo, in which case I might pursue a similar story. I'll look at a number of possible stories, try and find an angle or detail that will interest the audience or picks up on a current theme. I'll knock out one or two main stories – a mix of news and analysis then a few briefs. If I am lucky I'll get a tip-off about something a little more unusual.'

Middleton joined the Internet reporting ranks fresh from a course in journalism at the London College of Printing. 'I spent nearly two years temping in a mixture of tech support and enterprise procurement roles before a postgrad certificate in journalism,' he says. 'The combination of the two set me up for my first job, on a networking technology weekly. I went for the trade press and got into writing straight away. Other students with somewhat higher journalistic aspirations went for big-name broadsheets – but most are still copy-editing. I moved from *Network Week* to a US tech news service, then to *Tornado-Insider* [a start-up magazine covering the European Internet scene – Middleton edited the website].'

In many ways, the life of the on-line journalist can be pretty rewarding, Middleton says. Unlike well-established publications or news outfits, Web companies or departments tend to be less hierarchical, and more likely to give a chance to an enterprising young journalist.

'In most on-line publications, the editorial structure is pretty flat. You tend to take a greater degree of responsibility for your own writing, so you have to be fairly confident in what you are producing,' he says. 'Trying to find and substantiate a strong story can involve a fair amount of work. And there are constant interruptions from PRs – some of which might be useful. I think if you are working in print with pages to fill and you are understaffed it can be quite demanding – certainly some of my colleagues who work primarily in print have heavier workloads than I do. The Internet, on the other hand, is relentless – there is no end to the number of revisions you can make.'

As with all things Internet-related, Web journalism is still evolving and changing. On-line news organisations are pressing for higher standards in reporting, and beginning to give recognition to journalists who work for websites, rather than seeing them exclusively as reporters-in-training for the more exclusive preserve of off-line journalism.

In the meantime, journalists covering the industry wonder how long the good life can carry on. Salaries have risen steadily since the Internet came to town, but few journalists are willing to make bets that good salaries, plentiful jobs and free lunches are permanent fixtures. We may be back to sleeping under the editor's desk before too long, but it's a good ride while it lasts.

SKILLS YOU'LL NEED

Good reporting skills, writing ability, some technical knowledge, and an understanding of the Internet industry. Interest in the topic helps immeasurably, as does a strong dose of scepticism to temper the wild hyperbole with which the industry tends to view itself.

GETTING THE JOB

- The best way to get a writing job is to show 'em you can write. Try pitching articles to commissioning editors. Once you build up a portfolio of writing, you are more likely to attract interest for staff jobs.
- Make a list of sites and magazines that cover the industry. Most of these will have a 'jobs listing' on their website. Top ones include *Wired*, *News.com*, *Tech Web*, *Business 2.0*, the *Industry Standard* and *Red Herring*. Check these regularly.
- Mainstream press covers the Internet too. Check national newspapers and other media outlets to see who the media and Internet correspondents are. You may want to e-mail these people to see if any jobs are going or if they have tips or advice.

TIPS

- Basic research skills are imperative. You should know how to conduct interviews in person, over the phone, and also by e-mail. Always know a company's history before engaging in any dialogue with them. Tough questions earn respect.

● Electronic research is one of the basic tools of the Internet reporter. On-line databases, as well as basic search engines, are used for researching every story. Become familiar with all the available resources on-line.

● Early in your career, start a database of expert sources you can contact. Tend this database as though it were a garden. Take it with you everywhere you go. A journo is nothing without his or her contacts.

● Develop a speciality within the industry. Becoming an expert makes you a hot commodity.

● Read the competition. Every good story can't be yours, but keeping an eye on other publications and sites covering the industry means you'll know what to be looking out for.

GLOSSARY

● **Deadline**
The point at which an article is due, but also a handy excuse for putting off enthusiastic PRs. 'Can't talk now, I'm on deadline!'

● **Feature (or profile)**
A longer story that isn't necessarily tied to any timely news or event. What PRs propose you write to try to get coverage for their client when the client has done nothing newsworthy.

● **Flack**
Pejorative term used by journalists for PRs, as in 'that [Company X] flack won't stop calling me! I think it's time for a **smear piece**.'

● **Junket**
A free trip paid for by a company, bringing a crowd of journalists to some distant location to hear about the company's products, on the premise that journalists will feel obligated to write about them if they've accepted a gratis holiday.

● **Smear piece**
Negative article on a company that goes above and beyond the call of duty (and sometimes accuracy).

USEFUL ADDRESSES

● Business 2.0, 30 Monmouth St, Bath BA1 2BW, UK.
TEL +44 (0) 1225 442 244.
FAX +44 (0) 1225 732 262

● European Journalism Centre, Sonneville-lunet 10, 6221KT Maastricht, Netherlands.
TEL +31 43 325 40 30.
FAX +31 43 321 26 26.
www.ejc.nl; secr@ejc.nl

● Freelancers.co.uk (on-line only).
www.freelancers.co.uk/; queries@freelancers.co.uk

● Industry Standard, 315 Pacific Ave, San Francisco, CA 94111, USA.
TEL +1 415 733 5400.
FAX +1 415 733 5401.
www.thestandard.com; info@thestandard.com

● Media Guardian, 119 Farringdon Rd, London EC1R 3DJ, UK.
TEL +44 (0) 20 7239 9685.
FAX +44 (0) 20 7837 2114.
www.mediaguardian.com

● News.com, 150 Chestnut St, San Francisco, CA 94111, USA.
TEL +1 415 364 8900.
www.news.com; tips@news.com

● On-line Journalism Association, Annenberg On-line Journalism Program, University of Southern California, 3502 Watt Way,

Los Angeles, CA 90089-0281, USA.
TEL +1 213 740 1786.
FAX +1 213 740 8036.
www.on-linejournalism.com;
tips@on-linejournalism.com
• Recruit Media, 20 Colebrooke Row,
London N1 8AP, UK.
TEL +44 (0) 20 7704 1227.
FAX +44 (0) 20 7704 1370.
www.recruitmedia.co.uk;
info@recruitmedia.co.uk
• UK Press Gazette, 19 Scarbrook Rd,
Croydon, Surrey CR9 1LX, UK.
TEL +44 (0) 20 8565 4200.
FAX +44 (0) 20 8565 4462.
www.pressgazette.co.uk
• Wired, 520 3rd St, 3rd Floor,
San Francisco, CA 94107-1815, USA.
TEL +1 303 945 1910.
FAX +1 303 684 9182.
www.wired.com/wired;
info@wired.com

LAWYER

MONEY: Starting at about £40,000–£60,000 for qualified Internet lawyers, but the top e-commerce and mergers and acquisition lawyers make much more.

HOURS: If you're working on deals, or a hot issue, expect 12–15-hour days. In an advice-giving position, the Internet lawyer can lead a much more relaxed life.

HEALTH RISK: 2/10. Lawyers are in such high demand in the Internet economy that they can make their lifestyle suit their wants.

PRESSURE RATING: 7/10. Legal issues on the Internet abound, and the decisions made in the early years are expected to have ramifications for decades to come.

GLAMOUR RATING: 2/10. Do lawyers in any industry have a good reputation?

TRAVEL RATING: 6/10. Lawyers in more junior positions tend to travel more, as the senior types need to be locally accessible to the clients.

Few other fields have been as affected by the Internet as law. As a communications tool, the Internet raises issues of copyright and trademarks. As a business tool, it raises the issue of the legality of electronic transactions and exchanging goods across national boundaries. As an instrument of criminal minds, it is one of the most complex enemies law enforcement has ever tackled. And let's not even get started on how it has affected government and policy makers. All in all, the Internet revolution has made for some very happy lawyers.

Three investors are trading stock tips on an on-line bulletin board. They make pejorative comments about a certain stock. The company's lawyers sue for defamation of character.

A famous American radio personality, known for her rigid puritanical views, sues a pornographic website that bought and then published photographs she had brazenly posed for ten years earlier (oops). The website then proceeds to sue seventy other pornographic websites, which had easily copied the electronic representations of the photos and posted the snaps themselves.

Makers of an infamous drug that enhances male sexual prowess hire a team of lawyers to track down the people behind a website that sells 'Herbal Viagra'.

Luxury car manufacturers Porsche and 'lifestyle' magazine *Playboy* make a public legal crusade against so-called **cybersquatters** by tracking down and filing injunctions against anyone who registers a domain name with 'Porsche', or 'Playboy' in it. Even car enthusiasts who gathered at Porsches.com to talk about their love of the automobiles were targeted.

An eccentric physicist makes a

public example of the UK's oldest Internet Service Provider by winning a legal suit against the company after a wag had mocked him in one of the ISP's bulletin boards.

A 19-year-old American constructs a piece of software that lets music lovers around the world download their favourite songs for free. Rock stars and record companies (and their lawyers) around the globe react as though it were the day the music died.

Needless to say, the Internet has wreaked havoc on legal systems all over the world. From cybersquatters to **digital signatures**, lawyers have found a brand-new (and wholly lucrative) area of expertise. Since the mid-1990s, Internet and e-commerce law has become less a specialist field and increasingly a part of every lawyer's job. Some of the main areas where law and the Internet have clashed include personal privacy, intellectual property, trademark infringement (so-called cyber-squatting), and digital transactions. Legal groups in every country have had to appoint special committees to study Internet issues, and to attempt to establish how old laws can be applied to new media.

Trademark infringement has been one of the highest-profile legal tangles, and also one of the earliest to emerge. There are no regulations that govern who can register a domain name (Internet address), an oversight the ramifications of which weren't identified until it was too late. Large companies were very slow to move to the Internet, and some of the world's most famous brands found that when they tried to register their company name followed by a '.com', someone else already held the name. Not that those nefarious pranksters who became known as 'cybersquatters' or 'domain name speculators' weren't willing to part with the title ... for a price. Network Solutions, the company that administers the domain name registry, had a hard and fast policy of refusing to interfere in disputes, so the large companies were forced to take their issues to the courts. Thus did trademark infringement mark the beginning of a beautiful relationship between lawyers and the Internet. Few of the issues have any practical legal precedent, which poses fascinating possibilities for legal contemplation (and billable hours).

Privacy was another legal dragon that reared its ugly head early in the evolution of e-commerce businesses. Companies realised that by tracking what consumers did while on-line, they could form a better perception of who their customers were and what they might buy. They happily set about building software and tracking devices that collected information, but had their hopes dashed when consumer groups and private individuals objected to the 'Big Brother' tactics. Another body of law, this one focused on what businesses could and couldn't do with information they collected about consumers on the Internet, was established.

Intellectual property became a headline-grabbing issue when the multibillion-pound recording industry realised that their artists' works were being regularly copied and traded for free on the Internet, thanks to a new format for compressing music files called **MP3**. 'But how will we keep our artists in limousines and hot tubs, let alone lucrative recording contracts?' cried the industry. And another bevy of lawyers went to work. All this was made worse when a 19-year-old American college student wrote a software program called **Napster**, which allowed anyone to download music from other users' computers. MP3 trading went into overdrive, and the recording industry claimed sales had fallen because of Napster. Meanwhile, millions of people all over the world were frantically collecting music files, saved for once from paying a prohibitive £14.99 per album.

'Somebody recently said that if there had been as many lawyers around when the postage stamp was invented as there are today, we'd have all been waxing lyrical about the efficacy of sending documents in an envelope whose seal might easily come undone,' says Justin Ellis. Ellis is a specialist in Internet law with the firm Donne Mileham & Haddock in Brighton, West Sussex. 'However, we now live in a risk-averse world (probably of lawyers' own making), and our role is to ensure that our clients and their shareholders firstly don't put their investments at risk and secondly do as well as they can within the letter of the law.'

The daily life of the Internet lawyer is much consumed with these issues, and rather than reading law books they're forced to read the daily news to keep up with their field. Internet law changes from day to day, rather than year to year. 'Unlike much legal drafting, a lot of e-commerce work is on untouched ground, so there is a fair amount of free-hand drafting (i.e. making it up) as opposed to filling in the spaces (the banking lawyer's approach),' says Ellis. '[I read] a lot of news services to keep up with the market.'

Ellis read law in Brighton at the University of Sussex, followed by a year at law school in London. He then joined Clifford Chance, the world's largest law firm, eventually qualifying for their Media Computers and Communications Group in 1995. Three years later, burned out on London and the City, he moved with his family back to Brighton, which was becoming something of a haven for Internet and new media companies. 'I happened to visit Brighton with my wife, and we decided it would be good to come back here, so I got a job with DMH at the beginning of 1998, to build their non-contentious Intellectual Property/Information Technology Law practice, a large part of which focuses on e-commerce,' he says. 'I advise Internet start-ups on legal risk issues associated with trading on the Internet. Brighton is a media/Internet-rich area, so I see business plans about once a week.'

Like many lawyers in the Internet business, Ellis says, he is often used simply as a business adviser. In such a young industry, it's relatively difficult to find anyone who can claim to be an expert. Lawyers have spent as much time as anyone sorting out what risks might face a nascent Internet company, and often provide their expertise from that perspective.

'An important part of what I do is raising awareness of the risks, through seminars and newsletters,' Ellis says. 'I draft [companies'] on-line contracts, look at data protection, copyright and trademark issues. I also advise our corporate finance department when they are working on an acquisition, merger or flotation in relation to intellectual property and contract issues. Lawyers are increasingly becoming "business facilitators" (another horrible phrase – please don't quote me on it!) putting clients in touch with sources of investment and other contacts.'

Expertise of any kind in the Internet world commands a premium, but given the complexity of Internet law, lawyers are particularly in demand. '[My] days are very likely to be interrupted with a call from a headhunter – there's a dearth of e-commerce lawyers in the City firms and in industry,' Ellis says.

Ellis's advice for any budding lawyer with an ambition to enter Internet law is to head first for the big City law firms, as they have moved more quickly to develop specific divisions devoted to the area. 'Try to get a training contract with one of the big London firms, for three reasons. They'll pay you to get through law school, they'll pay you more when you start work, and they're the only places with large enough e-commerce practices to be able to dedicate training to that area,' he says. He also suggests building up a useful area of expertise beyond law. 'Do a university degree, but it doesn't have to be in law. It would be useful for an e-commerce lawyer to have some knowledge of the way the Internet, computers or telecoms work.'

While Ellis's life by the seashore – even as an Internet lawyer – is relatively peaceful, the life of the Internet specialist in a City law firm can be anything but. David Naylor heads up a group of e-commerce and communications lawyers within the corporate department at the London office of Weil, Gotshal & Manges, an international US firm, and he describes his days as 'hectic, pressured, fairly unpredictable and absorbing'.

'The e-commerce sector is so dynamic, there's really no kind of "average" day,' Naylor says. 'There's always something new coming in – actually, normally, several things at once. It's generally urgent and you have to be able to work it out rapidly as you go along.'

Naylor came to e-commerce law via a similar route to Ellis's, studying law at Durham followed by an MBA at Imperial College. He trained at Ashurst Morris Crisp, another international law firm with headquarters in the City. Also like Ellis, he qualified into the media and communications department in the mid-1990s, before moving to Weil, Gotshal & Manges in 1998. 'I also spent a year on secondment as a policy adviser at OFTEL, the UK's telecom regulator, working on introducing European competition law into the UK domestic telecom regime (which was pretty weak at the time) and on other projects including super-carrier alliances and so on,' he says. 'Most of the really impressive people in this area have done something other than go straight from law school into a law firm. The industry is desperate for well-rounded, commercial advisers. Although it may mean that you start your law career a year or two behind some of your contemporaries, in the medium to long term it definitely pays off to have done something business oriented as well.'

Internet lawyers who are working on well-publicised deals or issues can find themselves the focus of plenty of attention as journalists and others try to understand what particular changes a given Internet story will have on the world at large. Legal questions have become more central to the Internet, and the lawyers who focus on the area have seen their status rise accordingly.

'I do think I'm very lucky to have ended up doing what I do,' Naylor says. 'I guess it would be fair to say that I find my work demanding, stimulating and – within this particular sector – quite high profile. I'm sure there are more "glamorous" jobs – like being a film star or supermodel – but I doubt they're as consistently intellectually and commercially demanding and absorbing.'

SKILLS YOU'LL NEED

Legal training, flexibility and intellectual curiosity, interest in the industry and its related problems, and the ambition to have a hand in crafting the rules for a changing world.

GETTING THE JOB

- Familiarise yourself with important Internet legal issues.
- Get a relevant degree, either in law or a related field followed by a law conversion degree.
- Contact the top City law firms with communications, media or technology divisions.

TIPS

- Keep on top of the latest Internet issues. Read daily news feeds, particularly those relating to the industry (Wired News, News.com, FT.com, *Industry Standard* and other Internet-related news outlets).
- Participate in forums, conferences and organisations where legal issues related to the Internet are discussed. Non-profit groups like Liberty, Cyber-Rights & Cyber-Liberty and Privacy International hold discussions on relevant subjects. The Foundation for Information Policy Research also addresses the Internet and technology.
- Many law firms that specialise in the Internet also put out publications relating to their recent findings.
- Start your career with a large City firm, especially those that have developed a name for themselves specialising in e-commerce and the Internet.
- Keep regular tabs on the regulatory decisions made both domestically, in the European Union and in the United States. With the field changing all the time, the law is a fluid thing.

GLOSSARY

- **Cybersquatter**

A certain kind of Internet entrepreneur who takes advantage of large companies' lack of Net savvy by registering their domain names and selling the names back to them.

• **Digital signature**

A unique electronic identifier that can act as a legal verification for a transaction.

• **MP3 (Motion Picture Expert Group's audio layer 3)**

A combination of letters and numbers that strikes fear into the hearts of the recording industry. MP3 is the digital audio format that allows people to trade songs over the Internet for free.

• **Napster**

Software that keeps track of what Internet users have in their MP3 collection. The software, and its accompanying website, lets users view its database and download songs for free from other Napster members.

USEFUL ADDRESSES

• Ashurst Morris Crisp, Broadwalk House, 5 Appold St, London EC2A 2HA, UK.
TEL +44 (0) 20 7638 1111.
FAX +44 (0) 20 7972 7990.
www.ashursts.co.uk;
enquiries@ashursts.com

• Berwin Leighton, Adelaide House, London Bridge, London EC4R 9HA, UK.
TEL +44 (0) 20 7760 1000.
FAX +44 (0) 20 7760 1111.
www.berwinleighton.com;
info@berwinleighton.com

• Clifford Chance, 200 Aldersgate St, London EC1A 4JJ, UK.
TEL +44 (0) 20 7600 1000.
FAX +44 (0) 20 7600 5555.
www.cliffordchance.com;
info@cliffordchance.com

• Cyber-Rights & Cyber-Liberties, Centre for Criminal Justice Studies, University of Leeds, Leeds LS2 9JT, UK.
TEL +44 (0) 498 865116.
FAX +44 (0) 113 2335056.
www.cyber-rights.co.uk;
lawya@leeds.ac.uk

• Foundation for Information Policy Research, 9 Stavordale Rd, London N5 1NE, UK.
TEL +44 (0) 20 7354 2333.
FAX +44 (0) 20 7827 6534.
www.fipr.org; cb@fipr.org

• Privacy International, 666 Pennsylvania Ave, SE, Suite 301, Washington, DC 20003, USA.
TEL +1 202 544 9240.
FAX +1 202 547 5482.
www.privacy.org; pi@privacy.org

• Shaw Pittman, Tower 42, Level 23, 25 Old Broad St, London EC2N 1HQ, UK.
TEL +44 (0) 20 7847 9500.
FAX +44 (0) 20 7847 9501.
www.shawpittman.com

• Weil, Gotshal & Manges, 1 South Place, London EC2M 2WG, UK.
TEL +44 (0) 20 7903 1000.
FAX +44 (0) 20 7903 0990.
www.weil.com;
weil.london@weil.com

Marketing Director

Money: From £25,000 to £75,000. A few marketing directors will earn more in high-profile Internet businesses.

Hours: Apart from a few hectic nights checking the details of your TV advert, and the party to follow, you'll be working normal office hours.

Health risk: 4/10. Marketing people are most at risk from the long-term effects of long lunches.

Pressure rating: 7/10. You, and your marketing budget, are big expenses. You'll be under a lot of pressure to justify it.

Glamour rating: 6/10. Marketing directors get to decide how the rest of the world views the company, so they usually have a high profile to match.

Travel rating: 5/10. If you're doing marketing for a new multinational, fasten your seat belt, but if you're London-based, long-distance travel will be via black taxi.

Marketing people have a couple of key tasks: figure out who and where their company's customers are, and then make sure their customers know the company exists and how to buy its products. The role of a marketing manager in a new-economy company is often a lot broader than this. Marketing people promote the company to all kinds of audiences – not just customers, but also investors and partners. They also need to be financially minded to justify their budgets, which are often a big part of the company's spending.

Marketing people hate being in the office. Their job is to be out of the office, telling other people about the great company they work for. Because they're out and about so much, people have seen a lot of marketing directors. They're easy to recognise, since they will often fall into the following categories:

Gizmo Girl

She has come from somewhere in the company, like exhibition planning, and has been given a marketing job because she's young, pretty and has long blonde hair. Your 72-year-old Scottish chairman fancies her, and always approves her budgets with a smile. Her great joy in life is finding new gadgets to give away at company conferences: she's moved well beyond company golf umbrellas and coffee mugs, and now gives out full-sized replicas of the company's head-quarters, complete with toy people inside.

Avant-garde Boy

An art school graduate who didn't have the guts to be a film-maker. He is never in the office. He's also never in front of customers or potential business partners. Avant-garde boy lives at the offices of the ad agency, where he'd really like to work (though the salary isn't as good, and the hours are longer). He lunches with creative directors, admiring the other's use of words like 'panache' and 'seraph'. He wears Armani knock-offs because he's cheap, and unoriginal. He usually has a long-suffering member of staff who does all his work, and gets none of the credit.

Spreadsheet Geek

No one knows what gender this person is, or what they look like. They only communicate through e-mail. This person ended up in marketing because no one knew what to do with them. He/she sends out spreadsheets on **market segmentation**. He/she will eventually get frustrated at the lack of intellectual input, and go to work for an advertising research house. He/she won't be missed, except at budget time, since neither Gizmo Girl nor Avant-garde Boy knows how to put together a spreadsheet.

In an Internet company, the marketing characters are often very different. For one thing, the company is short on people, so there will be one person doing Gizmo Girl's exhibitions, Avant-garde Boy's managing of the advertising agency, and Spreadsheet Geek's budgets, and more. People who can do all these things are fairly rare, and are usually more experienced and older than your 'typical' marketeers, who tend to be in their early twenties.

In many companies, particularly those whose business is making physical goods, marketing is seen as a weak department that spends money without any results. For an Internet company, it's another story entirely: marketing activities like building a strong brand and accurate market segmentation are seen as critical to the company's success. A good marketing person is viewed as a key asset in the war to get customers to listen to what the company has to say, remember what the company has said, and trust the company enough to buy from them in the future.

Because of the range of their activities and the speed at which they have to work, the Internet marketing director is like the conductor of an orchestra. They work with a number of people inside and outside the company to set budgets, justify and promote the company in front of prospective customers or partners, set up exhibitions, manage public relations and analysts, and choreograph the company's brand. To get all of this done, directors work with specialists such as Web design companies, advertising or PR agencies, media specialists, and more. That explains some of the scale of marketing budgets, which keep growing. Marketing budgets for dot.coms are enormous: maybe a quarter to a third of all the company's cash will be spent here. A marketing manager will typically manage a budget of six figures, possibly seven.

All these responsibilities – big budgets, managing lots of suppliers, considerable pressure from customers and partners – make the marketing director's job both high-profile and high-stress. Since their job is to have a very clear idea of the company's strategy and of its benefits, the marketing director will need to know everyone in the company and what they do.

Because they know the company best, the Internet marketing director will find a bunch of other things falling on their already overloaded plate. Extra responsibilities may include account management (taking care of the company's best clients), business development (getting new clients), strategic planning (figuring out where the company's going), and everyday organising. The job may even extend to hiring business recruits, collecting information on competitors, helping define what the company is offering, and helping to negotiate with venture capitalists. After all, the person who knows the company best and has the greatest ability to present its good points is the person you want in front of the money!

A typical example of this 'new and improved' director is Kirkland Newman, marketing director of musiclegal.com. Newman's prior experience was very different from working with a small dot.com: she worked in New York with the Rockefeller Brothers fund, putting together grants for South Africa and eastern Europe, then Ogilvy and Mather, a large advertising and communications company, where she was strategic planner for Lotus and IBM. Newman says, 'My role has been much wider than PR/marketing, so I've had contact with funders, record labels, ISPs, and hosting companies. It's hard to give a focused answer to what a marketing director does. I am actually head of marketing and business development, so I'm stretched in terms of the number of things I have to do, and I constantly worry about letting things fall through the cracks. I need to take time out to recruit people also, which is just one more thing to add to the list.'

Claire Kerr is marketing manager of Proteus, the Internet consultancy. Kerr was well prepared for taking on this role, since she had taken on a marketing assistant role straight from university, and spent six years working her way up the marketing ranks before moving to a competitor and, now, a start-up. Her current role includes working with advertising, PR and marketing. She describes her days as 'really busy and very varied – jumping from high-level strategy and planning one minute to sleeves-rolled-up implementation the next'.

The ability to be flexible and learn quickly is essential for anyone who wants to be involved in Internet marketing. Stephanie Copeland of Level 3 describes her job as marketing and PR director as 'tedious, challenging, exciting. The amount of change that is occurring in this industry makes everyone an expert and novice at the same time. You never know how the market is going to swing because we are rewriting history.'

The demand for good marketeers for Internet companies just keeps growing. Fortunately, someone with initiative and talent can usually wangle their way in, since a key skill of the good marketeer is the ability to negotiate and present well.

SKILLS YOU'LL NEED

- A flair for communication, and a gift for the gab.

- A true love of your product, your company and your market (all of them will suss you out for a faker otherwise, and your best marketing plans will be wasted).
- The ability to plan, because you need to be looking forward to an eventual goal to support the company in its strategy.
- Negotiation skills come in very handy, because there will be frequent discussions with suppliers as well as with potential partners where the ability to exact more favourable terms may have significant impact.

GETTING THE JOB

- Keep in mind that recruitment tends to be very network-oriented, so get to know someone who does the job, and ask them to introduce you around.
- Try for an entry-level position, like marketing assistant – these are often advertised in the newspapers.
- Do a marketing degree that includes a year's placement. That way, you end up with a relevant qualification and some valuable experience.
- Demonstrating a personal interest in the industry would help – such as developing your own website or making sure you keep up with industry news.

TIPS

- You will need to be very versatile, and have a lot of patience. Ask yourself whether you enjoy working with lots of different people, as you will need to.
- Will you be able to put together a good case to convince the finance director that the money's worth spending on marketing?
- Can you balance analytic work and creative thinking? Both will be necessary.

GLOSSARY

- **Market segmentation**

The ability to look at a universe of potential customers (the market) and choose a sector of that market to target, based on such factors as age, socio-economic status or lifestyle.

USEFUL ADDRESSES

- Level 3 Communications, 66 Prescott St, London E1 8HG, UK.
TEL +44 (0) 20 7864 4444.
FAX +44 (0) 20 7864 4400.
www.level3.com
- Proteus: The Internet Consultancy, 26 Britton St, London EC1M 5UB, UK.
TEL +44 (0) 20 7689 6666.
FAX +44 (0) 20 7689 6667.
www.proteus.co.uk;
info@proteus.co.uk

MEDIA BUYER

MONEY: The typical range is £15,000–£40,000, unless you're a director, in which case you'll earn upwards of £60,000. Even as a junior media person, there are perks like free lunch, so at least you'll eat.

HOURS: More than 60 hours a week, including a lot of time spent negotiating over martinis.

HEALTH RISK: 6/10. All those martinis and cigars won't be good for you.

PRESSURE RATING: 7/10. Strict deadlines, large budgets, nervous clients. This can get very stressful.

GLAMOUR RATING: 5/10. As media owners get more desperate for your dosh, they'll spend a lot entertaining you. Expect some perks.

TRAVEL RATING: 2/10. Media buyers are generally glued to their phones, screens or spreadsheets. Unless you get the odd conference in Cannes, you'll be stuck at your desk.

Media buyers place advertisements for Internet companies in magazines and newspapers, on television, radio and the Internet. But while Internet companies are clients, dot.coms also try to sell advertising space to media buyers. As the purse-holders for advertising spend, media buyers get special treatment from websites, which are trying to up the amount of advertising budgets they receive, most of which is currently spent on TV and magazines.

Media buyers were once the Cinderella of the advertising industry. Advertising creatives, the ones who make the ads, got to wear black and take lots of money from clients for creating ads featuring dancing chocolate. Media people meanwhile were stuck at their computers, trying to eke out the pennies from the media budget, to make sure the punter saw this great ad at least once. Something changed. Lots more magazines, newspapers, cable television stations and the Internet came along. Today, the media buyer is a very important person, since clients began to realise that people seeing and remembering the ad may be more important than its quality.

The Internet has been a double whammy for media buyers. They have many more dot.com clients these days, but dot.com companies also sell advertising space on their websites ... to media buyers! The media buyer is a source of revenue to the Internet companies, since sites can sell banner ad space to them, but more often the media buyer acts as a consultant to such companies, telling them where to buy advertising to best promote themselves. The dual role the media buyer plays is only one of the weird idiosyncrasies that makes this industry such a convoluted mire of loyalties, favours and reciprocal back-scratching.

First of all, the Internet was a new medium which advertisers didn't understand and needed help with. Media buyers got to speak intelligently about page views and hits, advertising banners and buttons, and their corresponding impact on the media budget. But with the onslaught of new Internet companies and their need to make contact with customers, the media buyer is more important than ever. As Internet companies typically spend 25–30 per cent of their fledgling budgets on media, the right choices are critical, as is justifying the dosh they spend to results-hungry investors. The shrewd skills of media buyers are practically setting the **rate cards** for popular websites: an ad on the Internet is only worth what someone is willing to pay for it, and there's plenty of space on the Web going spare.

The job of a media buyer hasn't always been as high-profile as it is now. Part of this is because hitherto it was reasonably straightforward to buy media – there weren't many choices. Until recently, Britain had only four television channels, and two of them didn't take advertising. If a media buyer was told by a client to get some ads out to people, they'd pull their list down from the shelf and book the relevant time slot on the relevant TV channel. The media owner and the buyer would go out for a drink to cement the deal, and would most likely repeat it the same time the following year.

With the proliferation of television channels, magazines and newspapers, and the rise in advertising budgets, the media buyer's job has become far more complicated. This complexity has changed their working environment. Far from being stuck in dusty back-office rooms at the ad agency, media buyers often work for new, glamorous specialists who boast great track records at getting clients results from new media such as websites or interactive TV.

Since the job has become more challenging in recent years, people are staying in it longer. When media buying took place in advertising agencies, there was often nowhere to grow as a buyer. Now, with specialist agencies such as I-level springing up everywhere, there are more exciting opportunities – and the chance to start your own company once you have made your way up the ladder. Jon Wilkins of London-based media start-up Naked Communications has a convert's zeal about the new opportunities in media. 'We are at the leading edge of creative media planning,' he says. 'We are trying to change the market away from bulk buying to being creative and innovative.'

The background and personality of the people doing media buyer jobs have changed in recent years. The media buyer was traditionally seen as the barrow-boy at the sharp end of the advertising industry. Buyers were once hired without any formal qualifications, on little more than energy, youth and raw ability. Buyers' key skills were to negotiate sharp deals, detect fibs, and stretch a small budget. It would have been easy to hear the following conversation between the ad sales person (the representative of a publication who's trying to get you to buy space) and the media buyer:

Ad sales: 'Come on, it's the last double page left. I'll do a special price for you' (meaning: I've got tons of space left to sell and am trying to sell this one at an inflated margin, and I'm desperate to make my commission).

Media buyer: 'Well, I don't know, we're full up this season. Don't know if the plan had your publication in mind. Plus your rate card looks a bit steep!' (meaning: You must be joking, not at that price. What are you playing at?).

In recent years, with the proliferation of media outlets and their increasing complexity, the media companies have had to add a serious layer of analytical capability to what they require from their buyers. Media buyers (sometimes media planners, to reflect the fact that they have a strategic emphasis) often have degrees in psychology, statistics or economics. Often a team of buyers and planners work together: it's rare to find the combination in the same person, and the workload is fierce, so one person will decide where the ads go and the other will negotiate the best deal for them.

Most media buyers and planners work either for the media department of an advertising agency, in which case they work on behalf of the agency's clients, or for specialist 'independent' media planning and buying agencies, who team up with different ad agencies to service clients. Media buyers and planners work on specific accounts, which are client companies that the advertising and/or media agency represents.

The pressure tends to be high from important accounts. Today it is very difficult for advertisers to reach so-called 'desirable' audiences (youngish, full-time employed people with disposable income) through conventional means. With the rash of cable TV channels, and the fact that people are watching less of any of them, how do you get to your audience with that expensive TV advert? You have to adopt a strategy that uses, in addition to conventional media like TV and newspapers, a certain amount of **guerrilla marketing** and sponsorship to grab those eyeballs.

Imagine your media agency has the Bloggo Fast Food account. It will have a significant media budget (after all, it needs to compete with Wimpy and Burger King). Bloggo's budget to advertise its Bloggo Burgers is not as large as Burger King's, nor is Bloggo so well known. This is a typical challenge for a media buyer, who will think about such issues as market segmentation (which people are going to buy Bloggo Burgers?). Once the media agencies understand what kind of people they are trying to reach, they will use the **ratings** to figure out what combination of media, or media mix, they should use.

Ideally, the outcome would be that Bloggo Burgers were advertised to a likely buyer on his or her way to work on the car radio. At lunch-time, when the hungry person left their office, they would notice a poster for Bloggo Burgers, and think, 'Hmm. I'm kind of hungry.' With any luck, there would be a Bloggo Burgers outlet near by, where the lucky punter could redeem the coupon that had been in that morning's newspaper for a free Bloggo shake. The media planner and buyer would have been working away in the background to make sure that the punter was aware of Bloggo, and that they had an incentive (in this case, the coupon) to buy. They might also have chosen to hit the Bloggo target through magazines, newspapers, television, radio, outdoor outlets (posters and bus shelters, for example) and the Internet.

Alexandra Eidenschenk, senior media planner with New York advertising agency Mad Dogs and Englishmen (founded by two expat Brits), came to the job by accident. Having planned on becoming a doctor and studying medicine at university, she landed a job with the pharmaceutical division of an advertising agency. Recognising her analytical capability and eye for detail, a savvy manager placed her in the media area, where she's been for several years, despite moving agencies a few times. She describes the way the job is changing within a typical agency environment: 'Agencies are downsizing but taking on more business. We meet with media reps to keep up with changes in the media industry and to be aware of new media opportunities. We also have a lot of contact with clients, as the media department is becoming more and more strategic. We do a lot of grunt work like keeping budgets and executing media buys, but we're also part of the strategy development.' The shift from commercial buying to involvement in strategy is the reason why ever-smarter, strategically minded people are joining the profession. Those people who are involved consistently at a strategic level will sometimes call themselves media planners, and will work in teams with buyers.

The team approach works well, since while the media buyer is typically young, a lot of responsibility rests on their shoulders. The bulk of the millions of pounds in a typical advertising budget will be spent on media: television slots, advertising space, event sponsorship. The job involves a lot of complicated thinking, usually working to a tight deadline, and tends to attract people with a very high energy level, who are good with numbers, fast with facts, and able to communicate. Although it isn't a particularly people-centred job, you do end up dealing with a wide circle of folks, from media owners through to specialist researchers who educate you on, for example, the latest trends in interactive TV, and what product advertising would be most suitable for that environment.

Media buyers are in control of big budgets and represent several major advertisers. They are therefore mini-celebrities to the advertising sales people jockeying for their custom. They are given loads of free publications that they don't have time to read, are taken to lunch, dinner, drinks and the odd corporate jaunt. As the competition is getting fiercer and media outlets keep growing, the perks keep getting better. In America, the competition for the media buyer's attention is fierce, so American media buyers get wined and dined, given spa weekends and tickets to premières. 'We certainly get some wonderful perks,' Eidenschenk says. 'We get taken to all the best restaurants and get tickets to shows and sporting events from advertising reps hungry for business. Friends and family are definitely jealous when they see me front and centre at the US Open Tennis Tournament. That makes all the hard work worthwhile!' Even in the UK, Jon Wilkins says, you get 'lots of jollies and freebies. Visits to film premières, footy games, Cannes, the World Cup.'

Although media buyer salaries were not high in the past, the difficulty of finding people with the right knowledge is causing wages to rise. 'Right now, the money is very good,' Eidenschenk says. 'Media planners are scarce and in high demand, since many of us jumped to the dot.com and advertising sales worlds. People with two to five years of experience are commanding forty to sixty per cent increases on their salaries. Senior people are able to ask for nice salaries and some extras such as health club memberships and time off. It's definitely a good time for media people.'

Media buyers follow a traditional career ladder. The typical route is to join the media department of an ad agency or a media independent, such as Zenith Media, straight out of school or university. As an alternative, there are a number of specialist interactive agencies that specialise in buying and planning media across new distribution channels such as interactive TV, WAP phones, and the Internet. Usually, you will start out as an assistant (the job is often open to non-graduates who are commercially savvy). Subsequently, you will be a media buyer/planner, and progress through various levels of seniority until you are a board director of the agency and make business and management decisions for your company as well as managing big-client relationships. Since the advent of the Internet, people tend to move jobs more quickly, and there are greater opportunities to be more visible in front of clients.

Media buying is a difficult, stressful career with high burn-out. Many buyers go on to become owners of agencies themselves, leaving the detail to their teams. Some move on to the marketing departments of their clients, where they have lighter hours.

SKILLS YOU'LL NEED

- A healthy liver to stand up to all those drinks.
- Excellent negotiation skills. The media world is full of people who argued with their parents about bedtime when they were children, and kept negotiating for an extra half-hour.
- A very quick head for numbers. You will be dealing with stacks of media research and need to have the numbers at your fingertips.

GETTING THE JOB

- Any quantitative degree such as statistics or economics will be helpful. Alternatively, the evidence of commercial skill (running your own student business, for example) will get you in the door as a buyer.
- You can do a degree in marketing,

with an internship at a media-focused company.

- There are a number of specialist headhunters: check such trade publications as *Campaign* or *Mediaweek* for job opportunities.

TIPS

- Keep looking at problems fresh: the media landscape changes every year, so using last year's plan just isn't an option.
- Focus on the details and be patient when going over complex budgets with clients, who may not be as quick with the numbers as you are.
- Keep in touch with popular culture.
- Start with a big agency that has a lot of tools and technology in-house. Decide if the culture suits you and, once you have a few years under your belt and acquired some experience and contacts, consider moving to a smaller agency or a specialist.

GLOSSARY

- **Guerrilla marketing**

Unconventional marketing techniques that do not employ traditional media. An example is people at train stations dressed in costume singing a song. Usually more noticeable than traditional media, but not necessarily more effective.

- **Rate cards**

The published prices for media space that the media buyer consults. Of course, they *never* pay retail ...

- **Ratings**

The measure of how popular a publication or TV or radio programme is. Media are independently measured by ratings agencies, who publish lists of how many people buy, watch or listen to a particular media outlet. RAJAR is a ratings agency, and you would look to RAJAR to see how many people are listening to Classic FM, at what times of the day, and how likely those people are to buy a Volvo.

USEFUL ADDRESSES

- Campaign, Haymarket Business Publications Ltd, 10 Cabot Square, Canary Wharf, London E14 4QB.
TEL +44 (0) 20 8845 8545.
FAX +44 (0) 20 8606 7301.
www.campaignlive.com
- I-Level, 64 Vincent Square, London SW1P 2NU, UK.
TEL +44 (0) 20 7630 9002.
FAX +44 (0) 20 7630 1934.
www.i-level.com
info@i-level.com
- Mad Dogs and Englishmen, 126 Fifth Ave, New York, NY 10011, USA.
TEL +1 212 675 6116.
FAX +1 212 675 0340.
www.maddogadv.com
- Naked Communications, HMS President, Victoria Embankment, London EC4Y OHJ.
TEL +44 (0) 20 7353 2333.
FAX +44 (0) 20 7353 9444.
jon@nakedcomms.com
- Revolution, Haymarket Business Publications Ltd , 10 Cabot Square, Canary Wharf, London E14 4QB.
TEL +44 (0) 20 8267 4730.
FAX +44 (0) 20 8267 4696.
www.revolution.haynet.com
- Zenith Media, Bridge House, 63–65 North Wharf Rd, London W2 1LA.
TEL +44 (0) 20 7224 8500.
FAX +44 (0) 20 7706 2650.
www.zenithmedia.co.uk

PARTY PLANNER
(EVENTS CO-ORDINATOR)

MONEY: From £25,000 to £45,000.

HOURS: Office hours will be 9–6, but on party days the planner must be on hand till the wee hours overseeing.

HEALTH RISK: 5/10. Late nights entertaining can be trying, but the social whirl can be good for you too.

PRESSURE RATING: 6/10. With every detail of events falling on your shoulders, there's a lot of pressure to get it all right.

GLAMOUR RATING: 5/10. These are the people who plan the parties, not the people who get parties thrown in their honour.

TRAVEL RATING: 7/10. Events planners tend to organise events not just locally, but also for their clients in other places too.

Parties are a staple of the Internet industry. Dot.commers like to party more than almost any other business folk, given as they are to networking, and building up the biggest collections of business cards possible. It's an industry that has adopted the adage 'It's not what you know, it's who you know'. Party planning dot.com style has become an art form all of its own.

Party planning ... how hard can it be? Book a **venue**, order some grog, send out the invites, and you're set, right?

Wrong. The devil of parties is in the detail. The Internet industry is obsessed with partying, and has become increasingly blasé about what counts as a good time, and what should be given a miss. Companies have to try hard to make an impression with a party these days, and most believe it's worth the effort. Every detail makes an impression, from the initial invite to the theme to the drinks to the venue to the decorations to the entertainment to the **giveaway** gift handed out at the door on your guests' way out.

Planning a good party has become a key part of Internet companies' marketing budgets. A good turnout, good music and (most importantly) plenty of hooch can say a lot about a firm. Companies use parties to announce new products (the launch party), to announce an old product that's been redesigned (the relaunch party), to encourage their business acquaintances to acquaint with you (the networking party), or in times of bad publicity to reassure everyone the company will be okay (the feel-good party). There are also a fair number of event-driven parties: whenever there's a big conference or other event, companies will **sponsor** their own party to accompany it. At gatherings like the Cannes Film Festival, with all its connotations of glamour, dot.com companies line up to sponsor parties to try to absorb some of the excitement.

'Parties are extremely important in this industry, because there's a lot of young creative energy flying around,' says JoAnn Soo, an events co-ordinator for Excite PR in New York. 'They love networking because deals and relationships are created in a matter of days. It doesn't take a year to create a partnership, and the more heads there are, the more ideas there are.'

Events co-ordinators occasionally work within companies, but more often party planning will be only a portion of their job – they will have other duties like marketing or public relations. Smaller companies might use an external agency, or farm out the responsibility to their public relations agency. Whoever takes over, Soo says, the first task of the party planner is to get some answers from the client on what they are hoping to achieve from the party. 'Some questions include but are not limited to: What are your goals and objectives? What's the purpose of the event? Who are you trying to target? Why are you targeting these people? How much money do you have for this event? How many people do you have to staff this event?' she says.

Once Soo has answers to some of these questions, she can get started on the planning. She'll know whether to book a large or small venue, whether the event calls for a discreet chamber quartet, a nineteen-piece big band, or a trance DJ. She'll know whether to serve champagne in crystal flutes or Sex on a Beach, and whether the staff serving those drinks should be clean-shaven waiters in monkey suits or nineteen-year-old blonde girls in roller-skates and miniskirts.

Booking the venue will always be the first task. Popular locales are booked up months in advance, and a date for the party can't be set until the venue is confirmed. Once you have a date, and an idea of what kind of party you're laying on, it's time for the invites, which involve another rash of decisions by committee. Everyone will have an idea as to who the guest list should include and how the invites should read, and it's up to the party planner both to force consensus on the details and get the ball rolling.

'Your party needs to reflect your company in every way,' says Aimee Kessler Evans, director of marketing and publicity for MarketingSherpa.com. Evans plans all of MarketingSherpa's parties, and since the company's business is helping Internet companies promote and market themselves, their own parties need to be top-drawer. 'At MarketingSherpa.com, our style is very cheeky. So, needless to say, we won't be doing cocktails at Stringfellows for our next event. It's much more our speed to have an event at a chic club with funky music and no suits allowed. Moreover, we will carry that attitude into the promotional items that we give away at our events. Rather than hand out free travel alarm clocks, our attendees are more likely to leave with MarketingSherpa.com nail varnish. Carry your creativity over to your "widgets", if you have the budget for it. People love free stuff, and a great promotional gift – whether it's a tin of mints with your company's name emblazoned on it or just a really excellent pen – will leave your attendees with something to remember you by.'

As planning for the event gets rolling, it's important to remember that attendees will have a different agenda from the company who sponsored it. While your objective is to get publicity and attract attention to your company, the guests will be there to network and enjoy themselves. As much as the chief executive of the client company might want to spend an hour on a podium discussing the newest products, it's your job as party planner to suggest helpfully that this might kill the mood. Alternatively, if the party is just about ... well, partying, the company will have spent a load of dough with no results.

'There are many reasons why parties are important,' says Evans. 'The number-one reason is obviously networking. Whether you're looking for partners, advertisers, employees, a new job, or a sugar daddy for your start-up, Internet parties are a perfect place for schmoozing. It's all about networking for the attendees, but for the host, it's all about branding and publicity. A truly great party will ideally gain publicity for your company. Whether it's by members of the press who've attended the event or just via word of mouth, industry parties get your company's name "out there".'

Although there are hundreds of mistakes the sponsoring company can make in planning, attendees of an Internet party can fall into traps as well. Two mistakes you never want to make, according to Evans: '1) Not bringing enough business cards. Nothing spells "amateur" like the sheepish shrug and smile on your face when you're out of cards. Take about three times as many cards as you think you'd ever need, along with a pen or two to take notes on the backs of cards that are given to you. Really, forgetting your cards makes you look like a complete nobody (without the evidence to prove otherwise!) – and a networking zero. 2) Clinging to your co-workers. If you spend more than ten per cent of a party or event standing next to your girlfriend from Marketing, you're wasting your time. The little "clique" you're creating makes it intimidating to approach you – and harder for you to meet new people. If you're not out there shaking hands with a big smile on your face, why are you even at this party? Moreover, you're making your company look unfriendly and élitist, and I'm sure your boss won't be too impressed with that!'

For the company planning the event, one of the most embarrassing outcomes can be spending the budget unwisely. Nothing causes more red faces at an Internet company than spending millions on a launch party and having to report a month later that it has to go out of business. Spend enough to make an impression, but not enough to wipe out your marketing budget for the year.

'You can spend anything from next to nothing to thousands of dollars, and you can either end up in debt or with thousands of dollars in sponsor funds,' says Evans. 'It depends, again, on your goals, on your market. A launch party may not have any sponsors, and might return nothing more than some good press and a fun night for staff and investors. And it may cost big bucks to rent a venue for such an event. On the other hand, a weekly industry mixer may be held in a low-key bar and cost next to nothing, but it may have sponsors paying to have their brochures handed out at the event. These can be a profitable venture.'

So dependent has the Internet industry become on its networking parties that a number of companies have turned hosting parties into a money-making venture. In 1998, a group of four London-based Internet entrepreneurs were disappointed by the lack of any events or parties that would allow them to meet the influential investors they needed to further their business plans. At that time, London, unlike Silicon Valley, was devoid of an 'Internet scene', and entrepreneurs were hard pressed to find a community of support. The four began hosting a gathering on the first Tuesday of every month, called, predictably, FirstTuesday. The parties were blatant networking opportunities. Like the old traffic light parties, where attendees wear green if they're single, red if they're taken, and yellow if they could be talked round, FirstTuesday attendees have a green sticker on their badge if they're looking for money, red if they're investors looking for deals, and yellow if they're a service provider or member of the press. Over the next two years, the event grew until thousands of people were attending the London parties every month. FirstTuesday spread out into 85 other European and American cities. In July 2000, the company was sold to an Israeli venture capitalist for a reported $50 million. FirstTuesday, charging for sponsorship of these parties, had found that bad Chardonnay and a stellar invite list could spell profits in the Internet industry.

Sadly, though, the thing with parties is that it's so easy to become unhip. Yesterday's super-cool new venue is today's has-been, which only the most behind-the-times company would use for a launch party. FirstTuesday became mightily popular, but like anything that depends on being in fashion, as soon as everyone knew about it, it became passé. In the months before the company was sold, only a newbie would go to a FirstTuesday; the Internet Über-cool were on to something new.

'You don't want to be throwing a party in Le Bar Bat if every party last week was there,' says Evans. 'And you don't want to be throwing a party in Hell's Kitchen if everyone's hanging out in Soho.'

Soo says that the trouble with spending all your time planning events is that you rarely want to attend one when you're not working. There is an upside, though. 'I'm planning my own wedding right now, and I don't have to pay for anything!' she says. 'My suppliers are all doing it for free.'

SKILLS YOU'LL NEED

An eye for detail, good organisational capabilities, a friendly nature, and pleasure in working with people. It doesn't hurt to be a party animal, and know what people appreciate in a social occasion.

GETTING THE JOB

- Many party planners start out with entry-level positions in public relations or marketing. Volunteer for events duty, and get your feet wet working with experienced planners.
- You can learn a lot from planning social events in a volunteer capacity. An event for an amateur theatre company, volunteer fund-raisers for charity organisations, or the weddings of friends and relatives can all teach what it takes.

TIPS

(courtesy Aimee Kessler Evans)

- Know which clubs and venues are 'in'. Keep up to date on the 'in' clubs on a weekly basis. Times change quickly!
- Be creative – the scene gets boring when everyone's just throwing happy hours at the same six bars. Pick a new spot, and do something a little different.
- Be detail-oriented – from the signage to the name tags to the hors d'oeuvres, pay attention to every little thing. Those little things, like remembering that there may be vegetarians or non-drinkers at your party, make all the difference in the world.
- Wear fabulous clothes! Don't be the plain Jane at your own party – wear something wonderful that will make it obvious that you're the hostess (or host)! Give people something to talk about – or at least compliment you on. And be warm, gracious and friendly to your attendees. Make them feel like your guests, and they'll want to come back to your parties.

GLOSSARY

- **Giveaways**

The free toys a company will hand out at the end of a party, usually some knick-knack bearing their name and logo. It's all about the branding!

- **Sponsors**

A corporation that pays for the privilege of having their logo prominently displayed at an industry party. If a company knows that a certain party is going to attract the crème de la crème of the local Internet scene, they'll be keen to attach their name and logo to the event, giving the organisers a way to make a party profitable.

- **Venue**

The bar, club, hall or theatre in which your event will be held. Choice of venue says a lot about the party itself ... a key thing to get right for a successful do.

USEFUL ADDRESSES

- Awesome Events, 120 Wilton Rd, Victoria, London SW1V 1JZ, UK.
TEL +44 (0) 20 7233 5557.
FAX +44 (0) 20 7233 5260.
www.awesome-events.co.uk;
sales@awesome-events.co.uk
- Entertainment Corporation, 58 Tachbrook St, London SW1V 2NA, UK.
TEL +44 (0) 20 7233 7931.
www.entertainment-corp.com;
karen@entertainment-corp.com

- ExcitePR – Events Consulting Group, 1220 Broadway, Suite 706, New York, NY 10001, USA.
TEL +1 212 268 1646.
FAX +1 212 268 1734.
www.excitepr.com; info@excitepr.com
- FirstTuesday, 12 St James Square, London SW1Y 4RB, UK.
TEL +44 (0) 20 7849 6779.
FAX +44 (0) 20 7849 6226.
www.firsttuesday.com;
firsttuesday@egroups.com
- MarketingSherpa.com, 1791 Lanier Place NW#5, Washington, DC 20009, USA.
TEL +1 202 232 6830.
FAX +1 646 349 2846.
www.marketingsherpa.com;
subscriptions@marketingsherpa.com
- Premier Party Catering, 39 Upper St, Islington, London N1 OPN, UK.
TEL +44 (0) 20 7226 4380/3166.
FAX +44 (0) 20 7704 0381.
www.premierparty.co.uk;
julius@premierparty.co.uk

PRODUCER

MONEY: Between £18,000 and £60,000. A senior producer will have huge responsibilities and be paid accordingly.

HOURS: 50–60 per week, unless you are in charge of a team or on deadline. Which is often the case: expect to sleep at the office occasionally.

HEALTH RISK: 6/10. You get resentment when you're cracking the whip to make people deliver, and lots of love once it's all over. This is not the job for a natural paranoid.

PRESSURE RATING: 7/10. It is stressful, but at least you're the one with some measure of control.

GLAMOUR RATING: 6/10. Although it's nice to be in charge of the project, it won't necessarily get your name in lights.

TRAVEL RATING: 2/10. Producers are usually in the office, or in the basement trying to persuade technical people to work faster.

Producers are a special kind of project manager who co-ordinate creative aspects of a project, for example the launch of a website or the development of a new programme or channel by bringing together the varied personalities and skill sets – technical, business and creative – and trying to prevent people from killing each other in the process.

Producers in the heyday of Hollywood always worked behind the scenes, funded the film, and occasionally dealt with the ego clashes between directors and stars. The Hollywood producer was an important person with a big ego, who could walk around with a big cigar and talk about 'my new film'.

The new media producer's role is very different (especially the big ego bit). The responsibilities are serious: the new media producer will be in charge of a large budget, and have the responsibility of delivering a new website/interactive TV channel/ mobile entertainment portal. He or she will have to get lots of people together and persuade them to work together. Producers need to employ diplomacy and stealth, and keep their own egos firmly under control. They also need to be able to see through the detail and find solutions to problems, which may be creative or technical, or in such specialist areas as animation, illustration and design.

The job is not the most glamorous. Producers are too busy getting things done to talk about how important they are, so the job generally suffers from a lack of visibility in the industry. If a complex, leading-edge website was delivered on time and on budget, it had a stellar producer somewhere behind it.

Neil Kelly is a producer at Traffic Interactive. He landed in the agency world from a background of IT and project management. Although he is trained in project management, he admits that in the Internet world being a producer 'is a fairly new role, which is critical to get right', and there are no rule books.

Gary Prescod, of Eos Internet Ventures, has come through a background in production, including being responsible for British Airways' on-line activity, and working on other big clients for new media agency Syzygy. He describes the structure of a producer's role: 'Picture the stages: planning, design, technical build, integration, testing and launch. Each of these stages involves a different set of challenges, involves different working hours and a different set of diplomatic skills – from dealing with the client with enormous expectations to the designers or **coders**, all of whom need dealing with in a variety of different ways.'

Producers need a rare set of personal qualities combined with good natural organisational abilities. More formal qualifications often include a background in project management or technology. Some have realised that they enjoyed dealing with people more than they did contributing one part of a project from a solitary computer screen. Others enjoy the impact they are able to have on a tangible outcome: a great website.

Prescod describes the stage where the producer sees an impact: 'In the planning phase, one must lead the client in setting and prioritising requirements, thereby agreeing the scope of the project, drawing up the overall project plan ... all this is usually carried out in a very short timescale. It is here that the producer can really have a great impact on the end product. The producer can act as the customer champion, and tutor the client in best-practice customer experience, navigation and product positioning, and drawing out some complex on-line services such as registration, personalisation and e-commerce.'

A typical day is spent establishing the tricky balance between making sure you have everyone's input and opinion, and moving on to executing. It can be all too easy for a weak producer to end up with a stack of notes outlining various opinions as people move off saying 'Great meeting' without having committed to delivering anything by a due date. Getting people to agree to meet deadlines, by whatever method, is where the producer shows his or her mettle.

There is a lot of compromise and cajoling involved, with the producer as chief negotiator. Prescod says, 'Invariably you're asking people to compromise on the quality of their work. Designers may wish to get everything on a page **pixel**-perfect – this simply may not be possible in the time available. It's your job to convince them to compromise. Not easy. Equally, the client will have to be strongly encouraged to sign off designs in a timely manner. If they cannot do so, it is the role of the producer to point out the implications of their actions – whether a slip to the plan, more costs, or something else.'

Production people at large interactive agencies often move on to become a team leader, or head of production, which brings a corresponding increase in responsibility, visibility and pay. The production manager will do a lot more working with clients, and will be responsible for any project that goes off the rails (which happens frequently in an area where so much is new and uncertain).

Although the job is neither glamorous nor high-profile, producers tend not to mind. They have a sense that their job is critical to the success of the new media industry. As Prescod points out, 'The producer, being involved both in product and service definition as well as in project management, has a unique and very important role. Satisfaction comes from both pushing the boundaries of customer experience on-line, and the pleasure of seeing something delivered on time and within budget. The role will always be critical – an effective interface between the client and the builders, which can cut across any type of project, whatever the interface, be it Web, interactive TV, mobile phones.'

SKILLS YOU'LL NEED

- An incredible amount of maturity and patience, to make up for the lack of it around you.
- The ability to be firm with and manage difficult personalities, including the client's.
- Generosity of personality: you need to let other people hog the limelight and be secure in what you've accomplished.
- Excellent insight into what customers need: you are, after all, working for them.

GETTING THE JOB

Take relevant courses such as information technology management or project management.

TIPS

- Keep a balanced perspective, and realise that you won't get much praise until after the job is delivered, successfully.
- Keep up your knowledge about technical or creative excellence in the field: you'll need to prove your street cred with designers and coders.

GLOSSARY

- **Coder**

Slang for the technical bod whose job it is to write or customise software using computer languages such as C++.

- **Pixel**

The smallest possible unit of your computer screen. Pixels are made of one or more dots of colour, which contribute to the look of a Web page.

USEFUL ADDRESSES

- Eos Internet Ventures, 8–14 Vine Hill, London EC1R 5DX, UK.
TEL +44 (0) 20 7239 0000 .
www.eosventures.net;
info@eosventures.net
- Syzygy, 4th Floor, Elsley House, 24–30 Great Titchfield St, London W1 7AD.
TEL +44 (0) 20 7460 4080.
FAX +44 (0) 20 7460 4081.
www.syzygy.co.uk

Programmer

Money: From £20,000 to £40,000 for starting programmers.

Hours: A lot, but they are flexible. Most work 'programmer hours', which means showing up at 10 or 11 and working through till midnight.

Health risk: 8/10. Programmers do not tend to be healthy people. Expect **carpal tunnel syndrome**, insomnia, poor diet, lack of exercise ...

Pressure rating: 5/10. Programmers never have enough time to do what they'd like to do, and there is frequent pressure from the bosses to deliver.

Glamour rating: 1/10. No glory, no glamour in the programming world.

Travel rating: 1/10. A deskbound job.

If the hi-tech industry has a jobsworth, the programmer is it. Behind all the hype and buzz and whiz-bang multimedia of the Web are teams of hard-working technicians, writing the code that makes the whole industry tick. Programmers take what has been dreamed up by the marketing people and designed by the creatives, and actually make the Web pages. A small Web icon that takes two minutes for marketing to think up and 20 minutes for the art staff to design could take two weeks for the programmer to code. Every minute piece of every Web page is the result of some programmer's sleepless night.

Programmers are often the least involved in planning an Internet project, but the most involved in executing the plans. The business people have their say, and the artists have their say, and the project managers create a schedule for when the site will be delivered, and then the whole thing is handed to the programmers, and they are told to get on with it.

Although it isn't the most glamorous job in the world (okay, it isn't glamorous at all), without programmers there would be no Web. 'People like me are the nuts and bolts of the industry,' says Justin Williams, a Web programmer with Aktiv Technologies, a Web design agency in Brighton, Sussex.

The basic language of the Web is HTML (Hyper-Text Mark-up Language), a text-based programming language that uses an established set of commands to tell the Web browser what to display. These commands are known as tags, and appear in HTML code like this: <tag>. If the designer has dictated that a certain line of text should appear as the title of the page, then the programmer will type the tag <title> before the text. HTML uses a back slash to indicate where a command finishes, e.g.: </tag>. If this book were a Web page, one of the first lines of code would be <title>How to Make It on the Internet</title>.

This tag-based way of thinking has spilled over into programmers' social life as well. In e-mails to friends, you might see the following:

From: a.programmer@adot.com
To: another.programmer@another.com
Subject: Re: How's life
Date: Thu, 24 Aug 2000 18:50:24 GMT

Hey, man, back on the job today after a measly five days of holiday. Had to come back early to repair the search function on the site. <rant>My so-called boss, who's supposed to have hacked so much code that he's worth two hundred grand a year, couldn't even find a dropped colon that screwed up the install. </rant>

See you soon ...

HTML is the most basic programming language the Web has to offer, because it was the first. When it was developed, most websites only displayed text, and perhaps a few pictures, which was well within the capabilities of the language. In the vernacular of the Web, these were **static** pages, which meant that the information they contained didn't change very often. To change a static page, the programmer had to change the code by hand.

Gradually, websites became more complex. People in the growing Internet industry began to realise that Web pages would attract more attention if they changed more often. Thus began a practice of building **dynamic** Web pages with content that changed all the time. The more dynamic the Web pages became, the more complex was the programmer's job. HTML was no longer adequate (in programmer-speak, it wasn't 'robust'). New programming languages developed: **Java**, **XML**, **ColdFusion**.

Companies are always pushing the limits of what the Internet can do, so programmers are always being pushed to keep up with the latest trend. They might start out knowing only HTML, learning other languages and tools as they go. Most programmers are constantly upgrading their knowledge, through reading, taking courses, and attending conferences. They also share information constantly through on-line bulletin boards and chat rooms. With so many programmers connected to the Internet all day long, they have built a worldwide virtual community for trading tips, seeking counselling from other programmers, and more often than not engaging in on-line 'flame' wars. A 'flame' is a particularly aggressive or abusive e-mail or message that castigates a colleague for saying or doing something stupid. That 'something stupid' might be meaningless to an ordinary human being, but in the élite community of programmers is worthy of derision. 'Can you believe it? That moron thought you could import SQL code into an SGML format! I'm totally gonna flame him.'

Many websites cater to this community of programmers, but one of the most famous is a news site called Slashdot (www.slashdot.org). People around the world send e-mails to Slashdot when they see an interesting story that the programming community will care about. Usually, this consists of a brief description of the story, as well as a link to another news site where the full story is posted. There are so many Geeks logging onto Slashdot every day that they are often blamed for clogging up other news sites that Slashdot links to. They even use their group power to lobby governments and companies to do things their way. This is known as 'the Slashdot effect', when thousands of angry Geeks use their collected might to force change.

Programmers by design are extraordinarily detail-oriented. The code they write is made of millions of commands, and one misspelling or misplaced comma could mean the whole Web page won't function as intended. Since they spend their days elbow deep in minutiae, it's no wonder that they tend to argue the finer points when among their peers. In the early part of a project, they are given instructions on what to build, but once it's built they begin a laborious process of checking and rechecking their code. And inevitably, some bright idea from the marketing or creative departments will force them to rebuild everything at the last minute.

'Often stress is caused by underestimating the time it will take to achieve a given goal,' says Dan Corbin, a Java programmer at OneSwoop.com, an on-line automobile sales site. 'As is the nature of development, things don't always go to plan. Problems arise which must be solved before you can get on with what you thought was the true task in hand. This adds time pressure, and this can lead to stress.'

Justin Williams works with external clients, rather than on internal projects like Corbin. With multiple projects going on at all times, he says the pressure is constant. 'There's never enough time to finish jobs to full satisfaction. Unforeseen events are always putting us behind schedule.'

Programmers will generally report to the project manager, or in some cases the chief technical officer. Programmers with lots of experience tend to move into these roles as they get promoted, but a good programmer doesn't always make a good manager. Although the promise of more money will lure many programmers to make the leap, they may miss 'the good ol' days' back in the trenches of programming. 'Typically, I have a team of four to five junior and senior staff working on a functional area of our website,' says Patrick Simpe-Asante, who heads up the development team at OneSwoop. 'Coming from a pure development background, I prefer to get my hands dirty with programming periodically. Sadly, this is not always possible. Most of my time is spent managing projects.'

When a project is conceived, the project manager will break up what needs to be done into specific jobs, which are handed out among the programming team. The size of this team will vary depending on the project: for very small websites or small additions to websites it could be just one person, but it could be hundreds for very large projects.

'Projects are broken down into smaller tasks, and these smaller tasks form the basis of a day's activity,' Corbin says. 'The hours I put in will tend to vary widely as project life cycles elapse. In the early days, hours put in will not be excessive. However, as deadlines loom, so the pressure grows, and hence the working day becomes extended. The working week is likely to extend by as much as twenty-five per cent before an important deadline.'

Corbin is a software programmer who evolved into Web coding, like many in the Internet world. 'In my formative years I was always interested in programming, although this was purely on a recreational basis,' he says. 'Through A-level and university my attention turned elsewhere. But I then taught myself Java to a basic level from books and the Internet before applying for a role as a trainee programmer at a software house. Here I gained fantastic experience in all stages of the development life cycle over a period of two years, before being approached by an agency looking for prospective [employees] with my skill set.'

Williams had an even more abrupt career change that led him into programming. 'I was a nurse who got disillusioned,' he says. 'I had a friend who worked in Web development and he got me interested. I started at the bottom of the heap.'

The bottom of the heap is where most programmers start out, but knowledge is valuable in the Web industry. If you can teach yourself a useful and relevant programming language, there is high demand for your services. Most polytechnics and universities teach courses in coding, and you can pick up programming skills from books and continuing education classes as well. Anyone who has tinkered with computers for a while will have the basic skills to pick up coding, as long as they're committed to endless hours perfecting their knowledge.

SKILLS YOU'LL NEED

Programmers need to be strongly detail-oriented, and patient, as well as have all the relevant technical qualifications, including knowledge of one or more programming languages, and the software tools used to design and develop Web pages. More sophisticated programming languages like Java are in particularly high demand and hard to find, so some companies are willing to train less skilled programmers.

GETTING THE JOB

Programmers are in high demand. If you've got the right skills, getting a job is just a matter of finding the right company to hire you. Check typical job listings, but also contact Web companies directly. Most will maintain a 'jobs' listing of their own on their website. Make sure you can refer prospective employers to examples of your work.

TIPS

- Keep developing your skill as a programmer by learning as many languages as possible.
- Become familiar with development tools and new trends in Web design and development.
- Develop a speciality, and participate in discussion forums and news groups

that cater to that speciality. You'll learn more from on-line bulletin boards than you will in a classroom.

GLOSSARY

- **Carpal tunnel syndrome**

A condition where pressure on a nerve (the median nerve), where it passes through the wrist into the hand, causes pain, pins and needles, weakness and numbness in the hand. Caused by repetitive motion such as heavy keyboard use. A badge of honour among programmers, but also a death sentence on their career.

- **ColdFusion**

A programming language and software tool from Allaire Corporation that helps Web programmers integrate their Web pages with databases.

- **Dynamic content**

Content on a Web page that changes frequently.

- **Java**

A programming language developed by Sun Microsystems that can ostensibly run on all kinds of computers, as well as the Web. Java was responsible for introducing animation, multimedia and data-driven dynamic content to the Web.

- **Static content**

Content on a Web page that doesn't change, or changes infrequently.

- **XML**

Short for Extensible Mark-up Language, XML is a tag-based language similar to HTML. However, programmers can extend the language by adding their own tags and definitions, whereas HTML is more limited.

USEFUL ADDRESSES

- Builder.com, 150 Chestnut St, San Francisco, CA 94111, USA.
TEL +1 415 364 8900.
www.builder.com
- Slashdot, 50 Nagog Park, Acton, MA 01720, USA.
TEL +1 978 635 5300.
FAX +1 978 635 5326.
www.slashdot.org;
malda@slashdot.org
- Sun Microsystems, Inc., 901 San Antonio Rd, UMIL03-06, Palo Alto, CA 94303, USA.
TEL +1 800 786 7638.
www.java.sun.com/;
javahelp-comments@sun.com
- Webmonkey – Designers Resource, Lycos-Wired Digital, 660 Third St, San Francisco, CA 94103, USA.
TEL +1 415 276 8400.
FAX +1 415 276 8500.
www.webmonkey.com/designers;
webmonkey@wired.com

Project Manager

Money: £30,000–£50,000 for project managers with a few years' experience. This rises dramatically for more experienced managers.

Hours: At least 50 hours per week, and usually some weekends.

Health risk: 7/10. Lots of interruptions and lots of requests coming from all sides might drive you mad, on top of the inevitable problems of stress.

Pressure rating: 8/10. As the nexus of all activity, the project manager carries a big responsibility for the success of the project.

Glamour rating: 2/10. Hard work, but it's behind the scenes. Few project managers see the limelight.

Travel rating: 2/10. You'll be chained to the office, in preparation for emergencies.

For all the hype surrounding dot.coms, something a lot of people forget is that someone actually has to do the work. Web projects can be a lot more complicated than they look, combining as they do complicated technology, editorial content, artistic elements, and finally some kind of business plan. The project manager sits at the junction of all this activity, both directing traffic and enforcing rules, but most importantly making sure the thing gets finished.

A newly started dot.com, or an established company looking for a new market, prepares to launch a website. Someone must decide on a name and a Web address for the site. Someone must plan how the site will be marketed. Someone must write the content. Someone must design the appearance of the pages. Someone must decide how the site will make money or serve the intended audience. Someone must figure out what technology will be used to develop and maintain the site. And someone must figure out how all the people involved will work together.

That someone is the project manager, probably the most crucial person in any Web venture. The project manager oversees staff, plans the development cycle, listens to the ideas of the creative team and the business team, and generally makes sure that everything gets done. A successful project manager has to be everyone's best friend, since most of his or her time will be spent cajoling work out of recalcitrant **techies**.

Project manager roles generally take two forms in the Internet industry: either they are an external manager, working for a consultancy or Web design practice, or they are appointed internally to supervise the project for their employers. If they are working at an external agency, their client is the company commissioning the work. If they are working on an internal project, the client is the department or executive who has appointed them to supervise the website development effort. 'In brief, [I am] responsible for delivering the client's requirements and providing advice on best practice,' says Anna Barsby, a project manager for Red Banner, a Web design consultancy in London.

When a project is conceived, one of the first things a company has to do is put someone in charge. A project manager should have a hand in the planning stage. Often, the job in planning meetings is to temper the enthusiasm of the marketing department, who will be requesting heaven handed to them on a plate, unaware of technological limitations. Of course, the technology director will be telling the marketing manager that *nothing* is possible, so the project manager must walk the line between these two, encouraging the technologists to raise their estimates, and marketing to lower theirs.

After these early planning meetings, the project manager will sift through the wants of the marketing, technology, business and creative planners, and come up with a development plan that takes into account the entire team's desires. This usually means drafting a planning document that lays out how the site will look, when it will be delivered, what the technology requirements and spending will be, and what pieces of the pie will be delivered at what time. This document isn't cast in stone; in fact, it may as well be written in disappearing ink, since plans will change on an almost hourly basis.

After the planning is done, the project manager's role is to make sure the schedule is adhered to, or at least some attempt is made to do so. All sorts of havoc are guaranteed to break loose at all stages of the project, so a degree of flexibility and calmness in crisis are called for in this job. '[Every day] is hugely varied, which is a great appeal of the job,' says Barsby. 'At the start I visit clients frequently to discuss their requirements and provide advice on the way forward. Once the requirements are more firmly established, the emphasis shifts to spending time with the technical team in-house to work out the best way to deliver the system. During the implementation period my time is split between the client and the technical team to ensure that all is progressing well and resolving any issues that arise. Upon project close-down I help with the system hand-over, producing any documentation required.' Some project managers will stay with the project after the development is complete, monitoring progress and maintaining the site, but these are generally in-house managers. For external consultants like Barsby, the norm is to hand the site over to an internal administrator once development is complete.

Barsby spent three years with another consulting firm as a project manager before joining Red Banner, eventually working on one of the most high-profile Internet experiments in Britain – the Prudential's launch of Egg, an Internet bank. She says project management has its highs and lows, and keeping the stress manageable is a critical challenge. 'It is an exciting area to work in and does appear glamorous to the outsider,' she says. 'However, it involves a lot of hard work and the confidence to work at all levels within a client organisation, through to director level. Project management is essential to any industry that is continually growing and changing. [We] deliver change in a controlled way in order to meet time and budget commitments – both of which are vital to any Internet company.'

Of course, all that control and order can go down the drain if the client continually changes their mind about what the site should look like. The more people become involved in the planning process, the more complicated things become for the project manager. 'The worst-case scenario is when your client has no experience of IT, which can happen in small dot.com start-up teams,' Barsby says. '[For example] we visit the client – tease out their actual requirements with them, get sign-off on requirements and start system design and build. Then another client member gets involved and has "a lot of ideas" for the system, so we revisit the requirements (putting build on hold), redesign the system and start build (again). Then the client's boss gets involved and has "a lot of ideas" for the system, etc., etc. This can go on and on. Then two weeks later the client expects the system to be built!'

Barsby says only oodles of patience allow a project manager and her team to escape the nightmare client unscathed. 'The responsibility of the project manager in this scenario is to document everything, manage client expectations (giving coaching where possible) and give counselling to the development team.'

Working as part of an internal team doesn't mean the nightmare client scenario never happens, but it does give you a slightly higher measure of control. Marina Psaros, who has led Web projects internally for Microsoft, Netscape and Web news provider iSyndicate, says that for many of her projects, *she* is the client, beholden only to top executives.

'I own the overall vision of the product, which means that I am responsible for everything from functionality to user interface to target markets to comparative analyses to market research,' she says. 'I work with business development, marketing, production, sales and engineering to find out their various requirements with my product, and then translate that into something which is **buildable**.'

Even though the internal project manager doesn't need to continually sell the client on the right way to produce the site, a certain amount of energy has to be spent on keeping the team motivated and interested in the project. 'Talking to people all day is actually kind of stressful, because I'm essentially selling to my co-workers,' Psaros says. 'I have to build consensus and get everyone excited about what we're working on. I have to force them to meet deadlines, because the ultimate success or failure of the product is my responsibility.'

Psaros says that, unlike some project managers, she comes from a technical background, and could easily fill in as a programmer on her team. This can be a distinct advantage. 'Since my background is technical, I have an advantage when building product plans because I don't have to waste time wondering whether or not something is technically possible,' she says. 'I already know that.'

Of course, she still needs her crew of techies so she can focus on the big picture of the project. In fact, what with all the people she has to talk to and oversee, those spare minutes just to plan and think are inevitably elusive. 'Some companies, like where I am now, have a very open and communicative culture. This means that people stand around my desk all day and ask me questions which totally distract me from whatever I'm attempting to accomplish,' she says. 'It also means there are lots of meetings – meetings with the international group to talk about high-level strategy, meetings with engineering to go over back-end issues, meetings with marketing to try to explain what the product does, meetings with project managers to talk about scheduling. All this communication is good and bad – we don't hide information from each other like many traditional industries do, but it's also harder to find more than a solid hour where you can just think. Since most of my job is thinking, I often wind up working weekends or evenings.'

Project managers in all industries face this kind of stress, but in the Internet business the fast pace of change means that there's added pressure to get projects done quickly. 'Internet companies have a culture of urgency,' Psaros says. 'Everything has to get done yesterday.'

SKILLS YOU'LL NEED

Strong management training, exceptional organisational inclinations, understanding of Web design, editorial production, and business practices. Flexibility, confidence and a vision of the 'big picture'. Most importantly, ability to stay calm while chaos descends!

GETTING THE JOB

- Start out by working on small Web projects, either for a company trying out a first, small website, or by volunteering for a community organisation. They'll appreciate the free labour, and you'll learn what it's like to oversee a Web project.
- Try to work in an administrative capacity on a professional Web project, and to work closely with the project manager to learn how they operate.
- Make sure you can discuss your understanding of the company's business as well as their technology in the interview.

TIPS

- Learn formal project management skills. Many professional schools now teach courses – it never hurts to brush up on the basics.
- Clients quickly see through a fake. Never try to blag your way through a situation by pretending to know more than you do. Get the answers, and then come back with the whole solution.
- Try to develop mentors while you're starting out. Having someone to turn to in a crisis will help.

GLOSSARY

- **Buildable**

Adjective meaning that a website in the planning stages is actually feasible technically. Most often used in the negative by techies to explain to marketing staff that whatever it is they want to do simply isn't possible. 'Well, sure it sounds nifty, but it just isn't *buildable*.'

- **Techies**

A broad term that refers to all workers at an Internet company who have anything to do with technology – whether they be programmers, Web designers, system administrators or developers.

USEFUL ADDRESSES

- Avraham Y Goldratt (UK) Ltd (project management courses), 13 Bridge Ave, Maidenhead, Berkshire SL6 1RR, UK.
TEL +44 (0) 1628 674468.
FAX +44 (0) 1628 623811.
www.goldratt.co.uk;
info@goldratt.co.uk
- Hydra Development Corporation Ltd (project management resources), Wharfebank Business Centre, Pennyhole Entrance, Ilkley Rd, Otley, West Yorkshire LS21 3JP, UK.
TEL + 44 (0) 1943 858 858.
FAX + 44 (0) 1943 858 859.
www.hydradev.com;
info@hydradev.com
- Mirasol Project Management Consultancy, Raddenstile Lane, Exmouth, Devon EX8 2JL, UK.
TEL +44 (0) 1395 266761.
FAX +44 (0) 1395 273864.
www.mirasol.co.uk;
webs@mirasol.co.uk
- Monster.co.uk, 163 Eversholt St, London NW1 1BU, UK.
TEL +44 (0) 800 1695015.
FAX +44 (0) 20 7391 4701.
www.monster.co.uk;
sales@monster.co.uk
- Recruit Group, 10 Lloyds Ave, London EC3N 3AX, UK.
TEL +44 (0) 20 7480 7400.
FAX +44 (0) 20 7480 7411.
www.recruitgroup.co.uk;
info@recruitgroup.co.uk

Public Relations

Money: From £18,000 to £25,000 in most positions. Executive PR salaries can reach £60,000.

Hours: Fairly typical office hours, except when you're preparing a big press launch, or responding to a really dreadful story.

Health risk: 2/10. Unless a particularly nasty journalist or particularly pushy client comes along, PRs can stay mentally healthy.

Pressure rating: 4/10. The pressure can change from day to day – periods of calm punctuated by bursts of activity.

Glamour rating: 4/10. A fun job to the untutored eye, but boot-licking journos and clients can take their toll.

Travel rating: 5/10. Beyond the odd press trip, most PR work is in the office, chained to a phone.

The Internet is the story of the decade, covered in massive detail in every media outlet. Much of this is thanks to aggressive public relations, which Internet companies have used more extensively than any other industry. Corporate PR in other fields mostly means protecting clients from a bad news story, but for Internet firms corporate PR means pushing your company in front of every journo you can get your hands on. And lots of times, it pays off.

In late 1999 and early 2000, Martha Lane Fox's face was everywhere. The co-founder of Lastminute.com, a website that sells travel packages and gifts for procrastinators, Fox became famous almost overnight, renowned as one of a camp of 'e-millionaires'. Only 28 years old, she was heralded in every major British newspaper as the emblem of a new era of business.

Behind the scenes, Fox's public relations company, Gnash Communications, was credited with making a myth of Martha. Lastminute was nowhere near profitable, and deemed only a moderate success by any financial standards. Still, in the eyes of the press and the public, Martha Lane Fox was a whiz kid worthy of deification.

Companies like Gnash have become increasingly important to outfits like Lastminute. Public relations have become a key part of any Internet company's plan for success. Creating a public perception of the company as interesting, cutting-edge and revolutionary means more Web traffic, more customers and, ultimately, a better share price if the company goes for an Initial Public Offering on a public stock market.

PRs (or **flacks**, as journalists derisively refer to them) are now key players in the Internet industry. Companies, even in their earliest stages, tend to make the hiring of a good public relations firm a top priority. The practice dates back to Silicon Valley in 1994, when Netscape Communications, the first big success story of the Internet, was getting off the ground. Acting chief executive Jim Clark insisted that the company hire an on-staff PR to tout the Netscape story to every journalist who would listen. Gradually, the world became familiar with the infant history of the company. The stories written about Netscape weren't focused on the technology, or the business plan, but on how Marc Andreesen, a 22-year-old recent graduate, had brought his idea to a seasoned Silicon Valley executive (Clark, who had founded and run Silicon Graphics) and given rise to a revolution called the World Wide Web. In short, with good PR, Netscape managed to tell the human side of its story, winning the attention of journalists everywhere, and ultimately of the stock market.

'Tech companies tend to take PR very seriously, as they need to establish a credible reputation quickly, not only with the media, but also with current and potential investors,' says Kate Warwick, a senior account executive with Miller Shandwick, a well-known technology public relations company with offices worldwide. 'We often get involved at a very early stage in the company's life and assist them with raising their profile to the press and investors.' Internet companies following in Netscape's footsteps have stuck to the same approach.

PRs have become very choosy about the clients they work with. Good PR firms that have a strong reputation for getting press coverage for their clients tend to be approached by prospective clients, rather than the other way around. Media coverage tends to be one of the holy grails of the Internet industry, and a good PR, who is trusted by and has access to journalists, is worth every penny of the millions that companies fork out every year.

'PR is extremely important to the Internet industry,' says Fran Matthews, an account executive with Gnash Communications. 'It is without doubt the most cost effective marketing technique available to the many thousands of Internet companies, to ensure that they distinguish themselves from their competitors and that their messages are communicated effectively. The old saying that PR gives you credibility, while advertising gives you visibility, is significantly important in the current market climate.'

As any journalist will tell you, there is a huge amount of competition among companies to get coverage. There are a limited number of magazines, newspapers, websites and radio and TV programmes that cover Internet-related issues, so PRs spend a lot of time trying to come up with a unique angle or story that will put their clients head and shoulders above the competition. The Internet business has a certain amount of cachet, but isn't as attractive for some PRs as working with more mainstream media. This, combined with the difficulty of finding a PR who has good contacts in the Internet press, and who understands the technology and business, means that the salaries for public relations people in the Internet industry are higher than in consumer PR.

'There are masses of companies trying to say very much the same thing, so expertise in understanding the company and its marketplace really well is important,' says Giles Fraser, a founder and PR man with brands2life, a communications consultancy. 'My job is to do three things – to help companies articulate what makes them and their products or services special; to help them put together the right plans and supporting resources to communicate those plans based on research and market intelligence; and then to execute them.'

Once clients and PRs have settled on each other, the PR firm will begin to work out what the best approach for the company will be. 'PR tends to have a glamorous image for those who don't know much about it – lunches, parties, etc.,' says Fraser. 'The truth is that most of the work is office-based – lots of writing, phone work and meetings.' The PR will interview the founders of the company, get to know the management team, the product, and the line of business the company is in. They will draft a plan that suggests ways the media should be introduced to the company, and what media outlets they will target. The PR might start out by introducing the chief executive around to various journalists as an expert source, or may wait for some event like a product release or a crucial corporate milestone to put out a **press release**. Depending on the size of the company, an employee at a public relations firm might find themselves doing only one small portion of the work on any given account, or handling the whole account on their own.

'The company I work for has a very flat structure with little hierarchy,' says Matthews. 'The result is that my day is spent on every account handling activity from media relations, strategic planning and reporting, right through to the management and direction of the account. My day could be spent on the phone **pitching** a story to a journalist, taking a client out to meet a journalist face to face to discuss a new business announcement or service, writing a press release or a PR plan, or co-ordinating and organising an event such as a press trip or the press office at a conference.'

Fraser, after fifteen years in hi-tech PR, left the well-known firm Hill & Knowlton to found his own company with several colleagues. 'It is quite a change to go from managing over forty people to working in a small office with two or three people. There is no typical day. There is a wide range of things which need to be done. The bulk of the day is spent working with clients to formulate plans, developing materials such as messages, positioning statements and press releases and then talking to industry contacts – press, analysts, experts – about your clients and what they are doing. Networking is very important in this area of the business and it is also one of the most enjoyable things about it. Virtually everyone you meet can help you and vice versa.'

As with any job in the media, the work of the PR person can differ greatly from one day to the next, and can suffer ups and downs at the whim of both clients and journalists. In the worst case, a client with no story to tell, no interesting product to push, and a gift for offering up revealing indiscretions to journalists is harassing the PR for front-page coverage in every national newspaper while journalists either ignore him or write scathing pieces. On the other hand, the PR could have a genial, well-spoken client who is the darling of the media and gets nothing but glorious coverage. The days could be short, satisfying and positive for all involved, or could involve a midnight-oil-burning session that ends up with short tempers and an even shorter night's sleep.

'The stress levels are usually reflective of the companies you're representing,' Matthews says. 'In the Internet industry, the work tends to be fast-paced and unpredictable. You might have written a business plan and a communications strategy to match at the beginning of the year, but this could all change just a couple of weeks into the plan. What's more, any job in a service-related industry is high-pressure as you're at the call of the client. If you've got a big announcement or a conference coming up then you simply have to work the extra hours and deal with the stress in order to meet the deadline.'

The days will generally be split between dealing with clients and dealing with journalists, often arranging interviews between the two, or sitting in as an interview is taking place. Although it might seem awkward for the PR to be baby-sitting executives as they talk to journalists, he or she is there to make sure the message the interviewee is sending out is coherent and in line with the company's plan.

'We are working with intangibles much of the time, so how people perceive what you do is important and those perceptions are often less controllable,' says Giles Fraser. 'However, once one accepts that you can only do what you can do, then the stress is much more manageable.'

Of course, stress is amplified by rude, dismissive journalists and demanding clients, but with the increasingly important role that public relations plays for companies, the job has a higher status in this industry than in most. 'Working in [the Internet industry], one has a ringside seat to watch and participate in history in the making,' says Fraser. 'When I started doing work for technology companies, friends would look at you blankly when you described your work, but now of course you can't move without people talking about the Internet. This reflects the popularity of this sector as a career choice too. It used to be bottom of graduates' lists but now it is the top!'

For graduates, the field of public relations holds a lot of options, as there are opportunities on all levels that don't require specialist training: just good communication skills, good writing ability, and tenacity. Public relations tend to be more fragmented than most fields in terms of the backgrounds of people working in the profession: Matthews holds a degree in Environmental Management, and got into PR through a job as personal assistant at a PR firm. Warwick has a

Bachelor of Arts in English and Linguistics, and worked as a secretary in a PR firm after a temp job on the *Daily Express* news desk. Fraser has an arts degree and an MBA from Oxford. He took a job as a trainee in consumer PR, later moving into business and technology PR. 'This is not a profession with high barriers to entry. An enquiring mind and a will to do good work will take anyone a long way,' he says. 'The key is be prepared to try things with some experienced guidance and learn from mistakes. People shouldn't be afraid to try new approaches – there are no rules. Talent is short in this industry at the moment so now is a good time for people to enter the business.'

SKILLS YOU'LL NEED

A friendly nature, writing ability, good conversation and communication skills, and the ability to react quickly in an emergency.

GETTING THE JOB

- A number of PR agencies specialise in hi-tech PR, and all large international groups have a technology or Internet division. Contact those agencies to see if they have any openings.
- Large companies usually have a division devoted to public relations, some of which have internship or work experience programmes. Contact interesting companies in the industry to see what openings are available.
- Familiarise yourself first with any recent stories that have been written about the company before approaching them about a job. Show you know the industry and understand their business.
- Know what publications cover a specific company or client. Be able to discuss coverage in these outlets before approaching them for a job.

TIPS

- Cultivate good relations with journalists. Networking is the favoured pastime of the industry, and each journalist you meet is a potential pitch target in future.
- Make sure your story pitch is refined before making that crucial phone call to a journalist, and that you know the answers to the obvious questions they might ask. Nothing will make them lose interest quicker than 'I'm not sure, can I give you a call back?'
- Keep track of what stories are getting written. If you can understand the kind of piece a particular reporter is interested in, you'll be able to target your pitches better.
- Publications like *Media Map* and PR Newswire's *PRN Media* track reporters and editors who move jobs. Make sure you keep your information on who has what job up to date.

GLOSSARY

- **Flack** Pejorative term used by journalists for PRs, as in 'that [Company X] flack won't stop calling me! I think it's time for a smear piece.'
- **Pitch**
An effort made by a PR to attract a journalist's attention. 'I wanted to pitch you on this great new client we've got.'

- **Press release**

A document produced to promote a client's company or product, and sent out to news organisations in hopes of attracting coverage.

USEFUL ADDRESSES

- Edelman, 1500 Broadway, 26th Floor, New York, NY 10036, USA.
TEL +1 212 768 0550.
FAX +1 212 704 0128.
www.edelman.com;
new_york@edelman.com
- Gnash Communications, 5 Lambton Place, London W11 25H, UK.
TEL +44 (0) 20 7243 4443.
FAX +44 (0) 20 7243 4442.
www.gnash.co.uk; info@gnash.co.uk
- Media Map, 215 First St, Cambridge, MA 02142, USA.
TEL +1 617 374 9300.
FAX +1 617 374 9345.
www.mediamap.com;
info@mediamap.com
- PR Newswire Europe, Communications House, 210 Old St, London EC1V 9UN, UK.
TEL +44 (0) 20 7490 8111.
FAX +44 (0) 20 7490 1255.
www.prnewswire.com;
public_relations@prnewswire.com
- Text 100, Power Road Studios, 114a Power Rd, Chiswick, London W4 5PY, UK.
TEL +44 (0) 20 8996 4100.
FAX +44 (0) 20 8996 1200.
www.text100.com; jobs@text100.com
- UK Press Gazette, 19 Scarbrook Rd, Croydon, Surrey CR9 1LX, UK.
TEL +44 (0) 20 8565 4200.
FAX +44 (0) 20 8565 4462.
www.pressgazette.co.uk

Security Expert

Money: From £20,000 to £150,000 for big-name sites.

Hours: All of them. When you're not in the office, you've a pager strapped to your belt, a mobile in your pocket, and a homing device in your shoe.

Health risk: 9/10. If the required diet of sugary cola and pizzas doesn't do in your heart, the constant stress will give you an ulcer.

Pressure rating: 10/10. You're the last defence between your website and the grubby underworld of hackers, scam artists, fraudsters, and corporate espionage.

Glamour rating: 8/10. True, in the looks department the security expert isn't much, but when you have one finger on the pulse of power at all times, the job has its share of glamour.

Travel rating: 2/10. Unless your company has head offices in Tenerife, don't expect too much glam travel. Most trips are visits to a darkened **server closet**, lit by the exotic light of flickering monitors.

The big black eye on the face of the booming Internet industry is security. Most of the World Wide Web is as about as secure as a sieve, and it's the job of the security expert to keep websites protected. A highly technical job, with a little bit of witchcraft mixed in.

They go by many names, but security experts live at the heart of Web companies, protecting sites from Internet **vandals** and fraudsters.

Most websites, particularly ones that are handling financial information like credit card numbers and personal data, put security as one of their top priorities. The trouble is that the marketing dreamers who decide what kind of site will be successful don't always know the limitations of technology.

The Internet was designed as an open system: anyone could get on, trawl around, and find out information. A multibillion-pound industry has grown up around the Web to help companies keep sensitive information secure from prying eyes. Every site needs its own security expert, someone who can build a technical fortress around private data, while still making sure that the bulk of the site is accessible to the public.

The main threat to security is the much-publicised teenage hacker – kids out looking for **street cred** who hack websites instead of vandalising the neighbourhood library. Security experts are often former hackers themselves (although few will admit it), and make use of their knowledge of hacking tricks to try to prevent the new breed of youngsters from causing damage to a site.

The importance of a security expert to any site depends on the type of information the website houses. For sites that contain pure content like news and information, the security expert's main job is to keep hackers from defacing pages. In 1998, a famous hack of the *New York Times'* website caused untold embarrassment to the stodgy old paper when a group called 'Hackers for Girliez' blasted profanity across the home page.

The *Times'* hack showed the world that defacing Web pages could be embarrassing, but it wasn't until the growth of electronic commerce in ensuing years that Web companies realised that hacking could hit the profit line as well. As websites have been fashioned into electronic storefronts, companies increasingly worry about hackers causing more than just embarrassment. With consumers happily typing in credit card numbers to order all manner of frivolities on-line, Internet companies have had to add the possibility of fraud to their list of concerns. The fear is that hackers will use their skills to gather credit card information from a website, putting the customer at risk and, in some cases, making the company liable.

Security experts for these sites have a much more elevated status within the organisation. Their job is to construct a complicated series of passwords and **firewalls** to keep the information in and the hackers out.

A corporate security expert doesn't need to worry only about securing data virtually, but also physically. This means making sure that the rent-a-cops patrolling the front door aren't taking overlong ciggie breaks, that the receptionist is checking the identification of any jump-suited visitor passing himself off as a workman, and that employees aren't absent-mindedly giving out company passwords down the pub.

'Sometimes I lie in bed at night, unable to sleep, wondering "Did I close the fire door? Did I lock it?"' says John Wood, the head of security for a Silicon Valley Internet company.

Wood's insomnia comes not only from his own responsibility to the company, but also from the fact that he himself is being watched at all times. For companies whose paranoia about security is matched only by their stock market valuation, the security expert is sometimes the most obvious suspect when data goes missing.

To keep an eye on their own security people, companies often use outside consultants to audit both their trustworthiness and their competence. A failure on either count can result in dismissal, so internal security experts try to stay on their toes, keeping one eye out for the bad guys and one eye out for the good guys posing as bad guys. (Hackers divide themselves into **white hats** and **black hats**. The white hats are security experts working on the side of good, and the black hats are the criminal types.)

The consultants who perform security audits have a much easier time of things than the corporate security expert. They are even more closely tied to the world of hackerdom, given that they spend most of their time pretending to be hackers themselves. They get all of the rush of criminal activity and a nice fat pay cheque to boot.

These consultants go by a range of names, but the popular term is 'tiger teams'. They try everything a hacker might in order to gain access to the computers. First they try to hack in from the Internet, then they try to breach the physical security measures that have been put in place by the internal expert.

'Our server closet has floor-to-ceiling bars around it, so you can't just go in,' says the director of security for an e-commerce company in California. The company was recently put under tiger team assessment by Price Waterhouse, a large multinational consulting firm. 'They went in through the ceiling panels. I knew physical hacking goes on but the thought that someone would crawl through the ceiling tiles had never crossed my mind.'

Needless to say, there's considerable animosity between the two groups, particularly when the smug external expert shows up with a full report on all the places where the internal staff have left gaping holes for would-be hackers. But according to one external security expert, it's well worth it for companies to invest in their services. 'Many times the cost is only a fraction compared to what we could have gotten for the info we gained access to,' says Pete Shipley, chief security architect for consultants KPMG.

SKILLS YOU'LL NEED

Full knowledge of computer networks, an understanding of security practices – physical and virtual – and a competitive nature to help you wage war on malicious hackers. It never hurts to have spent your teenage years glued to a computer, attempting to break into corporate networks.

GETTING THE JOB

If you have the networking knowledge, the job is yours for the taking. Contact big accounting firms like KPMG and Ernst & Young to see about job openings in the security divisions. These are great foot-in-the-door jobs, and help you attach a big name company to your CV. Some of these firms also offer training courses for security experts.

TIPS

- Go to conferences where both white hat and black hat hackers are in attendance. Notably, the Defcon series and Black Hat conferences are good places to get security training, learn about Web vulnerabilities, and meet other people in the business. Learn from the good guys, and the bad guys.
- Try cracking a few websites yourself. There are tons of security consultants who do nothing but crack sites, send the companies a documented list of vulnerabilities, and make a name for themselves in the process. Try to stay away from the vandalism, though.
- Familiarise yourself with the various off-the-shelf software products used to keep networks secure. Companies like Baltimore Technologies and Network Associates specialise in security. You'll need to know their products to do the job. Network Associates also run a series of workshops training security experts.

GLOSSARY

- **Firewall**

The layer of computer security between the outside world and the inside of the company. All secure data lives 'inside the firewall', and the security expert's mandate is to keep intruders 'outside the firewall'.

- **Server closet**

Home of the security expert. Usually buried deep in the bowels of the corporate headquarters, filled floor to ceiling with computers, barricaded behind bars, locked doors and snarling Dobermann pinschers.

- **Street cred**

Making a name for yourself on the hacker scene, usually by defacing a famous website, or getting access to a top-secret government agency.

- **Vandals**

The politically correct way to refer to malicious hackers. To the old school, a 'hacker' is someone who innocently programs in computer language. Nowadays, the media has made 'hacker' synonymous with 'criminal', a fact that irritates old-time, non-criminal hackers. They're running a campaign to get the press to refer to malicious hackers as 'vandals'.

- **White hat/black hat hackers**

The two camps of the hacker world. White hats are those who delve into computer security for the intellectual challenge (and usually a consulting fee) while the black hats are more interested in illegal activities.

USEFUL ADDRESSES

- Baltimore Technologies, 61/62 Fitzwilliam Lane, Dublin 2, Ireland. **TEL** +353 1 647 7300. **FAX** +353 1 647 7499. www.baltimore.com; info@baltimore.com
- Black Hat - Amsterdam. www.blackhat.com; blackhat@defcon.org
- Defcon. www.defcon.org; dtangent@defcon.org
- Ernst & Young, 7 Rolls Buildings, Fetter Lane, London EC4A 1NH, UK. **TEL** + 44 (0) 20 7951 2000. **FAX** +44 (0) 20 7951 4001. www.eyuk.com; webeditor@cc.ernsty.co.uk
- KPMG, 8 Salisbury Square, London EC4Y 8BB, UK. **TEL** +44 (0) 20 7311 1000. **FAX** +44 (0) 20 7311 3311. www.kpmg.co.uk
- Network Associates, 227 Bath Rd, Slough, Berkshire SL1 5PP, UK. **TEL** +44 (0) 1753 217500. **FAX** +44 (0) 1753 217520. www.nai.com;:sniffer@nai.com
- l0pht Heavy Industries, PO Box 990857, Boston, MA 02199, USA. www.l0pht.com;:business@l0pht.com

STRATEGIST

MONEY: £40,000–£100,000-plus. Help people make good decisions and you'll be well paid for them – same goes for helping them not make bad decisions.

HOURS: 50-plus per week. Good strategists are obsessed by the industry, and spend most of their time reading, thinking and meeting people.

HEALTH RISK: 2/10. People are usually too much in awe of you to give you a hard time.

PRESSURE RATING: 7/10. You are never allowed an off day, or to say anything dumb when hung over. You're only as good as your last recommendation.

GLAMOUR RATING: 4/10. You're helping other people make smart decisions, which means they will take the credit.

TRAVEL RATING: 8/10. Your clients, and your inspiration, are all over the world. You'll have lots of frequent flyer miles, and an intimate knowledge of airport lounges.

Managing an Internet company brings two major challenges: how to act quickly, and how to act intelligently. The strategist helps with the second. Strategists are like brains for hire: they have a ton of information and insight into a particular business area, which is helpful for companies in deciding how to treat the future.

Strategy is a much-abused term. It has come to mean anything that's vague, woolly and based on thinking rather than 'practical' stuff. Strategy also generally involves expensive consultants and complicated diagrams. It should be something that's central to every company, because strategy is really about what options a company has, and how its managers choose what to do next.

For Internet companies, strategy is particularly important and difficult. Because much about the Internet industry is new, it is often hard for people to figure out what to do next. There's not much point in saying 'Well, in 1977 we decided to go into this market area, and we didn't do well, so we won't do it this time'. So much changes every month that looking to historic examples from ten or fifteen years ago is all but irrelevant. The newness of the area has been a problem for companies, but a great benefit to a small, lucky group of smart people – the strategists.

Strategists help companies prepare for the future. Since businesses have many decisions to face, a strategist will tend to specialise in helping companies make one particular type of decision. Some strategists specialise in advising companies on which markets they should operate in, how much it will cost, and how they should launch. Other strategists focus on helping new companies establish brands for themselves; look at the best kind of design for an organisation, and help to set up teams; restructure companies that are facing significant changes. Companies need help in other specialised areas like technology (which systems should they use to meet the business needs?), human resources (which people should they hire and how should they be compensated and assessed?), and partnerships and acquisitions.

A strategist gets involved with a company when the management starts to face questions it doesn't know the answers to. For example, imagine a company that currently operates in the UK, with a UK website and UK customers. They may be under pressure from investors to expand into other European markets, but how do they decide which ones and when? Should they have one office, or several? What will all this cost? Which markets represent the easiest targets for their product? Enter a particular kind of strategist, someone who specialises in **market entry**. The market entry strategist might advise them to locate their corporate head office in Ireland (where there are low taxes) and their sales office in Scandinavia, where there is a known demand for this product and an educated consumer base that won't need much convincing to buy.

Strategists are distinguished from other kinds of consultants because they do not get involved in **implementation**, or the actual doing of something. They help to set a direction for a company, and advise it on which way to go, but don't stick around to navigate the company through. And unlike gurus and other overall industry commentators, their advice is always focused on helping a particular company solve a particular problem. They get their credibility by having a track record of helping other companies do the same thing.

An Internet company needs the help of strategists even more than a well-established company. Because there is little established knowledge, and the industry is relatively young, there is often a shortage of people who have seen a particular problem before and understand what needs to be done. Big companies can afford to have a department of strategists in residence, often known as 'strategic planning' and headed by a 'director of strategy', but this isn't a luxury that a small Internet company can afford. Therefore, Internet companies call in strategists when they are facing a particular problem, because they can trust a strategist to understand the problem and put together some recommendations to solve it.

Strategists are big-picture people. Although they are clever enough to understand their areas of expertise in several layers of detail, they prefer to take a wide view. They are also quite independent, enabling them to go from project to project, taking their skills with them. Working independently is a good way for a strategist to maximise their income, since they will tend to work in short bursts on key projects. A strategist will often command day consulting rates of over £500, and usually closer to £1,000 for someone with rare technical or business expertise.

Companies sometimes use strategists to sort out the difficult issues the management doesn't wish to deal with directly. Monica Ali has been working with a number of Internet companies on helping them establish their brand strategy. She has seen brand strategy treated in extreme ways: either it's critical, or it's irrelevant. She says, 'Strategy is either the overpriced bit which the CEO likes because he gets to pontificate about his company – or it's the really tricky and essential bit that lays the foundation for brand building.'

Although there are many independent specialists, there are also a number of prestigious niche consultancies that specialise in strategy. The most famous of these are companies like McKinsey and Booz Allen & Hamilton, which have specialised in strategy for years and have recently moved into the Internet area. Several strategy specialists focusing on e-commerce and the Internet have sprung up, including companies like Decipher. Also, some analyst organisations have consultancy divisions, including Gartner Group and Ovum Ltd.

Shirley Brown is a strategy consultant with IT analysts Ovum. Although she began her career with a music and German degree, she moved into working with early electronic publishing and then to consulting with a multimedia specialist before joining Ovum. Her efforts are focused on helping companies decide what, when and how to launch, using her own and the company's resources. Brown describes her main output for clients as 'proposals, presentations, research, analysis, strategic thinking, and reports. The job involves a lot of writing.'

Paul Dickinson started his career in graphic design, and became a strategist through an early fascination with electronic media. He defines the work of a strategist as 'becoming a researcher. A good researcher absorbs information like breathing, day and night, all the time ... and then becomes an expert about the future, which hasn't happened yet.' Dickinson has chosen the less well paid but fun route as a strategist working with new companies, betting on his strategic nose to point him in the right direction. As he says, 'As a strategist you take bets on dot.com and other kinds of technology companies. In two years I will be very rich from these, or be out of a job!'

There is no typical background for people who become strategists. They need to have a field of knowledge that is valuable to others, and the ability to communicate well and analyse huge amounts of information. Many strategists have had only brief spells with large companies, and tend to be experienced at working either in a consulting or a think-tank environment instead. Many simply realise they have a skill which others need, and set up a structure to exploit it. Ali states frankly, 'I don't know how I came to be in this position. It wasn't planned and I just drifted along doing whatever I felt like doing next. Which is much the best type of career plan.'

Ali suggests that those who wish to be strategists need to be prepared for a significant amount of uncertainty. She says the job 'depends on the client, project, location, team you're working with, deadlines, etc. At the beginning of a project a typical day is a bit like wandering around in a dark room – then (if you're lucky) all the lights start to come on as the project progresses.'

SKILLS YOU'LL NEED

- The ability to digest tons of information, and draw coherent patterns from what you've read.
- Being able to deal with people at board level and understand the pressures they face.
- Being able to deliver high-quality, intelligent work under great time pressure.

GETTING THE JOB

- Stress your interest in, commitment to and enthusiasm for the Internet and related areas to a potential employer.
- Freelance strategists often move from research organisations or consultancies.
- Consultancies advertise for associates on job sites such as Stepstone, or try consulting company websites for job opportunities.

TIPS

- Work for the strategic planning department of a large company in a related industry, so that you can get a sense of how strategy is put together.
- Make sure to get out and network in the industry: reading the press may give you some information, but it's better to get it from people who are facing the real challenges.
- Develop an expertise in a particular area, like technology selection or organisational structure.

GLOSSARY

- **Implementation**

The execution of a plan. Often refers to installation of new technology, but could just as well mean executing a communications or hiring plan.

- **Market entry**

The process of deciding how and when a company should begin operating in a particular national or regional market. Market entry involves understanding the market conditions (things like the number of available customers, and the level of available spending) and infrastructure conditions (political stability, economic health).

USEFUL ADDRESSES

- Booz Allen & Hamilton, 7 Savoy Court, Strand, London WC2R 0EZ, UK.

TEL +44 (0) 20 7393 3333.
FAX +44 (0) 20 7393 0024.
www.bah.com

- Decipher, Bowater House, 68–114 Knightsbridge, London SW1X 7LT, UK.

TEL +44 (0) 20 7225 3698.
FAX +44 (0) 20 7823 8428.
www.decipher.co.uk

- McKinsey & Co., 1 Jermyn St, London SW1Y 4UH, UK.

TEL +44 (0) 20 7839 8040.
FAX +44 (0) 20 7339 5000.
www.mckinsey.com

- Ovum Ltd, Cardinal Tower, 12 Farringdon Rd, London EC1M 3HS, UK.

TEL +44 (0) 20 7551 9000.
FAX +44 (0) 20 7551 9090/1.
www.ovum.com; webinfo@ovum.com

System Administrator

Money: From £25,000 to £150,000. The bigger the system, the more complicated the administration, and the more qualified the system administrator or 'sysadmin' needs to be. Bigger companies will pay towards the higher end of the range, while small dot.coms will pay towards the middle or lower end.

Hours: System administrators work typical office hours, but often need to put in time in the middle of the night as well, when the rest of the office is sleeping and the **network** isn't in use.

Health risk: 2/10. Unless you suffer a major system outage, your health should remain intact.

Pressure rating: 5/10. When the system is working like a well-oiled machine, there's no stress. When the system is down, get ready for the firing squad!

Glamour rating: 0/10. Never let it be said that IT was a glamorous profession.

Travel rating: 0/10. The sysadmin can't travel too far from the office, lest a major emergency occur.

Systems administrators are crucial to an Internet company. They keep the computer systems up and running – everything from the e-mail used to communicate with customers to the website that is the central part of the business. System administrators usually have a broad range of computer knowledge, and are intimate with every aspect of a company's technology: software and hardware are the system administrator's bailiwick, and the company depends on them for every answer to every technical cock-up that comes along.

In the parlance of the techie, the 'system' is the network of computers that runs all the business operations: from e-mail to hosting the website to the internal software that runs the accounting and customer databases. The system administrator is the Über-techie who makes sure all these computers are functioning. Administrating a network is like being a parent: you don't just birth a child and send it out into the world; you nurture it, take care of it every day, kiss it better when it skins its knee, and go to conferences with its teacher when it misbehaves at school.

System administrators are the unsung heroes of the dot.com world. They get none of the glory that falls to the entrepreneur, none of the money that falls to the venture capitalist, and none of the free lunches and endless drinks parties that fall to the marketing team, the advertising staff, or the PRs and journalists. What they do get is frantic phone calls in the middle of the night when the computer systems inexplicably crash, angry hordes crowding into their offices when the e-mail **server** stops serving e-mail, and plaintive visits from the boss who has somehow forgotten his computer password and needs an override.

'Day to day, I ensure the integrity of all the data of the company which is stored in an electronic format,' says Saint Man, system administrator for Meome.de, an Internet company that has brought together experts in hundreds of fields to provide on-line expertise to Web users. 'Without this a dot.com is worth as much as thin air. It is the data that makes a dot.com valuable. Systems are important and a running system is vital. I must make sure all resources like printers, data storage and e-mail are available and running without a hitch. On a good day I could do very little, but on a bad day I could be needed by everyone, and the systems could be down at the same time.'

System administrators work with all departments of the company on their technical wants and needs. They work with website developers to help the development team figure out how the site will be hosted and what capacity of computer is called for to run the type of site they are planning. They also work with departments like human resources, accounting and marketing to find out what their technology needs are. If marketing wants to build a new database to track how customers are liking a new website, or what potential there is sell to chocolates on-line in remote South Pacific island nations, the system administrator will be one of their first ports of call. If the accounting department wants to launch an automatic bill collection scheme, the system administrator will help implement the new software. Any time a department within the company decides it needs a technological solution, the system administrator must decide how those computing resources will be allocated, and if new computing power is needed.

The life of a system administrator might be similar whether they are working for a small Internet outfit or a large company that has nothing to do with the Web. However, at Internet companies, where technology is integral to the business, the system administrator tends to play a more central part, rather than being simply someone who is stuck in a back room tinkering with computer parts, only brought out to be yelled at when something goes wrong. 'IT and the Internet industry are inseparable,' says Man. 'One without the other is a misnomer. You wouldn't get very far as an Internet company if you had no IT presence. My job provides all the platforms the Web designers and Web developers need to get their side of operations working. A Web server being down is the same as having the closed sign in a shop – except worse because people expect a website to be open twenty-four hours a day, and being down is as good as being non-existent. Same with a mail server – if that's gone, you lose an important line of communication between your site and your visitors or customers.'

Aside from new projects, the sysadmin also keeps the system healthy on a day-to-day basis. This means dealing with crises as they arrive, but also running regular checks to make sure everything is moving smoothly. 'Users give you grief about not being able to do this or that, or this is not working, that not working,' says Man. 'Apart from that, stress is pretty minimal if you know what you have to do and how to get it done. Though sometimes if things go wrong, they go wrong in a big way. Then it's stressful, as it's generally accepted that systems being down for an Internet company is a big no-no.'

The sysadmin also runs regular **back-ups** of the system, creating a duplicate copy of the entire computer network. This is because not even the best administrator can prevent things like natural disaster. By maintaining a copy of the network, the company can rest easy that, should lightning strike the building or a volcano erupt over it, or a tidal wave flood the entire locale, they can still be open for business on the morrow. Because the network changes regularly, the system administrator must also update the back-ups.

'It's hard to stick to a schedule as most of the important pieces of work I do can only be done when no one is interrupting the network and servers [i.e. at night],' says Man. The task of system maintenance is made particularly difficult for sysadmins at Internet companies, where employees tend to work all hours, often long into the night. 'People work late and having systems availability makes it hard to take down a server for maintenance,' Man says.

System administrators generally get their training on the job, although a fair few have computer science degrees. Man, like many, got an accreditation as an **MCSE**. A trained system administrator can work in any field, since nearly every kind of business these days is run on a computer network. But working for a dot.com can be energising: the systems are usually designed from the ground up, with the latest, greatest state-of-the-art equipment. In other fields, the company usually has some older (or 'legacy') computers that often do more to complicate the network than they are worth.

'I landed on my feet, really, as all the dot.coms I have worked for have offered a job to me without me ever looking,' Man says. 'Working for a dot.com, I can really have a better control of the design and **architecture** of the systems, which is the most satisfying. I would never have had these kinds of responsibilities in a large corporation. Here I'm allowed to experiment a lot more than elsewhere.'

SKILLS YOU'LL NEED

A system administrator needs to know everything about a computer network, and how all the pieces inter-operate. Sysadmins should be extremely patient, detail-oriented people, who don't mind carrying the weight of the company on their shoulders should a technical meltdown occur.

GETTING THE JOB

Get certification and advanced training in network administration. These skills and knowledge base are imperative for the job.

TIP

● Become familiar with all systems. The system administrator should not just be a jack of all trades, but a master of all trades as well.

GLOSSARY

● Architecture
In sysadmin lingo, architecture refers not to the company's office building but to the computer network, and how it is built. Architecture describes how all the various computers in a company are connected together. A bad architecture is one that is terribly complex, poorly designed and difficult to maintain. A good architecture is simple, elegant, and doesn't give the sysadmin tension headaches.

● Back-up
Both a noun and a verb, back-up is the act and the result of creating a duplicate copy of a computer network which could come in very handy should the building burn to the ground. The back-up is kept in another, secure location, often held by a specialist company that does nothing but provide back-up facilities for a number of firms. These facilities are secure, climate-controlled, and often look more like a futuristic military intelligence compound than a warehouse.

● MCSE
Stands for Microsoft Certified System Engineer, a certification programme that gives advanced training in system administration and maintenance. Many lower-level computer technicians become system administrators by passing through an MCSE programme.

● Network (system)
A collection of computers connected together. This can be either within a company (an Intranet) or in the world at large (the Internet). An internal network, also referred to as 'the system', is the responsibility of the system administrator.

● Server
A powerful computer within a network that serves up software programs to client computers (i.e. PCs). A server holds information that is used by the whole company, like a database or an e-mail program.

USEFUL ADDRESSES

● Microsoft, 1 Microsoft Way, Redmond, WA 98052-6399, USA.
TEL +1 425 705 1900.
FAX +1 425 705 1831.
www.microsoft.com/trainingandservices

● Sun Microsystems, Inc., 901 San Antonio Rd, UMIL03-06, Palo Alto, CA 94303, USA.
TEL +1 800 786 7638.
www.sun.com/; info@sun.com

Venture Capitalist

Money: From about £50,000 to well into seven figures at the top of the tree.

Hours: Usually long and hard, including time for learning financial modelling and other magic, time spent with companies, time spent travelling.

Health risk: 4/10. Not too many dangers other than food poisoning in business class on short-haul European flights, or coping with taxi drivers in Rome.

Pressure rating: 8/10. How would you like significant amounts of money depending on your judgement? Not to mention the emotional pressure of hungry entrepreneurs wanting you to fund them.

Glamour rating: 6/10. You can't usually tell a VC from an investment banker or corporate financier. Besides, no one will ever understand exactly what you do, and you'll either wear a grey suit or Gap software casual. Few household names in the business (unless you're in Silicon Valley).

Travel rating: 9/10. Generally, lots of travel. Will also be particularly handy for anyone writing a book called *Boardroom Decoration of the World*, or a guide to checking your e-mail in every country, on the side.

Venture capitalists are mysterious, intelligent individuals who are loved or hated for controlling access to capital that makes or breaks thousands of Internet companies. In Europe, venture capitalists are emerging from a heritage as 'risk capitalists' to become the most interesting flavour of finance, and to impress emerging dot.coms with their insight and wisdom.

Venture capitalists were once an arcane, grey-suited group who worked on such low-profile projects as management buy-outs (MBOs) in the nut-and-bolt industry. They were known as 'risk capitalists' because, unlike banks, they would invest money in something that did not guarantee a return. How times have changed! The Internet and its associated pace of change and need for large stacks of cash have transformed the VC into a casually dressed talent agent to the stars of the Internet revolution.

The venture capitalist as hero is an American creation, played in real life by powerful individuals such as John Doerr of Kleiner, Perkins or Ann Winblad of Hummer Winblad. VCs belong to partnerships which have as many names or initials as advertising agencies, with the significant difference that they are very well known. VCs have been credited with creating an enormous amount of wealth, and have acquired a certain amount of mystique for their prescience (as in, 'Did you know that VC who invested in Amazon when they were a five-person company?' Much shaking of heads in awe and disbelief).

Of course, that is California. What is the venture capitalist like in the rest of the world?

Venture capital is rapidly moving into the public consciousness and into the headlines. VCs are now viewed in the UK much as prophets would have been viewed in biblical times, and such high-profile VCs as Thomas Hoegh of Arts Alliance and Tim Jackson of Carlyle Venture Partners are interviewed as often as film stars. According to the BVCA (British Venture Capital Association), the UK industry is the largest and most developed in Europe, and invested nearly £8 billion in over 1,300 companies during 1999 (over £1 billion of that was in hi-tech, by the way).

But just because they are higher-profile than they once were, are venture capitalists any less mysterious? What, for example, do they do? And where does the money come from?

Part of the mystique arises from the fact that venture capital firms are mainly partnerships, and keep a deliberately low profile. Unlike the investment banks, even the largest venture capital firm employs only a few hundred people. In the case of Simon Cook's company, Elderstreet, the firm has only four professionals, all of whom have 'a cheque book' (the authority to make investments).

Also, as Toon den Heijer of Dutch venture capital firm Gilde explains, when credit comes along for a job well done, 'credit will go to the entrepreneur (which is okay and it should be that way), but when the investment fails it is our fault!'

VCs are often managing their own money: many partners were former entrepreneurs who took their stake and decided to help other companies grow, not wanting the day-to-day hands-on responsibility of focusing on one company. Tim Jackson, the entrepreneur who founded QXL, and Simon Murdoch, the former managing director of Bookpages (now Amazon UK), are two first-wave UK Internet entrepreneurs who decided to take their cash (post-acquisition in Bookpages' case, post-IPO in QXL's) and use it to help other Internet companies find funding.

What do venture capital firms do, exactly?

They invest money in companies, after much consideration. They spend much of their time evaluating the risks involved in doing so. A VC will know far more about the industry he or she is involved with than most financiers: the speed and complexity of technology investments make it essential to understand the market, or at least a small piece of it. As Po Bronson's fictional venture capitalist is described in *The First $20 Million Are Always the Hardest*: 'Each of Marquee Ventures's eight full partners and four associate partners had his speciality. Andy's main contact, Travis Grissom, was a hardware man: he could quote the labour costs in Singapore, the memory refresh times of RAM, and the cost per square inch of flat-panel displays.'

The VC is a bit like a banker, or

corporate financier, on speed. As Toon den Heijer describes it, 'a VC always has an opinion ... that's why our profile is between consultants and entrepreneurs'. The key differences between VCs and other finance professionals is their appetite for risk and the timing of their involvement with a company. VCs have historically become involved at times of major change. A company would approach a VC with a plan for an MBO, or to take the company public, or a need for cash to fund other kinds of growth such as acquisition. The VC would get to know the company and make a decision, set commercial terms for the investment, and join the board.

These days, living on Internet time and dealing with Internet entrepreneurs, VCs have found their (never leisurely) timescales compressed, and the pressure rising accordingly. VCs make everyone else's post seem manageable: most have been on the receiving end of hundreds of business plans per month in recent times. Often, it is a matter of luck that some of these plans get seen at all. Ashley Tott of 3i tells of receiving thirty to forty business plans per week, and spending huge amounts of time reading them. One day, as he was about to head out the door for a flight, he realised he had nothing to read, and grabbed a business plan from the stack on his desk. He read this lucky plan on the flight, got very excited by it, and 3i ended up funding the company: Paragon Software, now acquired by phone.com for $500 million.

Of course, reading business plans that will make your company lots of money, and flying around spotting opportunities and holding meetings with companies, are only two of the things VCs do. They actually spend a great deal of time with the companies in whom they have invested: most VCs serve on several boards, and may act as interim finance director or take on another management role for a fast-growing company.

'Entrepreneurs sent themselves to business school just to learn how to make a good pitch to a venture capitalist, but Andy just picked up the phone ... he was customarily transferred to some junior partner who had just graduated from business school, where he had been taught a hundred and one ways to turn down an entrepreneur' (Po Bronson, *The First $20 Million Are Always the Hardest*).

Apart from possibly going to business school, and undergoing the training for '101 ways to say no, nicely, to someone who wants a million', what other training or background might a VC have?

VCs are as much talent agents as spreadsheet whizzes. Although a big part of their job is the analytical evaluation of business plans and market sectors, equally important is their ability to understand the dynamics of a management team and the individuals involved. As one VC puts it, 'If I fund a company I will end up spending a huge amount of time with them, so it's important for the sake of the business that I understand how the management team works. It's much easier to be stuck in a plane with people you like, rather than a dysfunctional team with different personal agendas.' Many come to be VCs following on from other jobs in the finance or consulting industry: as an analyst for an investment bank, or a consultant or accountant with a large professional services firm. Toon den Heijer's advice is to do this as a first step, then to 'try to find a VC fund that fits your personality and where your skills are complementary in the existing partnership'.

Many VCs stay in the industry and move on to become partners in their own organisations, or join other venture capital firms or the companies they have invested in.

SKILLS YOU'LL NEED

The ability to absorb and understand the underlying numbers. A knack for psychology and an understanding of how management teams work. A deeper knowledge of one or two industry sectors such as software or coffee bar chains (two major growth areas for VC investment). Stamina (for surviving all those aeroplane flights and food).

GETTING THE JOB

- Most VC houses are small places. Therefore the best chance of getting the job is knowing an individual firm, or doing a placement.
- Work beforehand for one of the big consultancies in their corporate finance or transaction services (people who do due diligence on deals) departments. These people have good contacts in the VC community.
- Become an entrepreneur: if you get funding and make a pile of cash, you can always start your own VC firm!

TIPS

Try to get an internship with a venture capital firm during university or business school. Read publications like the *Red Herring* and the *Financial Times* to spot what high-profile VC deals are being done. Learn another language and cultivate an international mindset: lots of deal opportunities for VCs are in emerging markets.

USEFUL ADDRESSES

- British Venture Capital Association, Essex House, 12–13 Essex St, London WC2R 3AA, UK.
TEL +44 (0) 20 7240 3846.
FAX +44 (0) 20 7240 3849.
www.bvca.co.uk;
bvca@bvca.co.uk
- 3i plc, 91 Waterloo Rd, London SE1 8XP, UK.
TEL +44 (0) 20 7928 3131.
FAX +44 (0) 20 7928 0058.
www.3i.com

Web Monkey

Money: From £12,000 to £20,000. Web monkeys can easily move up in an organisation, but it is essentially an entry-level position.

Hours: Usually 9–6, but Web monkeys need to be available in a crisis.

Health risk: 2/10. At the bottom of the heap, the only thing that could ruin a Web monkey's day is boredom at being asked to do too many mundane tasks.

Pressure rating: 4/10. It's a low-responsibility job, but does come with its share of frustrations.

Glamour rating: 2/10. If the Internet industry is a barrel of monkeys, the Web monkey is definitely bottom of the barrel.

Travel rating: 1/10. Seeing the other side of the office counts as long-distance travel for most Web monkeys.

Every company has one. Other members of the office might not know his name, but they all know him as 'the web guy'. He's the kid in the office who doesn't have an advanced degree, an expense account or even a suit and tie, but he does know the ins and outs of the website like no one else. He is a Web monkey, one of a vast community of Internet workers whose job is so loosely described that most Web monkeys couldn't even describe it themselves.

In the mid-90s, before most companies were trying to make money from the Internet, quite a few were already setting up websites. These were usually pretty amateur affairs – a few pictures and bits of text. Almost without fail, they were run by young, slovenly workers whose background consisted exclusively of playing with computers and video games until their skin turned a pallor closer to that of ash than that of flesh. Teenagers used the Internet and they used computers, and so they had a much better understanding of how to work with both. They didn't, however, have much concept of life in the corporate world, and so were surprised when asked to put a bit of spit and polish on their demeanour. In fact, it might be said that as the Web experts grew up a little bit, they changed corporate culture far more than corporate culture changed them.

At first they were called **Webmasters**, a strange title more of their own invention rather than one that appeared on the annual organisational chart created by the human resources department. Since no one within the organisation really had much of an idea how to use the Internet, much less build and maintain a website, there was a sense that 'Webmasters' had special powers. Most bosses thought they must be allowed to wear funny clothes, bizarre haircuts and multiple piercings to let those powers foment. As the Internet has become more mainstream, the single Webmaster has given way to whole departments and companies devoted to designing and building websites, and the process has become much more sophisticated. Now there are Web developers, designers, content managers, producers, writers and tech support personnel to handle the tasks that used to be the exclusive domain of the Webmaster.

But in many ways, the culture of the Webmaster has stayed alive in the hearts of website workers. In every organisation, there are still people whose official title might be any of those listed above, but who fall loosely into the category of Web monkey. They are young, often fresh out of school; they may not have any professional background, but they have a familiarity with the Internet and with computers (and, more often than not, with video games). They have assorted technical skills but no formal training, and are generally lower paid than their more exalted colleagues, the project managers. Company managers like having Web monkeys on staff because they are technically skilled in a huge variety of areas, and they don't cost the earth like more specialised programmers.

Web monkeys have different roles in different companies. In a dot.com, they tend to be handed basic tasks, since they are surrounded by specialists and Internet experts. In off-line companies, where the website is only one of many things the company concentrates on, the Web monkey might have a more elevated position, working on all aspects of the site and commanding a better salary to boot. In either place, they are likely to come in late and leave late, bleary from a night out clubbing and wearing yesterday's T-shirt and beard growth. Most say that they came by their job almost as a fluke: an interest in technology and the Internet accidentally turning out to be marketable skills.

'This job just sort of came to me,' says Philip Anderson, whose official title with Internet venture Meome.com is 'Internet Researcher'. 'I left home and moved to London after my A-Level exams. It was a Friday lunch-time and I decided that on the Monday coming I would start to look for a job. I just lazed around and logged on to the Internet, then I received a message asking if I wanted a job. I couldn't believe it, I thought it was some sort of scam.'

The note was from Ben Salm, a founder of Meome.com and the former UK managing director of auction site Ricardo.de. The company is built around the idea that, given all the information available on-line, most people could use a guide to help them sort out good information from bad. Meome.com recruited hundreds of experts who were specialised in particular topics, and helped them build sites devoted to their topic alone. The experts can guide interested users to other places on the Web that have information relevant to their topic.

'When we started Meome, we needed a student who knew about the Internet and would start identifying experts for us,' Salm says. 'Using an on-line chat system, we tracked down this young kid who promptly turned up the next morning. At first he didn't really trust us, but it turned out that he knew a hell of a lot about the Internet. This guy is now our kind of office whiz kid. He built our first website, contacted and recruited our first fifty experts, and is turning out to be a real addition to our team.'

Anderson, who was seventeen when he first started working with Meome, says the job has become a lot more interesting as he's acquired more responsibility. 'My title is Internet Researcher, but I do a lot more than that,' he says. 'I have to find people and e-mail them, I also spend time updating and maintaining and building the website and sign-up system for our venture. While doing this, I also get asked questions about things and I can usually come up with a useful link or something.'

It seems to be a Web monkey characteristic that throughout their education most monkeys had little interest in scholastic advancement, although getting to the next level in the new Nintendo Super Mario Brothers game filled them with seething ambition. 'I've always wanted to get into this industry but was discouraged by my exam results,' Anderson says. 'I seemed to be able to do everything but not prove it in the exams. For A-level computing, I only got a D. My plan now is to stay here for as long as I can and gain lots of experience. I was only seventeen when I got this job, and it is quite glamorous considering what most people my age are doing.'

But oh, how that enthusiasm can wear off after a few years in the job. Some Web monkeys do a complete about-face from this kind of youthful enthusiasm to hard-bitten cynicism in only a matter of years. Rob Manuel, who's been monkeying around the Internet since 1992, after attempting to write a description of what he does for a living in an e-mail, confessed, 'It's all come out a bit cynical. [My job] has all of the stress and none of the glory.'

Manuel's version of an average day:

9.15 a.m. Late for work. Boss says, 'We really need to develop some trust here, i.e. I trust you to turn up.' He's such a wit.

9.16 a.m. Ah, the boss wants a cup of tea.

9.30 a.m. Provide tea. Boss reading his e-mails, forwarding the dullest ones to me for my attention. Oooh. The client needs a press release put into the news engine. Cut and paste. The client needs the text changing on a graphic. Cut and paste. The client needs a report on the success of the last bout of search engine registration ... Hmm, interesting – we're getting more links from a porn site that has used us as the 'I don't agree button' than from AltaVista. Nice.

11.30 a.m. The boss is in a panic. The client has phoned up saying 'the **navigation** is jumping position on every page on the website'. I spend the next two hours using cut and paste to put the same navigation into every document. Yawn.

1.30 p.m. No time for lunch. The client's mate has just phoned the client to say that the text is too small to read on the Macintosh. I spend the next two hours pasting **commands** into the documents.

3.30 p.m. Ah, lunch-time.

3.32 p.m. Ah, back to work. The boss wants some research on how to make a button on a Web page play a sound effect.

4.00 p.m. It doesn't work. It crashes the Macintosh, and makes stupid windows pop up on the PC.

4.30 p.m. It's the client again. He's saying that the **redesign** has broken the back button.

5.00 p.m. Scramble, scramble, scramble.

Life as a Web monkey isn't all fun and games, although the fact that someone will pay you to 'play around with a computer' might make it seem that way at first. Web monkeys appear to display a higher rate of cynicism than most (certainly exponentially higher than anyone in marketing). But since the Internet was founded on building communities around the world, the Web monkeys have some salvation. Since they spend all day on-line anyway, they often corral in on-line chat groups or on bulletin boards to grouse morosely about their state. One particular favourite posting point is www.netslaves.com, where disenfranchised Web workers can meet and moan while their bosses across the room think the busy tap-tapping on the keyboard is a Web monkey struggling with a particularly nasty piece of code. NetSlaves even offers helpful tips on how to survive life in the Web world. Check out their *Combat Manual: Basic Survival Techniques for Web Workers*.

Manuel found his way to monkeydom much the same way as Anderson did, although he's had plenty of time to lose his enchantment with the role. 'I started playing with Usenet [on-line bulletin boards] and e-mail in 1992, and found it much more interesting than the college I was meant to be attending,' he says. 'By the time I needed to actually get a job I didn't have much choice, it was the only thing that I actually knew anything about.'

One upside, for some people, is that most Web monkeys don't have to manage anyone else, or take responsibility for more than their own small piece of the pie. As Manuel says, 'monkey see, monkey do' about sums it up. 'Mankind came down from the trees,' he adds. 'Then they chased us monkeys back.'

SKILLS YOU'LL NEED

Knowledge of all things Internet, the ability to stare at a computer screen for at least eight hours per day, and a gift for taking direction, being told 'do this' then putting your head down and doing it. Knowledge of Web design and Web programming languages, as well as an international ranking in the Doom computer game (this last is optional, but extremely helpful for gaining respect from your peers).

GETTING THE JOB

- Check on-line news groups and

bulletin boards for Web jobs.
- Every time you visit a site, look for the 'jobs' link that will tell you if the site is hiring.
- A CV is only peripherally necessary for a Web monkey job. You're better off building your own site to showcase what you can do.

TIPS
- Hone your basic Web skills, and keep track of new tricks of the trade.
- As soon as you notice a new Web fad, learn how to do it. Keeping fresh keeps you interested.
- Take an anger management course to avoid an unhealthy attitude towards the boss/client/marketing guy.

GLOSSARY
- **Commands**

The programming language that fuels the Web is written in a series of commands. Putting in a <colour> command controls the colour, a <font> command controls the font, and so on. Unfortunately, there is no <leave work early> command.
- **Navigation**

Tools that let a website viewer move from page to page, such as a 'forward' or 'back' button.
- **Redesign**

Whenever serious changes are made to a Web page, this is termed a redesign. A redesign is called for whenever there is some problem with the page. Inevitably, once the redesign fixes one problem, it creates another, which requires another redesign. And so on, ad infinitum.
- **Webmaster**

The former reigning monarch of the Web kingdom. The job of Webmaster has now been distributed among several people, the most lowly of these being the Web monkey.

USEFUL ADDRESSES
- Netslaves, 28 Thompson St, Concord, NH 03301, USA.
TEL +1 603 226 9178.
www.netslaves.com;
info@netslaves.com
- Webmonkey – Designers Resource, Lycos-Wired Digital, 660 Third St, San Francisco, CA 94103, USA.
TEL +1 415 276 8400.
FAX +1 415 276 8500.
www.webmonkey.com/designers;
webmonkey@wired.com

APPENDIX 1

THE INTERNET INDUSTRY: HOW IT WORKS

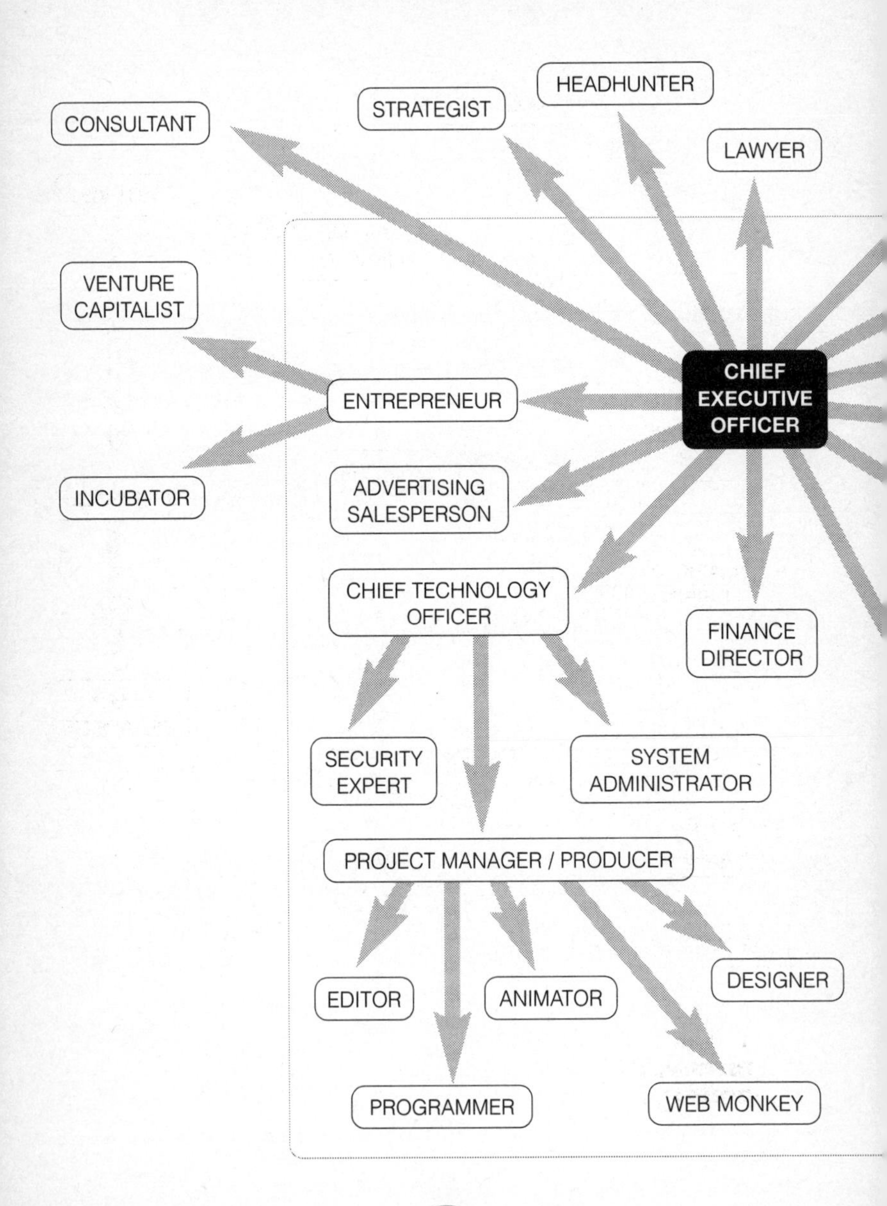

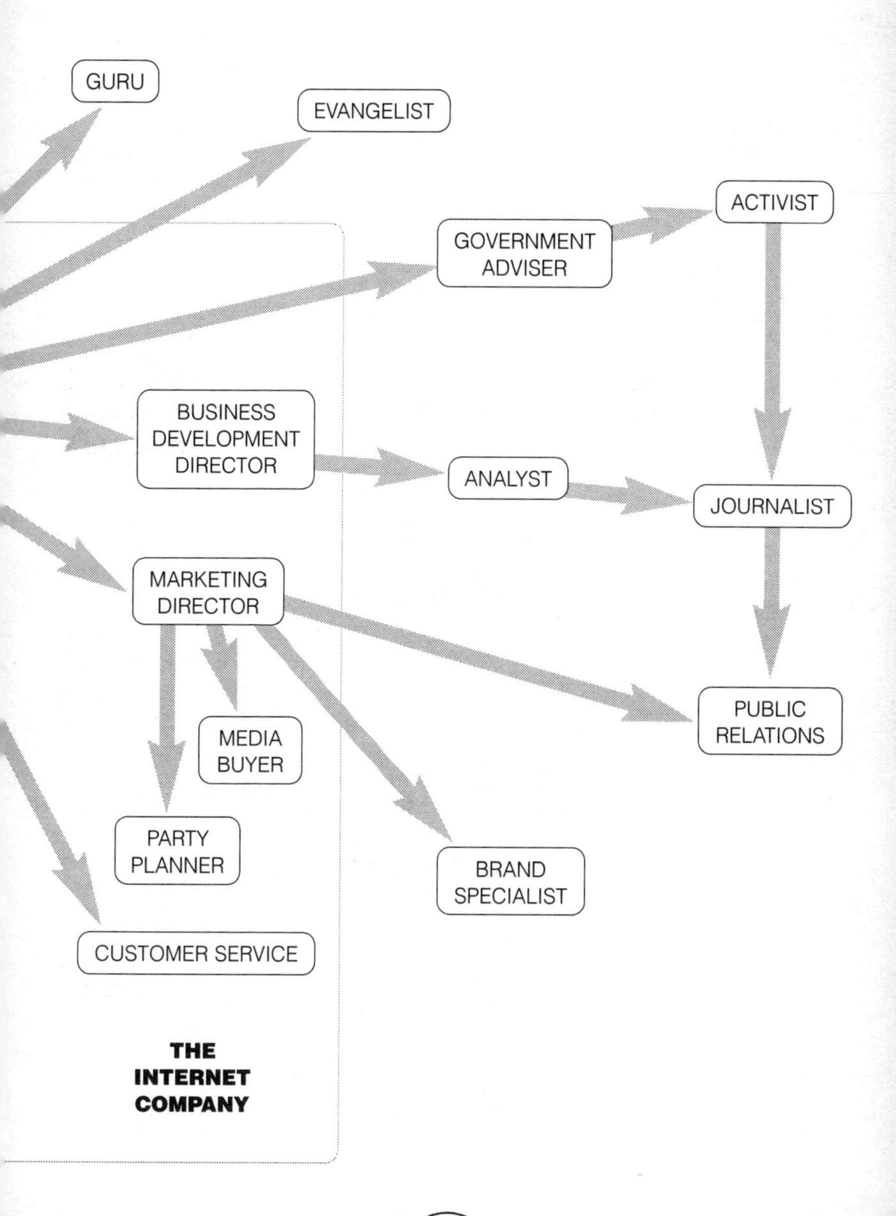
GURU
EVANGELIST
ACTIVIST
GOVERNMENT ADVISER
BUSINESS DEVELOPMENT DIRECTOR
ANALYST
JOURNALIST
MARKETING DIRECTOR
PUBLIC RELATIONS
MEDIA BUYER
PARTY PLANNER
BRAND SPECIALIST
CUSTOMER SERVICE
THE INTERNET COMPANY

APPENDIX 2

SPECIALIST RECRUITMENT WEBSITES

uk.classifieds.yahoo.com/uk/emp
www.bigbluedog.com
www.bwrs.co.uk
www.cerco.co.uk
www.cityjobs.co.uk
www.cvdirect.co.uk
www.eclipse.co.uk/camelot
www.greythorn.com
www.i-resign.com
www.jobdirectory.co.uk
www.jobmall.co.uk
www.jobs.com
www.jobserve.co.uk
www.jobsite.co.uk
www.jobzoneuk.com
www.mediajobs.co.uk
www.monster.co.uk
www.netjobs.co.uk
www.newmonday.com
www.recruitmedia.co.uk
www.reed.co.uk
www.stepstone.co.uk
www.taps.com
www.techpeople.co.uk
www.thenetwork.co.uk
www.topjobs.com
www.totaljobs.com
www.tsa-uk.com

BIBLIOGRAPHY

- Auletta, Ken, "How PointCast Lost It's Way – And $450 million", *The New Yorker*, 9 November, 1998

- Beard, Alison, "Partying on the DotCom Circuit", *The Financial Times*, 20 July, 2000

- Cullen, MaryAnne Motter, "Keeping Up With Cyberspace Law", *The Legal Intelligencer*, 26 April, 2000

- Evangelista, Benny, "Putting a Stop to Spam; IT's latest project for push-technology guru", *The San Francisco Chronicle*, 16 November, 1998

- Healey, Jon, "Animation is Booming on the Web", *San José Mercury News*, 20 March, 2000

- Piven, Joshua, "Push comes to shove for PointCast", *Computer Technology Review*, June 1999

- Roberts-Witt, Sarah L., "It's the Customer, Stupid", *PC Magazine*, 27 June, 2000

- Sceats, Caroline, "Online Advertising Grows Up: Exploiting a New Marketing Medium", *Fletcher Research*, March 2000

- Solomon, Karen, "Customer Service 2000. Customer Service is Getting Worse, Not Better", the *Industry Standard*, 17 July, 2000

- Sprenger, Polly, "Charles Cohen: He tried politics and PR before launching Beenz.com, so he knows the value of a freebie", the *Independent*, 20 September, 1999

- Sprenger, Polly, "Dirty Laundry Airs on Stock Site", *Wired.com*, 11 December, 1998

- Sprenger, Polly, "Dot-Cannes: the buzz at the world's most famous film festival is about the promise and threat of the net", the *Industry Standard*, 22 May, 2000

- Sprenger, Polly, "Dr. Laura Drops her Suit", *Wired.com*, 15 December, 1998

- Sprenger, Polly, "Porsche Sues Online Poachers", *Wired.com*, 13 January, 1998

- Sprenger, Polly, "Spike Decker: Sick & Twisted Web Pioneer", *TheStandard.com*, 17 May, 2000

- Sprenger, Polly, "Tracking Bogus Brands Online", *Wired.com*, 16 December, 1998

- Warner, Bernhard, "E-Christmas in February", the *Industry Standard*, 28 February, 2000

- Warner, Bernhard, "When Bad Ads Happen to Good Companies", the *Industry Standard*, 27 September, 1999

- Woodruff, Cathy, "Internet Law Spins New Legal Web for Firms", *The Albany Times Union*, 5 March, 2000

- Zgodzinski, David, "Cartoons Moving to the Web", *The Montreal Gazette*, 5 June, 1999